Curing their Ills

Curing their Ills

Colonial Power and African Illness

Megan Vaughan

Stanford University Press
Stanford, California
1991

Stanford University Press
Stanford, California
© 1991 Megan Vaughan
Originating publisher: Polity Press, Cambridge
   in association with Basil Blackwell Ltd., Oxford
First published in the U.S.A. by
   Stanford University Press, 1991
Printed in Great Britain
Cloth ISBN 0-8047-1970-5
Paper ISBN 0-8047-1971-3
LC 91-65562

To my parents

Zomba Maternity Ward (Two Decades After)
By Jack Mapanje

I was out of bounds, they said. Outside,
the corrugated iron roofing is crumbling
under rotting *mlombwa* leaves, the green
paint peeling to the rust of two decades
of dead dust. The windows are covered in
shreds of matting (to stop the scorpion
pneumonia of June!) Inside, some thirty beds,
a hundred pregnant women, top and tail on own
cellophanes; thirty others with babies are
cluttered on the cold cement, a family under
each bed, some in between. A fresh smelling
babe in the corner grinds; the mother suckles
him, labouring her tattered *chitenje* cloth. On
the floor, a tin plate with a piece of tripe
she could not chew.

      No one is fighting
the desert war here. These are refugees only
from child spacing, atoning for the ghost revolt
twenty years ago, repaired in this shrinking
hospital God knows how. And I gather, the doctors
who toil twenty-four hours (without drugs, with
blunt needles) offered to extend this wing, but
there was the usual hiccup about getting official
clearance. Yet this was the rallying cry of
the dais once. And when the authorities visit
the sick this Christmas, these women will be
jostled into neat lines, clapping their praises.
The floor will have been scrubbed brighter,
there will be one patient to each bed: another
dream done! But I hear, I was out of bounds.

NOTE: Dr Mapanje was still in prison at the time of going to press.
This may not be the final version of his poem.

Preface

When teaching at the University of Malawi in the early 1980s and researching on Malawian social and economic history, I became interested in the history of insanity, and, more especially, the history of the local mental hospital, founded early in the colonial period, before schools or hospitals for Africans served more than a minute proportion of the population. I was curious as to why the colonial administration had felt the need to define and confine the 'lunatic'. I think I was hoping for the colonial equivalent of what Foucault called the 'great confinement', a colonial story of massive institutionalization for the purposes of maintaining social control. I was to be disappointed in this, since the few dusty and depressing record books of the asylum which are kept in the National Archives show it to have always been a small and underfunded institution, populated by a few unfortunate individuals. If there was no 'great confinement' to be found in the records, there was, however, much of interest in the court records which provided a glimpse at the process of defining insanity in a colonial state. This process seemed to me to say a great deal about British colonialism in Africa. These courtroom dramas were presided over by a British district official, often under-informed and confused on legal matters, and understandably baffled by the problem of defining insanity in another culture. Often the evidence he heard seemed to be completely off the point – perhaps no-one really understood why they were there at all? Frequently he turned to African court assessors for a linguistic and cultural translation, which often muddied the waters further, making the often bizarre statements of the 'alleged lunatic' appear only normally strange and disconnected.

This book represents a development of the issues which emerged from thinking about those courtroom dramas. It is not a conventional history of medicine in colonial Africa, though I hope that I have provided a reasonably accurate account of some aspects of that history. My central interest has been not in weighing up the costs and benefits of biomedicine for Africa, but rather in examining the ways in which biomedicine as a cultural system constructed 'the African'. This has involved examining a disparate range of materials, from technical articles in medical journals to cartoon books on 'jungle doctors'. Despite the sometimes unorthodox nature of the sources, I have tried throughout to examine biomedicine seriously. Though I have sometimes been critical of its role in the creation of negative images of 'the African', I have been concerned to examine it with the same respect as is now commonly accorded by Africanist scholars to 'indigenous' healing systems. Biomedicine, like other healing systems, is comprised of a complex set of ideas and practices which need to be examined in their own right.

If this is not a history of medicine in Africa, still less is this a history of healing. There is now a large anthropological and historical literature on African healing systems. Any account of the history of healing in Africa would have to place at its centre the ideas, practices and discourses of these many systems. This study does not attempt to do that, but rather concentrates on providing for biomedicine the kind of account that is normally reserved for 'indigenous' healing systems. I hope that, incomplete as this account is, it might at least make the point that biomedical practices can be as ritualised and 'exotic' as any other healing practices.

In examining the biomedical discourse on Africa, I have tried to locate this within a specific set of historical circumstances. This is not a study based on detailed examination of any one African archive, but the vast majority of sources I have used refer to British dependencies in East and Central Africa in the period 1890–1950. The development of the biomedical discourse which I describe in this book seems to me to be firmly located within these particular geographical and political boundaries. Since the nature of colonial rule, and of the development of capitalism, were very different elsewhere in Africa, I would not expect the history of biomedical discourse to be the same outside my area of study. The history of biomedical discourse and practice in South Africa, for example, is rather different to that I have described, and those of French and Belgian colonial Africa are very different indeed. When I have ventured outside British East and Central Africa in order to draw out a comparison, I have done so hesitantly.

My concern to locate this study in specific historical circumstances is, in part, a concern to explore the limitations of a Foucauldian account of 'bio-power'. I have attempted, in this book, to examine how far colonial power, and colonial medical power in particular, was different from that described by Foucault for post-Enlightenment Europe. In order to answer this question it seems to me necessary to say something not only about the discourse of biomedicine which was produced through the colonial encounter in Africa but also about how this discourse and the practices associated with it were experienced by Africans. In this I have been continually aware of the limitations of my method. I can say nothing conclusive on the question of colonial subjectivity, but I hope that this study might at least stimulate further discussion on that issue.

I have been aware of many pitfalls in the course of writing this book. I have probably dived blindly into many others. One that I have recognized and have tried to avoid, but doubt if I could have avoided completely, is that by writing an account of colonial discourses and practices I might simply reinforce and reinscribe them in an academic discourse. This seems to me to be a particularly acute problem when dealing with the sometimes humiliating and dehumanizing rituals of biomedicine. I hope that I have avoided the worst kinds of prurience, and that my efforts to describe and analyse the representations which form the core of this book do not further dehumanize.

A great many individuals and institutions have contributed to my writing of this book. My first debt must be to my friends, students and former colleagues at the University of Malawi, and to the staff of the National Archives of Malawi. I owe a similar debt to many librarians and archivists in the National Archives of Zambia, Rhodes House (Oxford), the Bodleian Library (Oxford), the Radcliffe Science Library (Oxford), the London School of Hygiene and Tropical Medicine, and Nuffield College Library. The staff of the National Film Archive, London, were endlessly helpful, and amongst them I owe particular thanks to Fiona O'Brien. Tony Muscat of the Overseas Film and Television Service also kindly uncovered and screened a number of films for me.

I have been struggling with the substance of this book for several years and have benefited from the contributions of many students and colleagues at seminars in the Universities of Oxford, London, Cambridge, Sussex, at Columbia University, New York, and at conferences in Berlin and Maputo. I am particularly grateful to the organisers of the conference on health in southern Africa, held in Maputo in April 1990, for allowing me to present my ideas to a group of health workers from southern Africa who not only study biomedicine but are committed to creating better biomedical practices.

A number of individuals generously shared ideas and material with me. Luise White kindly allowed me to use her notes from files in the Kenyan Archives, and Richard Davenport-Hines sent me proofs of his book prior to publication. Dr Paul White and Mr Robert Hugh Stannus Robertson were generous with material. David

Arnold shared his knowledge of the medical history of India with me, and Charles Webster helped me to situate the African material within a wider context of the evolution of biomedicine. Karen Jochelson and I have discussed the history of sexually transmitted diseases in Africa at length, and I have gained a great deal from her work. Richard Rathbone encouraged me in the study of colonial madness when I was beginning to have doubts about the sanity of this enterprise, and bombarded me with references. I have also benefited over a long period from the work and insights of Shula Marks, Maryinez Lyons and Marcia Wright. More generally I owe an enormous intellectual debt to Ann Whitehead, who got me thinking about colonial history in a different way and whose insights have been invaluable to me. Henrietta Moore read the entire text and has managed always to couch her sharpest criticisms in the kindest terms. Elaine Herman gave me invaluable help in producing the manuscript. My daughter, Anna, encouraged me to keep writing despite the disruption this always causes to our household, and the friendship of my colleague Stanley Trapido has made Oxford a congenital place for me. David Held of Polity Press encouraged me to write this book in the first instance, and remained unfailingly supportive throughout its production. I also owe thanks to Pam Thomas of Polity Press for her calm and friendly efficiency.

Lastly, I would like to mention my ex-colleague from the University of Malawi, Dr Jack Mapanje. When I first began work on this book he and I wrote to each other on the subject of hospitals. Jack's final contribution to this correspondence, before he was arrested and imprisoned, came in the form of a poem entitled 'Zomba Maternity Ward (Two Decades After)'. In this poem he gently reminded me that it is poverty and repression, as much as 'bio-power' which is responsible for dehumanization and degradation in modern Africa. On completing this book I am reminded of how much I, and very many others, miss Jack's combination of warmth and incisiveness.

Megan Vaughan
University of Oxford

NOTE

An earlier version of the material in Chapter 6 appears in 'Syphilis in Colonial Africa: the Social Construction of an Epidemic', in T. O. Ranger and P. Slack eds, *Epidemics and Ideas* (Cambridge, 1991). Some material in Chapter 5 is contained in 'Idioms of Madness: Zomba Lunatic Asylum in the Colonial Period', *Journal of Southern African Studies*, vol. 9 (1983) and an earlier formulation of the general argument of this book can be found in 'Health and Hegemony in Colonial Africa', in D. Engels and S. Marks, eds, *Hegemony and Society in the British Empire* (Oxford, 1991).

1 Introduction: Discourse, Subjectivity and Differences

> Alone I walk the quiet ward
> Where shaded lamps long shadows cast,
> No noonday bustle – noonday sun,
> No noise of speech from anyone.
> Outside, the Stars of Africa
> Twinkle around the Southern Cross.
> The wards beyond may suffer loss –
> But mine is gain, as when I tend the cord
> And welcome into the night
> A dark-skinned babe whose palms are white.
> (P. G. Adams, 'Night Duty:
> African Hospital')[1]

Alone at night in the hushed wards of a colonial African hospital, the young white doctor contemplates questions of life and death. Dark shadows are cast over the death-filled wards, but from the window he catches a glimpse of a brilliant star-filled African night sky. The birth of a baby interrupts a night of death, and as he 'tends the cord', his eyes fall on the unexpectedly white palms of the black baby's hands.

In the late twentieth century, as in the late nineteenth, the European imagination is easily captured by the image of the white doctor in a dark Africa. In the nineteenth century this encounter would probably have been framed in a jungle-like setting, as in many pictorial representations of David Livingstone. The white doctor stands confronting both the 'nature' and the 'culture' of the dark continent, the boundaries between which are disturbingly ill-defined. Armed only with his faith and his medicine, he is stalked both by the animals of the bush and by men in animal skins. By the mid twentieth century the scene of the encounter has moved indoors to the hospital ward. Here the constant play of light and dark, lamplight and shadows, hope and fear, is used to inscribe the encounter. The wild Africa is still there, to be glimpsed through the window as something both beautiful and deadly, whilst inside the hospital the encounter with the other Africa goes on in struggles with disease and death. But, we are reminded, there is also hope – not so much in the birth of a black baby but in the miracle of its white palms.

The western medical discourse on Africa, as this example indicates, is not always marked by its subtlety. In the post-Enlightenment European mind Africa, it seems, has been created as a unique space, as a repository of death, disease, and degeneration, inscribed through a set of recurring and simple dualisms – black and white, good and evil, light and dark.[2]

In his book on *Difference and Pathology* (1985), Sander Gilman has described western discourses on sexuality, race and madness from the eighteenth century onwards.[3] His book is about objectification, and his framework a psychoanalytic one. All human beings, he argues, create stereotypes, and none of us can function in the world without them. The creation of stereotypes begins in childhood. The child can grow into an individual only through articulating a sense of difference between her or himself and the rest of the world. The development of a 'normal' personality, Gilman argues, involves the objectification and distancing of that part of the self which individuals are unable to control and through which they are exposed to anxiety. This part of the self, the 'bad' self, is distanced by being identified with some external, 'bad' object. Herein, he argues, lie the ontological origins of the development of stereotypes.

Stereotypes are necessarily 'crude representations of the world', for their function is to perpetuate an artificial sense of difference between 'self' and 'Other', and to preserve the illusion of control over the self and the world.[4] The need for stereotyping, however, takes place at the level of the 'group', as well as at the level of the individual, and functions in much the same way. The need for control, and the constant threat of loss of that control, necessitates the projection of difference on to some 'Other', and all images of the 'Other', he argues, derive from the 'same deep structure'. Central to this 'deep structure' is an anxiety over sexuality, and the relationship which develops between sexuality, pathology and 'difference' in the form of skin colour: 'sexual anatomy is so important a part of self-image that "sexually different" is tantamount to "pathological" – the Other is "impaired", "sick", "diseased". Similarly, physiognomy or skin colour that is perceived as different is immediately associated with "pathology" and "sexuality".'[5]

The relationships between these different categories and signs of 'otherness' are the focus of Gilman's work. In his chapter on 'The Hottentot and the Prostitute', for instance, he describes the development of a nineteenth-century discourse on black female sexuality, and its realization in the figure of the 'Hottentot Venus'. In this, as in other chapters, Gilman demonstrates the inter-dependence of many nineteenth-century scientific discourses. Discourses on 'blackness', for example, rely heavily on images of sexual difference, whilst discourses on white female sexuality draw on images of 'blackness'.[6]

Gilman traces the same kinds of connections in the nineteenth-century discourses on madness and on degeneration, and in the twentieth-century specialisms of sexology and psychoanalysis. It was Freud who, as Gilman points out, referred to contemporary ignorance of the nature of female sexuality as the 'dark continent' of psychology. In the use of this English phrase, writes Gilman, 'he tied female sexuality to the image of contemporary colonialism and thus to the exoticism of and the pathology of the Other'.[7]

My purpose in this book is, I think, rather different from that of Gilman, though our concerns clearly overlap at many points. Gilman takes a broad sweep over European and North American culture from the eighteenth to twentieth centuries, and draws on a wide array of cultural forms and texts for his evidence. These range from the iconography of prostitution in the texts of an emerging science of sexuality in the nineteenth century, through *fin-de-siècle* dramas and mid-nineteenth-century art works to close analyses of the texts of psychology. All systems of representation, he argues, can be analysed as 'texts' for the purpose of the study of stereotypes, and he quotes the following passage from Terry Eagleton's book *Literary Theory* to support this position: 'Discourses, sign systems and signifying practices of all kinds, from film and television to fiction and the languages of natural science, produce effects, shape forms of consciousness and unconsciousness, which are closely related to the maintenance or transformation of our existing systems of power. They are thus closely related to what it means to be a person.'[8]

Of course cultures as systems of representation are constituted by a very wide range of 'signifying practices', and Gilman traces the resonances of these as they apply to race, sexuality and madness in modern European culture. But by painting his picture on such a broad canvas, and by relying heavily on a 'deep' structural psychological analysis, he leaves us with a sense both of the coherence of this culture and of the inevitability of its form. There are few cracks or dissonances in the picture he paints. Images of race, sexuality and madness feed off each other to form a whole and, furthermore, they are all the product of a universal psychological mechanism of distancing and objectification, the function of which is to create 'normal' human beings.

Convincing as Gilman's account is in many ways, it neglects, in its broad cultural sweep, two central elements in the analysis of discourses mentioned by Eagleton. The first is the fact that they are 'closely related to the maintenance or transformation of our existing systems of power'; the second, that 'they are thus closely related to what it means to be a person'.

Gilman's work is primarily concerned with the process of objectification. As such, it does indeed deal with 'what it means to be a person', but it does so only in terms of the function performed by objectification in the development of the 'normal' individual and of group consciousness. Gilman does not discuss, as Fanon and other writers on colonialism have, and as a body of feminist work has, the question of the effects of this process on those who are so objectified. Neither can the process of objectification, within the chosen framework of analysis (the role of the 'stereotype'), raise the possibility that some discourses might operate less through a one-way process of objectification than through a more complex process of the creation of subjectivities.

In the chapters which follow, I attempt to analyse, within the specific historical context of British colonialism in Africa, the processes both of objectification and of the creation of subjectivities, through a delineation and discussion of biomedical discourses on 'the African'. I am less concerned with the psychology of these processes than I am with what Gilman calls their 'realization' in a specific social context. As such, my discussion is closely tied to the question of the nature of colonial power. By taking as my object of study a much more limited area of the production of knowledge (biomedical knowledge of 'the African') and a more closely defined social and political context, I hope to create a picture, not so much of the inevitability of insistent objectification and the endurance of images, but a more complex, and sometimes more blurred one, which can incorporate resistances and fractures. Though the sometimes crude simplicity of the biomedical discourse on Africa is much in evidence in the chapters which follow, I hope also to show that the production of that discourse was far from simple.

Social constructionism and the history of biomedicine in Africa

A number of overlapping literatures have informed my approach in this book. Firstly, and perhaps most evidently, I have been informed by a social constructionist approach to the history of biomedicine.[9]

One of my main concerns has been to analyse the ways in which medical knowledge was produced in colonial Africa. This exercise is of course premised on the assumption that all forms of scientific and medical knowledge are to some extent socially constructed. In the chapters which follow on the history of madness, on the construction of leprosy and on missionary medicine, I have viewed medical texts and medical theories rather as narratives which draw on a wide range of cultural signs and symbols for their effect.

The social constructionist part of my argument has both been informed by, and has developed in response to, recent literature on the history of biomedicine and of 'medical pluralism' in Africa.

In recent years a number of critiques of the role of biomedicine in the 'Third World', and particularly in colonialism, have emerged. These critiques take various forms, the most influential having been those which emerge from a materialist perspective and which provide a 'political economy' of health and disease in colonial and post-colonial Africa.[10] But there is another strand in these critiques which draws less on political economy than on a late-twentieth-century scepticism about 'science', and disillusionment with 'modern medicine'. The 'problem' with biomedicine as it emerged at the end of the nineteenth century is seen to be its reliance on a process of objectification of the body, and a resulting sense of alienation on the part of the person whose body it is, and who is constructed as the 'patient'. This scientific method, it is argued, has the effect of removing health and illness from the social context in which they are produced, and in which they belong, to another level, which is both internal to the individual but also outside her or his control. Not only does this cause those who are ill to feel powerless and alienated but, it is also argued, this way of viewing the production of disease is also inefficient. By focusing exclusively on the 'natural history' of disease, and on the interaction between 'hosts' and pathogens, epidemiology as a theory and medicine as a practice cannot understand the true origins of disease. These lie, according to this view, not just in 'nature', but, crucially, in the organization of society, and its constructions and manipulations of 'nature'. They lie in systems of production and of social reproduction and in exploitation; they lie in poverty and in the exercise of political power. Epidemiologists, with their biological blinkers, will never be able to account for patterns of disease and their changes over time, if they continue to focus on individual pathology, rather than on society and on politics.[11]

Many aspects of this critique have informed my own analysis in this book. I have little disagreement with the central idea that biomedicine neglects to address the fundamental social, economic and political causes of ill-health, and I agree that there can be no 'natural history' of disease. What I am less certain about, however, are the assumptions made about the nature of biomedical knowledge here. It is certainly true that many biomedical theories and interventions have failed in Africa because no account was taken of the social and political context, and there are many examples of such instances in this book. At the same time, what is striking about so much of the medical knowledge produced in and about colonial Africa is its explicit concern with finding social and cultural 'origins' for disease patterns. Biomedicine drew for its authority both on science and on social science. Biomedical knowledge on Africa was thus both itself socially constructed (in the sense that its concerns and its ways of viewing its object of study were born of a particular historical circumstance and particular social forces) and at the same time 'social constructionist', in that it often sought social explanations for 'natural' phenomena. Furthermore, and perhaps even more importantly, biomedical knowledge played an important role in the wider creation of knowledge of 'the African'.

The paradoxes and contradictions in a biomedical 'world view' have been noted by many writers. Amongst others, Jean Comaroff has discussed the nature of biomedical knowledge, arguing that, whilst it is ostensibly based on 'empirical objectivity', in practice its underlying epistemology remains a 'cultural construct', existing in 'dialectical relationship with its wider social context'.[12] Central to biomedicine's 'cultural construction', argues Comaroff, is 'rational individualism', a view of 'man' as a 'self-determining, biologically contrived individual' existing in a context of 'palpable facts and material things'.[13] Following Foucault and others, Comaroff links this ideology of self-determination with a capitalist mode of production and with modernity which, while it bestowed on its subjects a sense of self-determination, simultaneously removed them from direct control over the means of production. In times of sickness and affliction, Comaroff argues, the contradiction between our supposed self-determination and the reality of our lack of control over our own bodies comes to be starkly obvious, leading us to feel conflicted and alienated.

I will return to Comaroff's arguments, and to the 'rational individualism' of biomedicine later in this chapter. Unlike some critiques of biomedicine, and other comparisons between biomedicine and African healing systems, Comaroff's analysis demonstrates that biomedicine is itself a very complex phenomenon. A reliance on scientific rationalism in biomedical theory does not, as Comaroff shows, mean that there is no cultural construction going on in biomedical theory. It is not its scientific method so much as the particular forms of social construction used within this method which makes biomedicine different from other healing systems.

Social constructionist analyses of biomedicine take many forms.[14] Most do not stop at the 'biological fact', and do not uphold any division between the 'social' and the 'natural', this division itself being a social construction born of a particular period of European history.[15] In this book I reproduce and comment on a number of biomedical narratives produced in colonial Africa. In general I approach these narratives as constructions of reality, and try and understand why they take the form that they do. At various points, however, I have stopped short of a full-scale constructionist approach, and have assumed that there may be a more accurate, and for me a better, way of accounting for and describing a disease pattern, an epidemic or a rise in mortality. It will be clear to the reader that, whilst I have deconstructed many aspects of medical knowledge here, there are others which I have kept intact. I have committed what, for the social constructionist, is the cardinal sin of assuming some material reality to which medical constructs, at some level, refer. In Chapter 6, for example, I have described the social construction of syphilis in early colonial Uganda and, using a conventional historical methodology, have claimed that I can provide a more accurate account of the spread of this disease. My account of the history of syphilis in Uganda is one which makes abundantly clear how fluid, ambiguous and unstable many biomedical disease categories are, but at another level it also assumes that there was a disease, and that people were sick.

In general my approach has been that whilst medical discourses must themselves be seen as constitutive of the problems they describe, they may also reflect, albeit very indirectly, material and political circumstances outside the immediate realm of the medical.[16] For this reason they have to be viewed as both constitutive of, and constituted by, specific historical circumstances. In the case of the history of tuberculosis in South Africa for example, the complex interactive process between the political economy of mining labour and the medical construction of tuberculosis is very evident.[17] At one level this history, like that of syphilis in Uganda, shows that there is no disease 'essence', no tuberculosis in the abstract. On the other hand, the shape which the medical constructions on the disease took in South Africa can only be interpreted by reference to the fact of sickness and debility amongst black miners, and the problem that this posed for employers of black labour.

A number of writers working with a social constructionist view of medicine have tried to solve the problem of relativism and the dangers of reification of discourse inherent in this approach by referring to medical discourses as 'mediations' of class and other social relations.[18] Jordanova, for example, focuses on the ways in which biomedical sciences in the eighteenth and nineteenth centuries have 'mediated' sex roles, gender differences and social stability. The editors of a recent volume of feminist essays on science and medicine take a similar perspective, though without using the term 'mediation': 'Throughout the collection, individual essays concentrate on the interconnection between theories of production and theories of reproduction – on the relation between the fictions, discourses, and representations involved in scientific ideology and the practice or material effects of science in our society, particularly as they affect women.'[19] How medical discourses are produced, and how precisely their effects are felt, are clearly central issues in this literature, and they relate directly to the question of power. As much of this historical and sociological literature either draws on, or is written in reaction to, the work of Foucault on the 'medicalization' of power in the nineteenth and twentieth centuries, it is necessary to discuss the relevance of his work to the historical circumstances of colonial Africa.

Foucault in Africa?

My argument in this book is basically this: that in British colonial Africa, medicine and its associated disciplines played an important part in constructing 'the African' as an object of knowledge, and elaborated classification systems and practices which have to be seen as intrinsic to the operation of colonial power. However, there are important differences between this colonial power/knowledge regime and the power/knowledge regime described by Foucault.[20]

Much of Foucault's work is concerned with 'bio-power' and its operation, both on the bodies of individuals and on whole 'bodies' of populations. In his analysis of a range of discourses and practices, from the creation of the prison to the creation of sexuality, Foucault demonstrates how the body, in modern western society, has become both the site of, and constitutive of, power relations. His earlier work traces the development of 'disciplinary institutions' from the late eighteenth century – the lunatic asylum, the clinic, the prison. The power regime represented by these institutions, and by the practices which constitute them, was, he argues, radically different from what had come before, for their power is not 'repressive power', but 'productive power'. Pre-modern regimes, according to Foucault, function through repression and prohibition, but developments from the late eighteenth century (connected to, but in no way derivative of, industrial capitalism) created new, and more effective modes of power which did not act simply on the body but through the body in everyday practices. In *The Archaeology of Knowledge* and in the later work on sexuality, Foucault develops further the notion of 'productive power'.[21]

'Productive power' was generated at the end of the eighteenth century in part by a radical shift in European thought. From this period, Foucault argues, 'Man' began to conceive of himself as both an 'object' and a 'subject' of knowledge – 'thinking man' was born, who could not only know the world (through the new disciplines of history, geography and demography) but could also know 'himself'. In the modern power regimes of this period the state controlled its subjects not by repressing them but through the creation of the notion of the individual subject, and of 'human welfare'. Whilst the new scientific discourses objectified the human body and claimed to know the mechanisms by which the individual and whole populations functioned, at the same time, and crucially, they developed individual subjects who actively participated in the new discourses about themselves. This idea is developed most fully in Foucault's work on the history of sexuality, in which the function of speech figures centrally. The modern 'subject', according to Foucault, is not only enumerated, and written about, by the scientific experts of the modern state, but, crucially, she and he also talks about her or himself, and thus participates directly in the disciplinary regime.

There have been numerous discussions of the problems presented by Foucault's notion of the operation of modern power. Power, in Foucault's discussion, does not emanate from any identifiable social group, is not 'exercised' in any deliberate fashion, but is 'capillary' in its operation – it is there, constitutive, of every speech act and movement and practice of day-to-day life. Though, as modern subjects, individuals may think that they know what they do, in fact they can never know what the cumulative result of their actions is. 'People know what they do', said Foucault in an interview, 'they frequently know why they do what they do; but what they don't know is what it is what they do does'.[22]

Because power is not an external force but is constituted in the everyday actions of individuals, the idea that individuals or groups might be positioned in different relationships with power is not a possibility, since this would involve conceptualizing power as external to the individual. Thus, whilst Foucault sees power as operating in part through the minute determination and specification of differences between individuals (the classification systems of psychiatry and of sexology, for instance), there can be no discussion of the difference that differences make in relation to power. More generally, the idea of there being effective resistances to power is also ruled out, as many critics have noted, since the discourses of resistance are necessarily permeated with the very ideas of 'freedom' and 'liberation' which themselves help constitute the modern power/ knowledge regime.

Of course, there are many different ways of reading Foucault, and differing interpretations abound. Nancy Fraser, for example, points out that, since Foucault locates power in everyday practices, he might be understood as identifying with a 'politics of everyday life', familiar to feminists.[23] At the same time she demonstrates that, in his own social description, Foucault constantly employs words like 'domination' and 'subjugation', which are themselves the product of liberalism and which might indicate, despite his protests to the contrary, a lingering identification with liberationist politics.

In the chapters which follow I outline the history of medical discourses and practices, some of which are contemporaneous to some of those described by Foucault. Assuming, for the moment, that Foucault's description of these practices for Europe is roughly accurate (this is a whole other area of dispute over Foucault's work which we cannot enter into here), the question is, how different were these histories as they were constructed in a colonial setting, and if different, why should this have been?

In order to answer this question, one needs to look at both aspects of Foucault's power/knowledge regime – the creation of 'objects' and simultaneously of 'subjects' – and one needs to ask how far colonial states exercised 'productive' as opposed to 'repressive' power. My examination of the operation of biomedical discourse in Africa would seem to indicate that there are real differences between the nature of the colonial power/knowledge regime and that described by Foucault.[24]

The first is that colonial states were hardly 'modern states' for much of their short existence, and therefore they relied, especially in their early histories, on a large measure of 'repressive' power. Only in some cases, and then only in the later colonial period, and in their liberal, welfarist functions, did they create the systems of surveillance and control common to Europe.

Secondly, and closely related to the first point, the medical power/ knowledge complex was much less central to colonial control than it was in the modern European state. Colonial psychiatry did identify the 'lunatic' and sometimes incarcerated her or him, as I show in Chapter 5, but in general the need to objectify and distance the 'Other' in the form of the madman or the leper, was less urgent in a situation in which every colonial person was in some sense, already 'Other'.[25] This is a recurring theme in the literature on psychiatry in colonial Africa, in which the problem of definition of the 'normal' and the pathologization of that 'normal' African psychology is ultimately more important than the subsequent definitions of the 'abnormal'.

This is a simplification, and most of this book is concerned to desimplify this phenomenon, but it nevertheless seems to me to be an important point. The distancing afforded by racism served colonialism well through most of its history, and 'differences' between Africans, though elaborated in terms of culture in particular, were continually subordinated to the overriding difference of 'race'. The need to maintain this overriding 'Otherness' meant that other sites of difference, and especially class differences amongst Africans, were addressed only hesitantly, and with a great deal of ambiguity, by colonial administrators.

Thirdly, and again related to the last two points, the extent to which colonialism, and medical discourse as integral to it, created 'subjects' as well as 'objects', and thus operated through individual subjectivities, is open to question, I think. Although a great deal of what I shall call 'unitization' went on in colonial states, this is not the same as the creation of individual subjectivities. By 'unitization' I mean the procedures by which people were counted (sometimes over and over again) for tax purposes or in censuses, weighed and measured if they were labour migrants, and, in some cases, 'given' medical histories and medical records. In general, however, though colonial states unitized, this was only a preliminary to the more important task of aggregation. In colonial medical discourse and practice colonial Africans were conceptualized, first and foremost, as members of groups (usually but not always defined in ethnic terms) and it was these groups, rather than individuals, who were said to possess distinctive psychologies and bodies. In contrast to the developments described by Foucault, in colonial Africa group classification was a far more important construction than individualization. Indeed, there was a powerful strand in the theories of colonial psychologists which denied the possibility that Africans might be self-aware individual subjects, so bound were they supposed to be by collective identities. If modern power operates through the creation of the 'speaking subject', then this colonial power cannot be the power which Foucault is describing. As Nancy Harstock has argued from a feminist perspective, 'reading Foucault persuades me that Foucault's world is not my world',[26] and the same could perhaps be said for many colonial and post-colonial peoples.

Finally, it seems to me that the extent to which colonial power was different from that described by Foucault owed a great deal to the particular, and uneven, development of capitalism in Africa and its relation to the colonial states, and to discourses on the 'African'. Medical discourses both described and helped to create the 'contradictions' of capitalism ('mediated' them, if you like). Africans were expected to move in and out of the market, as conditions dictated. They were to be single-minded cotton producers at one moment, and at another they were prohibited from growing the crop. They were to be 'docile bodies' for mining capital when the conditions of the labour supply demanded it, but not for the whole of their lives. They were to be created as consumers of products for their new, modern bodies at one moment, and at the next they were told to revive their 'traditional' knowledge of soap-producing plants. By relying so heavily on older modes of production for its very success, colonial capitalism also helped create the discourse on the 'traditional', non-individualized and 'unknowing' collective being – the 'African', a discourse to which the idea of difference was central.

Differences, resistances and subjectivities

Colonial medical discourse, as the following chapters indicate, operated to a large extent through the articulation of notions of difference. What I have tried to do in these chapters is to unpack 'difference' and to look at the varied and changing ways in which 'difference' and 'differences' were articulated. One of my aims has been to provide an account which does not leave 'difference' intact. My problem with Gilman's account of the pathologization of 'difference' is that, by resorting to a psychological theory of the necessity and inevitability of stereotyping, it merely adds one more pathologizing discourse to the others, leaving intact the 'deep' and seemingly inevitable associations between sexuality, sickness and blackness.

Colonial medical discourse was, without a doubt, preoccupied by difference. In the earlier colonial period (and for much longer in some areas of the medical and psychological literature) the overriding difference was represented as one of biological 'race'. But more elaborate distinctions of difference were also formulated, through a process of inclusion and exclusion, and a shifting of the boundaries of difference. For example, the colonial medical literature on the diseases of industrialization articulates various intersecting differences – between 'black' and 'white', between 'ethnic' groups, and between 'primitive' and 'modern'. In the inter-war period there was a powerful strand of thinking which saw the erosion of difference as itself a factor which predisposed individuals and groups towards the contraction of certain diseases. The differential incidence of many diseases was attributed not to the material conditions of industrialization and urbanization but to 'maladaptation' on the part of Africans. The condition of being partly 'modernized', a condition in which the boundaries of some kinds of differences had become blurred, was itself seen as pathological. Where old differences were no longer satisfactory, new differences became elaborated. The point I am trying to make here is that though there was, at some level, an overarching difference being articulated between the colonial person and the colonizer, at another level the creation of differences was a complex and shifting thing which must be related to the specific circumstances of colonial Africa.

Medical discourse operated by locating difference and differences in the body, thereby not only pathologizing them but also naturalizing them. As the notion of biological 'race' came under attack, white liberals (amongst whom were many doctors), became uneasy with medical theories which relied on the embodiment of difference, and elaborated other theories to account for perceived variations in, for instance, the manifestation of a disease amongst different social groups. In these theories medicine demonstrated its ability to draw on 'social science' as well as on natural science for its authority. In the particular circumstances of colonial Africa it drew primarily on anthropology and substituted culture for biology in many of its accounts.

Liberal commentators, for example, in the debate over psychological theories of the 1930s–50s (see Chapter 5), sometimes argued against *any* articulation of difference, so heavily loaded had the notion of difference become. This had two consequences. The first was that the terms of the debate (sameness/difference) kept them locked into the language of difference, even whilst they were opposing it. The second was that, in throwing out cultural differences along with biological difference, they were left with a medical science which was totalizing, universalizing and which could take no account of variation. The liberal denial of differences, then, tended to imply a resort to a more 'scientific' medicine which, amongst other things, could take no account at all of alternative ways of explaining illness.

The 'politics of difference', then, lie at the heart of many supposedly technical debates amongst colonial medics. Clearly what is even more important, however, is how those who were the subjects of these debates themselves dealt with difference.

In several chapters of this book I have tried to indicate how those who were 'bestowed' with difference, through colonial medical discourse and practice, dealt with this. This is not an easy task, and some might even say that it is an impossible one. The main focus of this work is the colonial discourses themselves, and the methodology I have used is not one in which colonial subjective experiences and resistances can be easily discerned. I have taken the view, however, that subjectivities are made, not given, and for this reason I have thought it worth pursuing with what is bound to be the rather limited exercise of describing what seem to me to be areas in which colonial medical discourse, and particularly its Christian versions, attempted to construct identities. This can be seen in the case of leprosy where sufferers were first encouraged to think of themselves as having been quite literally erased by the disease, and then encouraged to adopt a new, salvatory and collective identity as 'the lepers' (see Chapter 4). How far African leprosy sufferers adopted and internalized this identity is, of course, another matter, and I have tried to indicate both in this case and in other chapters where there were clear resistances to imposed subjectivities.

One of the most powerful accounts of the experience of difference and of colonial subjectivity remains that provided by Frantz Fanon.[27] Writing as a practising psychiatrist as well as a colonial subject, Fanon was concerned to analyse the experience of the colonial subject as a necessary preliminary to liberation. Fanon locates himself at the receiving end of the objectifying practices described by Gilman, and there is no question, in his account, that these practices have a profound effect on subjectivity. Not only does the white man project all that is bad on to the black person, according to Fanon, but his gaze annihilates that person, turning her or him into 'nothingness'. At the beginning of *Black Skin, White Masks*, for instance, Fanon makes this statement:

> At the risk of arousing the resentment of my colored brothers, I will say that the black is not a man.
> There is a zone of nonbeing, an extraordinarily sterile and arid region, an utterly naked declivity where an authentic upheaval can be born. In most cases, the black man lacks the advantage of being able to accomplish this descent into a real hell.[28]

Liberation, in Fanon's account, can only come about when the 'black man' is liberated from himself, from the results of a 'series of aberrations of affect' brought about by colonialism, which have made him into a black man in the first place. Being black is a function of 'being for others', and any attempt to step outside the black/white dialogue, or to hide from the white gaze, results in a complete dissolution of subjectivity:

> Sealed into that crushing objecthood, I turned beseechingly to others. Their attention was a liberation, running over my body suddenly abraded into nonbeing, endowing me once more with an agility I had thought lost, and by taking me out of the world, restoring me to it. But just as I reached the other side, I stumbled, and the movements, the attitudes, the glances of the other fixed me there, in the sense in which a chemical solution is fixed by a dye. I was indignant; I demanded an explanation. Nothing happened. I burst apart. Now the fragments have been put together again by another self.[29]

Fragmentation and dissolution, dominant images in the colonial discourse on the 'modern' African (and now, of course, dominant themes in postmodernism) are, argues Fanon, realities of the subjective experience of colonialism. Liberation, both national and personal, involves putting together another identity, by first recognizing one's 'difference' and then validating it, using it to empower in the struggle against the coloniser.[30]

Fanon's analysis, as many critics have pointed out, is written in terms of binary oppositions – self/Other, colonizer/colonized, black/white. The opposition between colonizer and colonized is real, it constitutes the subjective experience of both white and black, and it overrides other forms of 'difference'.[31] The experience of being 'Other' is as profound for the middle class of the colonized society as it is for the poor peasant. In fact, the result of 'Otherness', the division and disintegration of the self, is most likely to be felt by the more educated.

Fanon wrote within, not outside, the existing colonial literature on psychology and psychopathology, and there are many resonances between his work and the work of colonial psychiatrists whose pathologisation of the 'divided subject' served quite different ends (see Chapter 5). Fanon is presenting one way of dealing with an imposed difference politically – to recognize the reality of its effects and to begin from that position of difference to create new, liberating identities which will effectively do away with both the psychological and political effects of colonialism. Such a strategy, which involves an acknowledgement of the power of colonialism to impose subjectivities, has for long been a matter of debate and controversy amongst African political activists and intellectuals. The question of how far difference can be reclaimed as a tool of liberation, rather than as an arm of oppression, is a debate that continues to resound through a number of different literatures.

In the field of colonial and Afro-American literary criticism, the analytical importance of difference and differences is a matter of much discussion. If literature is to be seen as a form of 'self-representation' for both individuals and collectivities, then the strategies adopted to deal with imposed difference can be seen to be crucial. Colonial and post-colonial writers have adopted varying strategies, from the affirmation of the distinctiveness of 'blackness' in the Negritude school through various levels of subversion and appropriation of colonialist discourses.[32] While some African writers have asserted the continuity of African cultures and have articulated the idea of 'indigeneity' as a powerful experiential force, others have concentrated rather on the 'hybridizing' experience of colonialism in which the binary oppositions of black/white and colonizer/colonized no longer hold centre stage. The kinds of subjectivities reflected and created through this writing, then, vary enormously. In part this variation may reflect the differential effects of colonial power in different parts of Africa but it also reflects the personal and political choice of individual writers.

More recently the influence of postmodernist theories of the subject has been felt in this area of the study of colonial and post-colonial literatures, creating another language in which the debate over difference has been conducted.[33] Drawing in part on Lacanian psychoanalytic theory and on linguistic theory, postmodernist theory problematizes the notion of subjectivity, denying that there is any essential, coherent 'self', asserting rather that subjectivities are fragmented, incoherent and constantly in the state of creation and recreation. Differences and dissonances are what constitute the self, fragmentation and fracturing constitute experience. The notion of a coherent, active and whole subject, the essential thinking person, is, according to these theories, the creation of a specific period of western European history beginning with the Enlightenment and elaborated in the course of the nineteenth and twentieth centuries.[34] Far from being liberating, post-Enlightenment subjectivity is, as we have already noted through a reading of Foucault, posited as the mechanism of oppression. By believing that we are active subjects of our own making, we internalize and make more effective our subjugation.

Following this through, any 'liberationist' politics which appeals to the need to restore the sense of self and identity which has been destroyed or distorted by colonialism must necessarily be misguided, since no such coherent self can exist. On the other hand since, according to this theory, all subjectivities are created rather than given, there are endless possibilities for the creation and recreation of individual and collective identities.

A number of writers on colonialist discourse have drawn on these theories, most notably Said, Spivak and Bhabha. The creation of colonial subjectivities in these accounts becomes a more complex, less straightforward, matter than it is in the accounts of Fanon, Memmi and other earlier writers on the psychology of colonialism.[35] In these earlier accounts difference was created in a set of binary oppositions, between black and white, colonizer and colonized. In postmodernist accounts, differences take the place of difference, and the 'colonial experience' becomes less homogenized. Once 'the difference' is done away with, it is possible to see how different colonial individuals and groups may have had different investments in the subjectivities created in the course of colonialism. The idea of replacing one discourse (the colonial representation of the 'Other') with its reverse (the liberationist self-representation) is superseded by a more complex strategy. Postmodernist writing proceeds by unsettling and disturbing existing representations, rather than by replacing them with what, according to this theory, could only ever be another false construction of identity. Inversion can never be sufficient.

There is a sense in which colonial and postcolonial peoples discovered postmodernist theories of the subject long before they were popularized by the French philosophers and linguists of the 1960s. Dissonance, fragmentation and fracturing of identity have been dominant terms in which colonial peoples have described their experience of oppression. As a number of writers have pointed out, it may not be coincidental that postmodernism in the West was born in the period of decolonization when the identity of the colonizer was destabilized, and when dissonance and uncertainty were experienced by white western intellectuals. In their book on postcolonial literatures, Bill Ashcroft and his colleagues make this point, and also demonstrate how writing on colonialism and post-colonialism has both anticipated, and been 'colonised' by, post-modernism:

> Given the extent to which European postmodernist and poststructuralist theories have invested in cultural relativity as a term in some of their most radical insights, it is ironic that the label 'postmodern' is increasingly being applied hegemonically to cultures and texts outside Europe, assimilating post-colonial works whose political orientations and experimental formations have been deliberately designed to counteract such European assimilation ... Thus the so-called 'crisis of (European) authority' continues to reinforce European cultural and political domination, as the potential relativisation of European systems of thought acts through such labelling once again to make the rest of the world a peripheral term in Europe's self-questioning.[36]

One of the major representatives of the postmodernist 'school' of colonialist studies is Gayatri Spivak. She is one of the few writers who have attempted to connect this literature on difference and colonialism with another literature on difference – feminism.[37] Western feminism has, since the nineteenth century, also been concerned with the question of how to deal politically with difference, and has also recently engaged with postmodernist theories of the subject.[38] The feminist project has problematized the category 'woman', and has demonstrated how, through a variety of discourses (most notably medical and scientific ones), 'woman' has been constructed. But feminists themselves, as Denise Riley has pointed out, have helped to uphold the very category 'woman' which they have simultaneously deconstructed: 'Equality; difference; "different but equal" – the history of feminism since the 1790s has zigzagged and curved through these incomplete oppositions upon which it is itself precariously erected.'[39] Since 'woman' as a gender has been shown to incorporate an enormously wide range of identities, so feminism incorporates a wide range of political positions on the subject of difference – from those who celebrate and extend an essential womanhood, women's language and sensibilities, to those who wish to do away with difference altogether through 'gender blending'. Given this range of views on what constitutes 'woman', there has been an equally wide range of responses by feminists to postmodernist theories of the subject. Whilst some feminist writers see liberation in the dissolution of centred subjectivities, others doubt whether women as a whole can afford the privilege of dissolution. Nancy Harstock, for example, has pointed to the fact that postmodernist theories of the subject came into vogue just at the moment when women were finding a more powerful, collective voice.[40] Women, it is argued, were never constructed as full post-Enlightenment active subjects in the first place, so what use to them can a theory be which deconstructs what they have never experienced?

Here, of course, the resonances with post-colonial literature are very clear. It is perhaps testimony to the imprisoning influence of one or other form of 'difference' that the western feminist literature has taken so long to come round to a recognition of these resonances and their implications. Nancy Harstock, in her discussion of where feminists stand in relation to postmodernist theories of the subject, refers to Albert Memmis's work on the psychology of colonialism. 'Those of us who have been marginalized', she argues, 'enter the discussion from a position analogous to that which the colonized holds in relation to the colonizer'.[41] Diane Fuss, in her defence of essentialism, has also made reference to the literature on colonialism and post-colonial writing.[42]

The relationship between feminist and post-colonial theories must, however, go beyond the indication of resonances and parallel lines of argument for, as many black feminists have pointed out, drawing these parallel lines has the effect of rendering invisible colonial and postcolonial women.[43] For as long as feminism constructs woman as white, and while the 'colonized' and 'black' are constructed as 'male', so black and colonized women slip out of the picture altogether and are effectively silenced. Where this silence has been filled by attempts, on the part of western feminist researchers, to 'recover' the voices of black and colonial women subjects, it has often created yet another exoticized 'Other' as a subject for academic discourse.[44]

That western feminism should have found itself in this situation is, I think, testimony to the power of the representations of the 'Other' which feminism both works within and seeks to undermine.

Colonialism, sexuality and gender

In Caryl Churchill's play *Cloud Nine* the interdependence of discourses on the African and on 'woman' is articulated through the character of Clive, the colonial officer. Clive's identity is totally encompassed by his masculinity, and this in turn is dependent on his ability to subdue both the African population of the district and the members of his family. Both 'woman' and 'Africa' are 'dark continents' for Clive. When a 'native uprising' coincides with his discovery of his wife's adultery, Clive's confidence is seriously threatened. When Clive discovers that his best friend is a homosexual he suffers another blow: 'Rivers will be named after you', he exclaims, 'It's unthinkable.'[45]

The medical discourse on Africa was, as much of the material in this book indicates, highly sexualized. This sexualization operates in two different ways. On the one hand, colonialist discourse on Africa, including medical discourse, was shot through with a male sexual imagery of conquest, penetration and subjugation. This was, of course, gendered imagery, for the colonialist was a male conqueror of 'Africa', a female body, ripe with both pleasure and danger.[46] But in addition to this, medical discourse played another and rather particular role, which was to specify and articulate ideas about African sexuality. Sander Gilman's work, as we have already seen, maps the history of this western discourse on black sexuality and links it with the deep psychological need for projection of 'Otherness'. Blackness and sexuality are, in Gilman's analysis, deeply inextricably intertwined.

In order to 'disturb' the apparent inevitability of this association, we need to look at the different ways in which colonialism sexualized and gendered the 'Other', and at the different representations of the 'Other's' sexuality. But we can also look at the question another way round through examining the ways in which representations of women and of female sexuality were, in nineteenth- and twentieth-century Europe and North America, permeated with images of colonial 'Otherness'.

In her book on nineteenth-century science, Cynthia Russett provides a number of examples of the ways in which anthropological and medical theory (and later, eugenics) constructed both the European child and 'woman' by reference to the 'primitive races'. Knowledge of the 'primitive', in other words, was used to 'make foreign', to construct both the 'child' and the 'woman'. Victorian scientists, argues Russett, needed to fit their data on the difference between the sexes into a wider comparative framework at a time when 'universal laws' were much in favour.[47]

One way in which this universalizing was achieved in the mid to late nineteenth century was through 'recapitulation theory'. Recapitulation theory linked the life history of the individual with the history of the species: 'In its simplest form the concept of recapitulation asserts that every individual organism repeats in its own life history the history of its race, passing through the lower forms of its ancestors on its way to maturity.'[48] Ontogeny and phylogeny, terms that we owe to the architects of recapitulation theory, are therefore directly related: 'Ontogeny recapitulates phylogeny'. Victorian anthropology was, according to Russett, much taken with recapitulation theory.[49] Women, children and 'savages' were said to have much in common. Consequently, this theory brought forward statements not only on the 'childlike' qualities of 'savage races', but also on the 'primitive' qualities of women. The white female skull was supposed, for example, to resemble that of the 'Negro'. The European woman's physiology, like the black man's, preserved primate qualities.[50] As Donna Haraway's work on the history of primatology shows, late twentieth-century science also has a propensity to associate the white woman with the non-human primate through the construction of powerful and highly sexualized images.[51]

Sex specialization and sexual difference became, in the eyes of the Victorian scientists discussed by Russett, a mark of the evolutionary advancement of societies. Differences between the sexes, then, were said to be less marked in 'primitive societies', and this included differences in physical sexual characteristics, as well as in other measures such as brain weight. Writing by physical anthropologists of the mid nineteenth century continually drew parallels between 'woman' and the 'primitive races', and the question of women's role in society became associated with the issue of slavery and its abolition. For physical anthropologists, then, 'the issues of race and sex were intimately related – not two separate problems but two aspects of the same problem'.[52]

Women from the 'primitive races', then, were less differentiated from their men than were women in 'advanced' societies. Sexual differences became more marked as one moved up the evolutionary scale. Sander Gilman's account of the discussions which surrounded the 'exhibiting' of the 'Hottentot Venus' in the nineteenth century gives a rather different perspective on this issue. Here specific attention was given to the 'primitiveness' of the black woman's genitalia, and to her supposedly equally 'primitive' and powerful sexual appetite. The black woman then, according to Gilman, became a signifier of the dangers of female sexuality in general,[53] whilst in the twentieth-century paintings analysed by Ludmilla Jordanova, a black man, rather than a black woman, seems to stand as the signifier of sexual 'Otherness'.[54]

Jordanova describes nineteenth- and twentieth-century scientific discourses as 'mediating' a set of ideas about gender roles and gender differences, and Donna Haraway describes how one scientific specialism, primatology, mediated ideas on nature, culture, race and gender. Jacobus, Keller and Shuttleworth, meanwhile, show how, in the nineteenth and twentieth centuries, the 'feminine body, as the prime site of sexual and/or racial difference in a white, western, political and sexual economy, is particularly the battlefield on which quite other struggles than women's own have been waged'.[55]

The discourses described by these writers are complex and elaborate. Deciding quite what they were primarily concerned with is not an easy task. Clearly, while concerns about sexual difference and gender mediated much of the colonial discussion of 'other races', it was also the case that the scientific and medical discourses generated by colonialism mediated issues of gender, sexuality, production and reproduction in the metropolitan countries.

Colonial discourses on the gender and sexuality of colonial subjects were not, however, monolithic. 'Africa' as an object of conquest in the nineteenth century was, as I have noted, often represented as 'feminine', as synonymous with dark and dangerous female sexuality. But, as conquest turned into colonization, so, I would argue, this picture changed. While Africa 'herself' remained female, her inhabitants were most definitely male. It was the 'maleness' of African sexuality which came to represent 'the African'.[56] This is not, of course, a generalization which holds for the whole of colonial Africa, or for the whole of the colonial period, and therefore must be treated with some caution. There were specific moments when, as in the debate on sexually transmitted diseases (Chapter 6), African female sexuality became an object of discussion in its own right. Christian missionaries were also responsible, through their concern with the family, for elaborating a discourse on the African woman (though woman as mother rather than as sexual object). In general, however, it seems to me that the medical discourse on Africa whilst heavily gendered and sexualized in its language, allows relatively little room for specification of the gender of its subjects. Whilst Orientalism elaborated a notion of the 'femininity' of its subjects,[59] the Africanist discourse bore many more resemblances to that described by Fanon, in which the 'Negro' represents sexual instinct, and is the 'incarnation of a genital potency beyond all moralities and prohibitions'.[58]

While 'Africa' and 'Africans' were sexualized in the European mind, the gendering of African subjects in the colonial discourse was shifting and unstable. In particular, the sexuality of African women only became a subject of distinct interest when it could no longer be contained by African men – when, for instance, women moved to towns and cities as migrants in their own right. The legacy of this very ambivalent colonial attitude to black sexuality is still felt in Britain and elsewhere. In a discussion on the 'Imaging of Black Sexuality', for example, Sunil Gupta describes the legacy of a colonialist discourse which at times described its subjects as 'sexual athletes', and at other times denied them any sexuality at all.[59] June Jordan's poem, 'En Passant' also describes the rendering invisible of the black woman and her sexuality as a result of the white mythology of black male 'sexual athleticism'.[60]

Whilst the medical discourse on Africa was very deeply concerned with sexuality, then, and whilst many of its metaphors were gendered ones, it was less concerned with elaborating on gender differentiation amongst its subjects, and tended therefore to make women invisible. In part this can be explained by the simple fact that it was African men, rather than women, who most often encountered the colonial medical services. These services were, as I have indicated, very thinly spread throughout most of colonial Africa, at least until the post Second World War period, and were concentrated at centres of labour. It was men who were weighed and measured by doctors whose job it was to weed out the unhealthy from the labour force, and although the diseases of industrialization, such as tuberculosis, spread very rapidly amongst women and children in the rural areas, relatively little attention was given to the rural dynamic of these diseases. It was men who, having behaved strangely or violently in an urban area or mining compound, found themselves defined as schizophrenic and confined to a colonial lunatic asylum. African women, by contrast, were said not to have reached the level of self-awareness required to go mad, and in the colonial literature on psychology and psychopathology, the African women represented the happy, 'primitive' state of pre-colonial Africa. In a period of rapid social and economic change, women came to symbolize, in a discourse shared by colonial administrators and many African men, 'tradition' and order.[61] It followed that when they stepped out of, or resisted, this role by becoming migrant workers themselves, they would become the object of a particularly heightened concern over social disintegration. This concern evidenced itself in the colonial medical literature in the inter-war period as a concern with low birth rates, infertility and sexually transmitted diseases – all of which were, to some extent, 'real' medical problems but which were analysed not in terms of poverty and poor living conditions but in terms of female immorality.

In missionary medical discourse, however, African women had always occupied a central position. Of course, the distinction between missionary and state medical services and personnel was often not a clear-cut one. Mission hospitals and dispensaries were frequently funded by colonial governments, and individual doctors and nurses sometimes moved between the two systems. On the issues of maternal and child health, and on 'women's issues', however, the missionary medical discourse has a long, and somewhat distinct, history. It was only rather late in the colonial period that a secularized version of this became evident in government documents and interventions. For Christian missionaries, African women, far from representing the welcome stability of 'tradition', were often the repository of all that was held to be dark and evil in African culture and social practices (see Chapter 3). Women as midwives, as controllers of initiation ceremonies and as central figures in 'fertility cults' and 'traditional' religions, were an early focus of medical missionary concern. Much of this concern was expressed in terms of the 'liberation' of women from what was seen as a position of servitude, but as with many such liberal expressions of concern, it was very double-edged. Medical missionaries made maternal and child health their 'baby', whilst governments quite systematically neglected it. For many African women these interventions were welcome, but they came incorporated in an ideology which represented women primarily as reproducers, which undervalued their productive role and which exalted 'domestication'.

My argument here is that, although colonial medical discourse was often very sexualized and gendered itself, it does not follow from this that it always gendered its subjects in a very direct way. The fact that gender was not always *the* dominant signifier and differentiator in the medical discourse on Africa does not, of course, in any way mean that African women might not have experienced colonialism in a distinct way. It does, however, make the need for a women's account of colonial medicine more acute.

Power and pathologization: how did colonial medical discourse work?

I have already indicated where some of the limitations of a Foucaultian analysis of medical discourse may lie when applied to colonial Africa. The extent to which colonial power set out to 'subjectify' as well as 'objectify' is, I think, open to question still. In the chapters which follow I describe both processes at work, but it is clear that 'objectification' occupies much more ground than 'subjectification'. It was Christianity, rather than colonialism per se, which was most deeply concerned with the latter and with the creation of new identities.

Much recent work on the social history of Africa would tend to support the view that colonialism had a limited impact on cultures and the identities they created. There is now a large and impressive body of work by medical anthropologists and historians on 'medical pluralism' in Africa which reinforces this view.[62] Biomedicine, when it 'landed' in Africa, confronted a wide range of different healing practices, more or less systematized, and often existing side by side. In some parts of Africa, and under certain circumstances, one or other system might have become formalized and closely aligned to political authority – but in general there was relatively little professionalization of the task of healing. Though some of the more politically powerful of these healing systems were dealt a severe blow by the incursions and prohibitions of early colonialism, in general, according to this literature, African healing systems showed themselves to be remarkably resilient and adaptive. Far from being destroyed by the joint assault of colonialism and biomedicine, they tended rather to absorb and internalize, to 'indigenize', those elements of biomedical practice which seemed most effective and most impressive – the most obvious being the injection.

Whilst colonial medical officers regarded this blending of methods to be highly dangerous, for a number of reasons not only connected to people's health, the more recent medical anthropological literature has tended to celebrate the pluralism and diversity of healing systems in Africa. Africans, it seems, have maintained a degree of control over health and healing in their communities which many late-twentieth-century Europeans and North Americans, oppressed and alienated by biomedicine, regard with envy. Modern Africans, according to this literature, have the enormous advantage of not believing in biomedical explanations – they can therefore derive benefit from its more successful operations, whilst escaping the combination of alienation and guilt which it is held to induce in its more vulnerable western subjects. Biomedicine, it seems, offered little in the way of a conceptual challenge to African ideas about health and healing, the continuities in which are more remarkable than the fractures.[63]

There is no space here for a detailed examination of this impressive literature. Many of its conclusions are, I think, highly plausible. Given the limited exposure that most African communities have had to biomedicine, and given its many failures as well as successes in Africa, it seems highly likely that African people would continue to depend, at least for some purposes, on a range of ideas and practices which are readily available. Of course it is not only Africans who remain sceptical about some of the practices and underlying theories of biomedicine, as the great increase in popularity of 'alternative' medicines in Europe and North America testifies. Equally it should be remembered that biomedicine is practised and interpreted by African doctors, nurses, and medical assistants, and as a practice is therefore as 'African' as any other healing system.

Nevertheless, what is evident from these accounts of 'medical pluralism' when placed next to the material presented in this book, is that the power of colonial medicine lay not so much in its direct effects on the bodies of its subjects (though this was sometimes significant) but in its ability to provide a 'naturalized' and pathologized account of those subjects. Biomedicine helped produce a concept of 'the African' and an account of the effects of social and economic change which was plausible and socially relevant to colonial administrators and, at various points, to individual Africans themselves. Though medical knowledge did not mean power in any direct sense, it certainly helped to make some people feel powerful.

The biomedical account of colonialism was not, as I have already indicated, a monolithic one. In the chapters which follow, I have tried to indicate some of the many points at which biomedicine argued with itself. There were always medical officers in Africa who were critics of aspects of colonial rule and colonial ideology, and they frequently made their voices heard. Most often these arguments were around the concept of 'difference'. In the course of many medical debates, as I have already indicated, it became essential to have a view on just how 'different' Africans were, with 'culture' replacing 'race' as a marker of that difference. The extent to which these debates and discussions are imprisoned by the notion of difference is very marked. To this extent, the liberal critique of colonialism did nothing more than reinforce many of its premises.

Whether it is possible to locate real 'resistances' to colonialism through this account of biomedical discourse is perhaps the more important question. I have already implied that the method adopted in this study is not one which readily locates resistance, and that therefore my conclusions on this subject must be very tentative. Apart from the direct resistance which African communities demonstrated to, for instance, enforced vaccination, there were many other positions on a continuum between overt resistance and internalization. An analysis of these positions depends, as I have already outlined, on an interpretation of subjectivities, and how far they were constructed by the colonial experience. Throughout the book, but especially in the later chapters, I try and indicate areas in which the practice of biomedicine may have played a role in the construction of new subjectivities. I also indicate that where this took place, this was not a simple process but one which was fractured by resistance and rejection. Given the limitations of my method and material, I can go no further than to indicate points at which this process of subjectification may have been taking place.

NOTES

1 *Central African Journal of Medicine*, vol. 3, no. 10 (October 1957), p. 431.
2 On the European discourse on Africa see V. Y. Mudimbe, *The Invention of Africa* (Mudimbe, 1988), and on the French Africanist discourse see Miller (1985). Though both of these works are very important, there seems nevertheless to be no equivalent for Africa of Said's study of Orientalism, Said (1978).
3 Gilman (1985).
4 Gilman (1985), p. 18.
5 Gilman (1985), p. 25.
6 On this point see also Jordanova (1989) and Russett (1989).
7 Gilman (1985), p. 107.
8 Terry Eagleton, quoted in Gilman (1985), pp. 25–6.
9 For a social constructionist approach to medicine see Wright and Treacher, eds (1982); Turner (1987). For an extremely useful critique of this approach see Bury (1986). I am indebted to Dr Ray Fitzpatrick for this last reference.
10 For a valuable review of the recent literature on health and healing in Africa see Feierman (1985). On the political economy of health in Africa see Turshen (1984); Packard (1989); *Social Science and Medicine* (1989).
11 For this argument see Turshen (1984), pp. 16–19 and Prins (1989).
12 Comaroff (1982).
13 Comaroff (1982), p. 57.
14 Bury (1986), pp. 140–7.
15 Wright and Treacher (1982): 'Introduction'; Bury (1986).
16 For a critique of the kind of approach I have adopted here see Figlio (1982), pp. 175–6.
17 Packard (1989).
18 Figlio (1982); Jordanova 1989, pp. 2–3; Cooter (1982).
19 Jacobus, Keller and Shuttleworth, eds (1990), p. 2.
20 Many of Foucault's writings are relevant here, though together they form an unstable body of work. There is no sense in which one can 'apply' Foucauldian theory to a set of historical material: Foucault (1976); Foucault (1989); Foucault (1979a); Foucault (1979b); and Foucault (1980).
    Foucault criticism is now a vast academic industry. Amongst this literature I have found the work of Dreyfus and Rabinow (1982) the most illuminating.
21 For Foucault's notion of 'productive power' see the discussion in Dreyfus and Rabinow (1982), pp. 126–42.
22 Michel Foucault in Dreyfus and Rabinow (1982), p. 187.
23 Fraser (1989), p. 26.
24 For a more general critique of the application of 'discourse theory' to

colonial situations see Parry (1987). For its application to South Asian history see O'Hanlon and Washbrook (1990).

25 This point was first made to me by Ann Whitehead. I am indebted to her for this, and many other insights.

26 Harstock (1990), p. 166.

27 Fanon (1986).

28 Fanon (1986), p. 10.

29 Fanon (1986), p. 109.

30 For a postmodernist reinterpretation of Fanon's views on subjectivity see Homi Bhabha's Foreword to the 1986 Pluto Press edition of *Black Skin, White Masks*, Fanon (1986). See also Parry (1987).

31 For the assertion of the importance of other forms of difference, especially those of gender, for colonial people see Spivak (1986).

32 Ashcroft, Griffiths and Tiffin (1989) provides a useful discussion of these debates. See also *Critical Inquiry*, vol. 12, no. 1 (1985), Special issue on race, writing and difference edited by Henry Gates; and Fuss (1989), chapter 5: '"Race" Under Erasure: Poststructuralist Afro-American Literary Theory'.

33 See Ashcroft et al. (1989), chapter 5 for a discussion of work by Spivak, Bhabha, Said.

34 Lyotard (1984). For a discussion of these theories and various feminist responses to them see Fraser and Nicholson, in Nicholson, ed. (1990).

35 Memmi (1990, first published 1957).

36 Ashcroft et al. (1989), pp. 172–3.

37 See note 30 and Spivak (1987).

38 See Riley (1988); Nicholson, ed. (1990); Fraser (1989); Fuss (1989).

39 Riley (1988), p. 112.

40 Harstock (1987).

41 Harstock (1987), p. 160.

42 Fuss (1989).

43 Hooks (1984).

44 See the critique by Mohanty (1988); Minh-ha (1989).

45 Churchill (1989), p. 41. Thanks to Jen Hornsby for introducing me to this play.

46 Stott (1989).

47 Russett (1989), p. 49.

48 Russett (1989), p. 50.

49 See also Gould (1977).

50 Russett (1989), p. 56. See also Comaroff (1990).

51 Haraway (1989).

52 Russett (1989), p. 28.

53 Gilman (1985), p. 90.

54 Jordanova (1989), p. 109.

55 Jacobus et al. (1990), p. 2.

56 Luise White has argued something similar in her study of masculinity in colonial Kenya: White (1990).

57 Said (1978), de Groot (1989).

58 Fanon (1986), p. 177.

59 Manuel, Fani-Koyode and Gupta (1989), p. 45.

60 Jordan (1989), p. 97.
61 See papers in Whitehead and Vaughan (forthcoming, 1991).
62 See Feierman (1985) for a discussion of this literature; also Prins (1989).
    For an extremely good example of the study of medical pluralism in
    Africa, see Janzen's study of Lower Zaire, Janzen (1978).
63 Prins (1989).

2 Rats' Tails and Trypanosomes: Nature and Culture in Early Colonial Medicine

On Sunday 18 September 1910, Dr Hugh Stannus, Medical Officer in Zomba, Nyasaland, sat down to write his regular letter to his sister in England. He wrote of his work:

As usual I am torn in different directions with many ideas being never content with any one thing. My native hospital is one of my chief delights and my notes on Native Diseases take a lot of time. I am always running about to catch some abnormality or removing something to be pickled or getting a photo of some oddity though my anthropological measurements and notes are getting rather left alone. Now there is some doubt whether we have the same sleeping sickness Trepanosome as in Uganda and I want in the next few weeks to get some work done on the rats to help settle the point though I am so handicapped I am afraid it will come to nothing.[1]

Enclosed in the letter was the timetable of work he had followed that day:

Sunday 18th September
7.45 three notes
7.50 breakfast
8.15 to office for daily reports
8.25 Native Hospital. Operate on big abscess of leg. Saw 20 other cases. Reported on a prisoner from an out-station, took photo of a deformity.
9.00 segregation hospital – took blood of sleeping sickness case.
9.15 European hospital
9.45 Dr Hearsey and a lady patient
10.00 a man with a dog – took its blood and microscoped it.
10.15–12.15 microscoped blood various

12.30 ordered my boy to produce 3 rats
12.45 lunch
1.45 rats produced
2–4 microscoped bloods – cow, rats, sleeping sickness etc.
4.00 tea
5.00 inoculated rat from sleeping sickness patient
5.30–6.00 reading room
6.00 fed rats
6.15 visited European people
6.45–7.30 developed photographs
7.30 dinner
8.00 I look at a pile of literature and wonder when it will get read.
Cigarette.

This somewhat extraordinary document inscribes the practices and concerns of 'tropical medicine' in Africa at the beginning of this century. Like many of his colleagues, Stannus had first arrived in Africa as a military doctor. From 1905 to 1910 he was medical officer to the King's African Rifles and based at Fort Johnston on Lake Nyasa. During these early years he spent his time 'investigating the endemic diseases of man and animals in the area, but also engaged in ethnological studies'.

His letters of this period reveal a wide range of interests and activities. In April 1906, for example, he had been placed under orders to go and investigate the 'causes of mortality among cattles two days from here'. In August 1906 he wrote of his efforts to grow strawberries, the presence of a predatory lion, and of nursing a European blackwater fever patient. In December 1906 he wrote at length about his hunting exploits. In June 1907 he was examining prospective labour migrants, and in July he was investigating sleeping sickness and thinking of buying a mule which he had had in quarantine for the 'tsetse fly-disease'.

What we might think of as straightforwardly 'medical' activities did not feature prominently in Stannus's work. He was obliged to minister to the British population of Fort Johnston at a time when European mortality rates were still very high in this part of Africa, but spent more of his time engaged in research. Some of this research, such as that into the 'tsetse-fly disease' was carried out on the direct instructions of the colonial administration, but the rest was motivated by Stannus's own curiosity and interests.

From the perspective of late-twentieth-century medicine with all its specialisms, Stannus's publication list from this period, like his Sunday timetable, is extraordinarily all-encompassing.

In 1910 he published a paper on 'Native Paintings in Nyasaland', another (in the anthropological journal, *Man*) on 'Alphabet Boards', and another entitled 'Notes on British Central Africa Natives'. In the

Figure 1 Dr Hugh Stannus at his microscope.

same year he published a paper on 'Piroplasmesis in Cattle', and continued to produce a 'Sleeping Sickness Diary'. During this time he had also been investigating the problem of pellagra which he had identified amongst prisoners in Zomba prison. He published a paper on this in 1911, and another in 1913, both in the *Transactions of the Royal Society for Tropical Medicine and Hygiene*. In 1911 he also published a paper on 'Human Trypanosomiasis in Nyasaland', another on 'Ovarian Cysts in an African women', and another (in the *Journal de la Salpetrière*) on 'Micromelio'. In the same period up to the First World War, he wrote on yaws, 'jigger disease', on 'Pre-Bantu Inhabitants of Central Africa', on 'Tribal Tattoos in Nyasaland', on 'Angoni Smelting Furnaces', on 'Blackwater Fever Suppression', on the 'Life Span of Negroes', on the 'Causes of Hypertrophy of the Lower Limbs', on 'Congenital Anomalies in Africans', and on 'Anomalies of Pigmentation – Albinism'. In 1922, as an outcome of this pre-war work, he published his major ethnological piece, 'The Wayao'.

Stannus was a great enthusiast for the modern aid to research – photography – and his photograph albums from this period also capture the breadth of his interests. One is the common tropical medic's catalogue of horrors, from elephantiasis of the scrotum to advanced cases of leprosy and yaws. Another features photographs

Figure 2   Photograph from Hugh Stannus's collection.

of cases of albinism, another shows women with lip plugs and
others with 'tribal tattoos'. Yet another is a collection of full-frontal
photographs of naked or near naked Africans, many of them young
and with what (in view of Stannus's ethnological interests) at first
look like more 'tribal tattoos' but which, on closer inspection, reveal
themselves to be chalk markings indicating the position and size of
the spleen. In addition there are more naturalistically posed photographs of village scenes and activities.

Though interpreting these visual images is hazardous, there are a
few things which can be said about Stannus's photograph albums.
Firstly, they expose the relentless empiricism of the early tropical
doctor. Everything that Stannus saw or touched in his time in
Nyasaland was photographed, catalogued and labelled, in the belief
that scientific knowledge would thereby be advanced. Secondly, the
Africans of Nyasaland are presented in these photographs as objects
of study and classification, like any other feature of the 'natural'

environment – head shapes, hair styles, and length of torso are all documented here.

The picture that emerges of Stannus's work and views is a complex one. The scientific objectification of the African subject is clear, as are the evolutionist premises of his work. Stannus was a product of a specific intellectual environment, and his attention to anthropometry is indicative of the concern with 'racial' origins and development which underpinned the biology and anthropology of the turn of the century.[2] But 'race', for Stannus, was inseparable from 'environment'. His interest in the 'racial' characteristics of Africans, then, was underpinned by Darwinian assumptions about adaptation.

The end of the nineteenth century saw a 'revolution' in biological science and medicine shaped by the discoveries of Pasteur and Koch. The discovery by bacteriologists of specific causal external agents of disease is widely regarded as a watershed in medical science. Germ theory focused the medical and biological gaze on the individual, on individual pathology and the behaviour of specific micro-organisms. As many writers have pointed out, the role accorded to the environment in this new theory of disease causation diminished as the focus on individual pathology increased. The discipline of epidemiology blossomed, but its unit of study was not the society but the individual, epidemics being described in terms of aggregations of individual pathologies. Meredith Turshen, in her work on the political ecology of health in Tanzania, sees the late-nineteenth-century bacteriological revolution as the source of many of the ills of colonial and post-colonial Tanzania and reflects radical critiques of western medical science more generally.[3] The failures, inadequacies and neglect of public health policies are attributed to the biological blinkers of the medical establishment. Epidemiologists may possess large amounts of information and analyse it using sophisticated statistical techniques but, say the critics, so long as they continue to view society as an 'aggregation of self-contained individuals', and to neglect completely the realm of social and economic relations, then epidemiology will always fail to address the real causes of much ill-health. The 'natural history of disease' in Africa is, argues Turshen, profoundly 'unnatural'; disease patterns of the twentieth century cannot be abstracted from the changes wrought by capitalism and colonialism in the modes of production and social reproduction.

The new medical science, whilst ill-equipped conceptually to deal with the social reality of twentieth-century Africa, did not fail to feed off Africa as a diseased environment for its research. 'Discovery' was what this science was about and the reputations of a new group of professionals – the tropical medical men – were at stake. Africa was a prime site for investigation of those insect-borne diseases which were misleadingly thought to be typically 'tropical', and great expectations were invested in the great medical expeditions of the turn of the century.[4] The new specialism of tropical medicine was, as Michael Worboys has shown, closer to being a branch of biology than a branch of medicine.[5] Tropical medicine was a postgraduate specialism as the turn of the century, and an attractive one for ambitious scientific medics. According to Worboys, an astonishing 20 per cent of British medical graduates then went on to practise in tropical and sub-tropical climates, most of them with the armed forces. Success in this new field depended as much on a knowledge of and interest in ecology and taxonomy as it did in human pathology. It was the triad of agent/host/environment which was seen to hold the key to the understanding of the diseases of Africa – sleeping sickness, malaria, yellow fever. This emphasis on understanding the environment gave some of the early tropical medics the all-encompassing interests seen in the person and career of Stannus and implies something of a qualification to the general characterization of post-1890s medicine as being obsessed with individual pathology. If the biological model was, as Turshen argues, a profoundly individualistic one, then this model was never fully applied to the medical problems of Africa and Africans.

To begin with, a pre-Pasteurian, holistic and sanitarian view of disease was not completely or immediately eliminated by the more reductionist, curative and laboratory-based school.[6] Worboys sees the triumph of the latter over the former in the field of tropical medicine as being epitomized by the differences and disputes between two famous 'pioneers' of tropical medicine, Manson and Ross. Though both were equally involved in the very individualistic pursuit of pathogens and the fame resulting from their discovery, their policy prescriptions were very different. Ross was a sanitarian at heart, with a strong belief in public health measures. This was, as we now know from the work of McKeown and others, a well-founded belief, for the sanitary measures of the early to mid nineteenth century had lowered mortality rates in industrial Britain (and amongst Europeans on the west coast of Africa) long before germ theory was proclaimed and the microscopes got to work.[7]

Notions of the environment and its control, born in late-eighteenth-century Europe, continued to exert an influence over the late-nineteenth and early-twentieth-century European mind. This view of the environment has been characterized by Ludmilla Jordanova:

a cluster of variables which acted upon organisms and were responsible for many of their characteristics. An understanding of human
beings in sickness and in health was to be based on a large number of
powerful environmental factors; climate, diet, housing, work, family
situation, geography and atmosphere. This notion of environment
could be split into two. First there were variables such as custom and
government which were human creations and were, at least in
principle, amenable to change. Second, there were parameters such as
climate, meteorology in general, geographical features such as rivers
and mountains, which were in the province of immutable natural laws
and proved more challenging to human power. In the first case environment denoted culture, in the second, nature.[8]

It was the tension and perceived struggle between 'nature' and
'culture' which, Jordanova tells us, dominated much medical discussion of the late eighteenth and nineteenth centuries. In the course
of this period the notion of culture had undergone a marked
change and had began to denote a state of civilization, identified
in particular with science, technology and the capacity for abstract
thought. Jordanova traces the effects of this shift on stereotypes of
women. Nature and culture become opposing forces in this ideo-
logical schema, and they are gendered concepts, women being
identified with nature, men with culture.

In the observations of early colonial medics like Stannus, however, there are strong elements of the early tradition of perceptions
of the environment, in which the separation of 'nature' and 'culture'
was less marked, and of an earlier tradition of medical science. By
the end of the First World War, the vestiges of this tradition had
been eroded by two developments. In the first place, the holistic
view of the sanitarian had been marginalized and its place taken by
the medical research 'campaign' and the relentless pursuit of the
pathogen. Secondly, 'culture' and the notion of cultural difference
had become reified, separated from 'nature' and conceived of as a
causal factor in disease. Medical research and practice in colonial
Africa drew on and investigated 'nature' in the form of the
pathogen, and 'culture' in the form of African cultural practices.

Stannus viewed African cultures as integral to a larger environment. Both the physical and cultural attributes of the Africans of
Nyasaland were, for Stannus, features of a larger landscape. He
approached the study of hair styles, lip plugs and basket-making in
much the same way as he approached the study of yaws, pellagra
and sleeping sickness. The effect of his classifications, measurements and photographs was, of course, to objectify, but this was
objectification without explicit reference to any supposed inferiority

on the part of his objects of study. Africans, in Stannus's view, were 'different', but this difference was to be explained by the nature of the environment they lived in, and could be investigated empirically as part of a wider study of that environment.

Stannus's holistic perception of disease and its causation did not bear much direct relation to medical practice in this early colonial period. Most early colonial doctors were attached either to Christian missions or to the military. The practices of mission medicine were to some extent distinct and are the subject of Chapter 3. The military doctors and a handful of government medical officers mostly treated the European sick in their stations, and performed very few curative services for Africans. Stannus's enthusiasm for his 'native hospital' and his attempts to provide some curative services for Africans were unusual at this time. When not treating European military and civilian patients, most doctors were involved in 'campaigns' of various sorts.

There were two sorts of early colonial medical 'campaign'. One was the large research expedition such as those which were conducted in pursuit of the cause of sleeping sickness; the other was the more direct attempt to prevent the spread of epidemic disease such as smallpox and plague.[9]

A contemporary of Stannus's in Nyasaland was Dr J. B. Davey, who had, as a young doctor, participated in the first type of 'campaign', the pursuit of the pathogen.[10] Trained at the Middlesex Hospital, he had served as a Civil Surgeon in the South African War of 1901–2, and had in 1902 been appointed by the Foreign Office as a medical officer in British Central Africa (later Nyasaland). During 1910–11 he worked with the Royal Society's Sleeping Sickness Commission, led by David Bruce. This, like many other sleeping sickness research expeditions in Africa, was a fraught affair, torn apart by the personal ambitions of its participants. Bruce, one of the many tropical medical men of this period to feel cheated of the recognition he felt he had earned, behaved imperiously, fought with his collaborators, and regularly flogged his African assistants.[11] Davey was a very junior member of the expedition and his desultory diary entries reveal that he spent most of this period catching, or more often not catching, tsetse flies on the shores of Lake Nyasa. Sleeping sickness research for Davey meant spending many hours scouring the lake shore with a net, aided by African assistants.

Of 15 January 1910 Davey wrote: 'After lunch I wandered about amongst the palms near the village. Thinking I heard tsetse I got the net and a boy and spent about an hour and a half catching only one *G. fusca* . . .' A similarly frustrating day was 18 January: 'Alifeya (houseboy and fly catcher) went around the village looking for *Glossina*. A boatman was however bitten on the hand by a *G. fusca* which he caught right amongst the huts as he was passing water against some bushes. This was about 4 pm. I then spent some time trying to find more without success.' Amongst his seniors in the world of tropical medicine, there was real excitement in the cut-throat pursuit of the 'secret' of sleeping sickness. For Davey, the only relief from the frustrating task of fly-catching was in a more conventional chase: 'After tea went out with man from village to dambo country to north-east of the village and got a male waterbuck brought down with one shot too.'[12]

The structure of these research expeditions was rigidly hierarchical and their focus narrow. At this stage in sleeping sickness research the complex interaction of people, animals, pathogen and environment which John Ford later found to characterize the disease[13] was obscured by a narrowly biologistic focus on identification of the pathogen, a focus just broadened sufficiently to take into view the insect vector. To this extent the sleeping sickness enquiries conformed to the picture painted by Turshen and others of medical science and its inability to address the larger 'political ecology' of disease. Though insects feature heavily in Davey's diaries, the human inhabitants of the shores of Lake Nyasa feature only as the 'boys' who are treated like extensions of the nets which they carry.

Sleeping sickness research represented the very biologistic end of 'tropical medicine' as described by Worboys, its leading figures being closer in their interests to parasitology and taxonomy than to medicine as more generally conceived and practised at this time. Tropical medical research of the Manson school was, as Worboys says, mission-oriented, and pathogen-obsessed. Africa was a laboratory in which the possibilities of the new bacteriology could be explored in a challenging way.[14] Africa was a place in which scientific reputations could be made. In the glamour of the early century research 'chase' in tropical Africa, the sanitarians like Ross lost out, as did the eighteenth-century holistic view of the environment, as held by Stannus and others like him. But we should not exaggerate the success and influence of the biologists, or imagine that public health issues were completely drowned out, for the other side of tropical medicine was represented by the 'great campaigns' against epidemic disease.

In the first half of the twentieth century any contact which the majority of Africans had with colonial medicine was likely to have been in the form of a 'great campaign'. Epidemics of smallpox, of meningitis, of plague, and sleeping sickness posed a constant threat to the economic (and political) viability of the early colonial state. The rise of tropical medical research was an outcome not merely of the elevation of germ theory, but of the continuing threat posed by epidemic disease to the entire colonial enterprise. As in India, so in

Africa, early medical provision was entirely oriented towards protecting the lives of the continent's new European inhabitants, particularly soldiers.[15] Philip Curtin has shown how deeply the nineteenth-century European perception of the west coast of Africa, and of the people of West Africa, was moulded by the experience of very high European mortality.[16] The representation of Africa as a place of disease, danger and death was one which survived the reductions in European mortality effected by sanitarian policies of the mid-century, and later advances in curative medicine.

In late-nineteenth- and early-twentieth-century East and Central Africa Europeans still perceived of themselves as grappling with a wild and uncontrolled environment, of which Africans were an integral part. In part this was an outcome of the extension of the separation of 'nature' and 'culture' described by Jordanova as characterizing the development of nineteenth-century European thought. The 'wild', whether in the form of the moorland, 'woman', or African wildlife was simultaneously romanticized and feared in European culture of the late nineteenth century. Recent work on colonial ecological history, and on the imperial hunting cult, has emphasized the process by which European male colonialists perceived and constructed 'Africa' and the African environment through this peculiar cultural lens, and has pointed to the European obsession with control.[17] The human and animal diseases of Africa were, of course, seen as integral to this environment waiting to be conquered and controlled, and the observations of early colonial medical men contributed to this larger European perception of the Africa as a continent waiting to be tamed.

But early colonial concerns over epidemic disease were not simply the product of the nineteenth-century hunting mentality which sought to capture and control, for it now appears that the early twentieth century in much of East and Central Africa was a peculiarly unhealthy time. The extent to which this unhealthiness marked a radical break from the period immediately preceding colonial rule is still a matter for debate, as are the demographic consequences of disease patterns of the late nineteenth and early twentieth centuries.[18] In some areas the mid to late nineteenth century had taken, through the war and social disruption accompanying the slave trade, and the spread of epidemic disease, a great toll on the health of African communities. In other places this pattern was less marked. But, in either case, colonial conquest facilitated the spread of epidemic diseases in a number of related ways.

In the first place, the mobility of the population increased enormously. Colonial states relied heavily on armies of human porters to move goods from one place to another. In some territories the movement of men as labour migrants began early in the colonial period. Some migrated to the industrial centres of southern Africa, bringing back with them the new diseases of industrialization, including tuberculosis and venereally transmitted syphilis, and facilitating the spread of other diseases. Secondly, the political and social disruption of the colonial conquest contributed, in some places, to the disruption of a complex set of beliefs and practices which had constituted a 'public health' system in pre-colonial African societies.[19] Thirdly, the colonial intrusion brought about the introduction of diseases which were new to most African societies. New diseases, such as measles, could sweep through whole regions, causing high mortality. Not only was there no immunity to these diseases but as new diseases their transmission was little understood and indigenous mechanisms of control were therefore lacking.

Early colonial administrations in this region therefore frequently faced a major epidemic of one sort or another. Most often the fear was that European populations would be affected. Africans were regarded as a 'reservoir' of disease and, as Maynard Swanson has demonstrated for the case of plague in South Africa, this often provided a medical rationale for racial segregation.[20] Settler economies were, of course, much more prone to this particular formulation than were the peasant-based economies of Uganda and Tanganyika, where the economic consequences of depletion of the African producing population was a focus of another kind of concern. In either case, there were only scant resources at the disposal of the colonial state to deal with the problem of epidemic disease. This was not, at this stage, because of the triumph of the 'individual pathology' model of disease and a resulting bias towards curative medicine. Rather it was because the early colonial state was generally impoverished, and in any case did not conceive of its role as providing health (or education) services on any scale, except to white minorities. The problem of epidemic disease threw this issue into relief for, though epidemics affected the poor most severely, they also showed an alarming tendency to cross race and class barriers. If one was going to protect the health of the European population, then the health status of Africans would have to be addressed, at least in a minimal way.

Far from being obsessed with curative medicine, the early colonial medical departments were taken up with prevention – more particularly with preventing the spread of disease from the African to the European. This did not mean that any enlightened and widespread public health system was instituted in British East and Central Africa. Rather, the public health of these territories was addressed piecemeal, through sporadic, militaristic 'campaigns' to prevent or treat one epidemic disease or another. In these 'campaigns' Africans were conceived of as an undifferentiated mass, part of a dangerous environment which needed to be controlled and contained. Prior to the elevation of the idea of 'cultural difference' in the inter-war period, there was a heavy strand of environmentalism, and even of 'political economy' in the medical discourse on African disease problems, and this was evident in the practice of some of the 'great campaigns' against epidemic disease of this period.

C. J. Baker was one of those early colonial doctors who had first arrived on African soil as a Civil Surgeon to the British forces during the Boer War, and then worked his way north.[21] In 1908 he supervised the running of a sleeping sickness camp in the West Nile district of Uganda, and by 1912 he was in Kampala and expressing concern over lack of sanitation in the town. In 1920 a serious epidemic of plague broke out in Kampala and Baker was in charge of an investigation into its causes, as well as directing measures for its control. His research uncovered a complex interaction of economic and social factors in the causation of the epidemic.

He began by investigating the rat population of Uganda and questioned local people about the species of rat to be found there. There were three species well known locally, and a fourth which people said was a new species in the area and which they associated with the rise of the cotton industry and the erection of ginneries. Baker became convinced that the spread of rats and of the plague had some connection with the cotton industry. He found the connection in the world market for cotton: 'The recent slump in the cotton trade caused the natives to store their cotton in their houses for months in the hope of obtaining a rise in the market price, and this cotton proved a great attraction to the rats . . .' This was not the whole story, however, for the differential incidence of the disease in different parts of Uganda could not simply be explained by the cotton industry – previous attempt to eradicate local rats had left some areas less protected than others: 'If the highly susceptible black rat invades such an area it will rapidly multiply, as it will have no competition to contend with, and eventually pick up the dormant infection from the surviving local rats and thus start epizootic plague.'[22] The causes of the epizootic were several, then. Firstly, a new species of rat had been introduced to Uganda, it was thought from the coast and via the railway. This species possessed little immunity to the disease, which was carried by rat fleas. Secondly, this susceptible rat species had multiplied rapidly in some areas owing to previous public health drives which had reduced the populations of indigenous, and more disease-resistant, rats. Thirdly, the cotton industry, and the economic slump, had combined to create conditions favourable for the breeding of these rats.

Understanding the epizootic was one thing, controlling the human epidemic quite another. At this time Baker was in correspondence with Andrew Balfour, Director of the Wellcome Bureau for Scientific Research and a great campaigner on tropical 'hygiene'. On hearing from Baker of the plague epidemic in Uganda, Balfour complained that this was yet another result of the colonial neglect of the 'sanitation' issue. He had been 'hammering away' for years, he wrote, at the need to appoint more British-trained sanitary inspectors in the colonies, but 'the Treasury seems always to be a stumbling block'.

In fact, as Baker has shown, the causes of the epidemic could only be called 'sanitary' in the wide, nineteenth-century sense of the word. The rest of their correspondence on the subject was highly technical, including recipes for rat varnish, and advice on the 'bird lime' method of rat destruction.

If Baker's understanding of the disease was sophisticated, the methods at his disposal for dealing with the immediate crisis were crude. He listed the following as preventive measures: the burning of infected houses (or disinfection in the case of brick-built houses in towns), the isolation of the sick, the segregation of contacts, inoculation of the population with Haffkine's prophylactic, distribution of information in the vernacular, and rat destruction.

Baker was apprehensive about enforcing what he feared would be unpopular measures on the African population. Inoculation proved popular, however, and a total of 57,016 inoculations were performed during the epidemic. The wholesale movement of people and the destruction of their houses, however, were, as Baker knew, likely to be viewed as highly provocative measures.

In Kamuli Baker held a conference with the District Commissioner and chiefs and urged them to organize a rat destruction campaign. But when he returned three weeks later he found that the epidemic had taken a firm hold over an area 25 miles in diameter, and that the death rate was increasing steadily. Segregating the infected population seemed to Baker to be totally impracticable, and it was impossible to keep control over contacts. The only remedy appeared to be total evacuation, 'but at first I hesitated to advocate such a drastic measure because I anticipated opposition from the inhabitants (in which I was wrong) and because if the people were removed to a distance famine might complicate matters'.

Despite fears of opposition, Baker did manage to remove people from the most heavily infected group of houses. The results of this evacuation were, apparently, very quickly seen in a fall in the death rate, such that 'it was possible to demonstrate to the Chiefs and people the necessity of applying the measure to the whole infected area'.

Meanwhile 'war' was waged on the rats. The rat destruction campaigns of early colonial Africa presented a bizarre spectacle. In

Kampala Baker addressed the European population on the necessity for organizing rat destruction campaigns. If the right words had to be found to persuade chiefs that their people should be moved, their houses destroyed and funerals suspended, so the right words had also to be found to persuade the European inhabitants of Kampala that rat destruction was not only necessary, but could also be fun. Baker appealed to the imperial hunting instincts of the male European population. Rat destruction drives could, he suggested, be organized like hunting parties, with a sweepstake thrown in. They would also be organized in such a way as would express the hierarchies of colonial rule:

> I suggest that we should get up a rat-catching sweep – I leave the details to you – whereby each European should write up say Rs5/-, take charge of a fixed number of men as rat hounds (if he can employ dogs as well so much the better) and see how many rats he can bring to me in a week, the winner of course to take the pool ... You will find it is not as exciting as Big game but not bad fun all the same and you will certainly be doing good to the community at large.

Snapshots of the Kampala rat destruction campaign show Baker and other officials proudly surveying piles of rat tails arranged to form the letters R A T S.

Rat destruction was a feature of anti-plague measures elsewhere in colonial Africa. James Brown has described the anti-plague measures undertaken in Zongo, Ashanti during the 1920s.[23] In Zongo large numbers of rat traps were set every day, and twopence offered for every rat brought to the authorities. Slogans with the message 'Kill Rats and Stop Plague' were whitewashed on buildings throughout the town. During the 1919 outbreak of plague in the north of Nyasaland, payment was also made to Africans for the destruction of rats. This made the campaign relatively popular amongst local people, or at least amongst small boys, who found it surprisingly profitable, as one medical officer reported:

> It is not, I think, realised how easily money paid for dead rats is earned by natives ... Trapping is carried out by small boys, and to some extent by women, who day after day troop in with their catches and at the end of the month must reap a reward exceeding far their wildest dreams of wealth. When payments were made in October for a period extending over three months it was a common sight to see a small boy of about 10 years of age receiving as much as 16/- to 25/-, the rate of pay of an ordinary labourer in this district being 4/- to 6/- per month.[24]

Here, as elsewhere, the plague epidemic highlighted the absence of any real public health system, and the need for an improvement in living conditions if epidemic disease was to be controlled.[25]

Many officials, both medical and administrative, understood that the real causes of epidemics lay in the major economic changes taking place in rural Africa. In northern Nyasaland the epidemic was most widespread in areas where people had grown a surplus of food for sale which was inadequately stored in houses and grain-bins, attracting large numbers of rats. Medics like Baker were not obsessivly 'bacteriological' in their outlook. Rather they were aware of the complexity of the production of the epidemics they had to deal with. Neither were they, like many of their successors, prone to attributing blame by alluding to predisposing 'cultural' factors. Rather, they regarded the problems of public health in colonial Africa to be much the same as those experienced in Victorian Britain and amenable to the same 'sanitary' solutions.

When it came to practice, however, the military type of campaign was the only model available, and in the colonial context such campaigns were liable be read as aggressive expressions of colonial power. Public health measures were, by definition, administrative as much as medical in their presentation. In colonial Africa what this meant in practice was that the medical officer became indistinguishable from the administrator in the eyes of the African community. There could be no convincing pretence of neutrality and, as Baker and others knew, this made the job of persuading people that it was in their interest to have their houses burnt and their crops destroyed all the more difficult. This was particularly so in many areas where the early colonial period was marked by the periodic raiding and burning of villages in tax-collecting drives and it may have been enhanced by the experience of the First World War when again the colonial state drafted thousands of Africans into its employ as porters and soldiers.

This was not always a straightforward encounter between the colonizer and the colonized, however. The agents of public health encountered by most villagers were not the white medical officers (of whom there were very few), or even the white administrators (though these did make an appearance when a crisis occurred) but rather African agents of the colonial sanitary state.

In early colonial Nyasaland 'smallpox police' were employed to tour the villages and enforce vaccination. They did not have an easy task in persuading people that vaccination was beneficial, or that it was more effective than their own systems of variolation. During the 1919 epidemic, the entire system of compulsory vaccination was called into question by the smallpox police themselves who were finding it impossible to prevent widespread evasion. Smallpox cases were not reported, and women hid their babies and children when the smallpox police were in their area. The task of these vaccinators was not helped by the fact that the vaccine with which they were provided was frequently inert by the time they came to administer it, and this had been particularly the case during the First World War. In general it was a mild form of smallpox which affected Nyasaland, and mortality was usually low. Vaccination, on the other hand, was often inexpertly administered and painful, and people complained that they could not hoe their fields for weeks afterwards.[26]

Most administrators felt that it would be easier, and less provocative, to use village headmen to control smallpox epidemics – a system which was to be further elaborated with Indirect Rule in the 1930s. The Resident at Chinteche, for instance, wrote that smallpox police had never been employed in that district, and argued, in the strange language of public health, that 'these people are quite capable of running a smallpox epidemic and looking after it well'.[27] The British colonial system of 'running epidemics' was characterized by this devolution of responsibility on to village headmen and chiefs, and the employment of African vaccinators. To a large extent control over these measures fell into the hands of the administrators, to whom the village headmen reported directly, rather than to the medical department and its officials. One District Commissioner in Northern Nyasaland in the 1930s made a point of vaccinating people himself.[28] One can only speculate as to how people received this direct exercise of colonial 'bio-power', and the association between political and medical control which it implied.

Medical officers in Nyasaland recognized that many of the real difficulties of controlling smallpox lay in the mobility of the population, and in the inefficacy of vaccination. In the 1929 epidemic, Sub-Assistant Surgeon Chetan Dev reported that in Dowa less than 10 per cent of the vaccinations performed had been successful. Arm to arm vaccination was almost universally a failure, and, as this was a tsetse area, there was no possibility of cultivating lymph in cows.[29] Here, as in Kasungu district, the Sub-Assistant Surgeon reported that labour migrants, making their way on foot from Southern Rhodesia through Mozambique, were spreading the disease:

> patients have been discovered walking with active smallpox from Kalindawulu's section in Portuguese East Africa to their respective villages in Kasungu district following the Fort Johnston–Kasungu road ... the immigrants are mostly from the Southern Rhodesia mines ... While suffering themselves they had not reported to the headmen or other authority but managed to work their way on to their villages

until discovered concealing the disease by following unfrequented ways during the day and calling in for food during the night.

The long-distance mobility of the male population probably meant that the scale of smallpox epidemics increased at this time, and made control all the more difficult.[30] Medical officers were aware that the problem was not likely to have a strictly medical solution, and their inability to deal effectively with smallpox was still evident in the late 1940s when an epidemic of a severe strain of the disease claimed thousands of lives.[31]

Smallpox, like plague, achieved epidemic proportions through changes in the political economy of this period. Though some control was effected through medical technique – inoculation against plague, for example, was an important feature of control of the disease – in general such means were bound to be ineffective without massive investment, and maybe not even then. The increased mobility of African people and the poor conditions in which they worked were, of course, the real problems to be grappled with. Unable to address the underlying problems of ill-health and susceptibility to epidemic disease, medical departments continued to respond to sporadic crisis through sporadic campaign. One can only feel sympathy for medical orderlies and vaccinators like Mr Sichimata who were sent to the 'front line' of the public health 'battle' inadequately equipped:

> I came alone to one village of Nyasaland [he wrote in 1936], I give them vaccination, 19 men and 15 women, and therefore I arrives at Dambo village, Northern Rhodesia, and asked him if they the Nyasaland people they infection for smallpox here and Dambo answer me said here my village have no smallpox and I say better bring all peoples nearby to me I want to see them how they are, and to give vaccination to their arms, and he say, We do not want your medicine because the medicine makes sores suffer much and again he said some year ago we was done that medicine and smallpox had comes in 1932 it was touched all of us and some of us has been death from smallpox, therefore we do not want again you better go off. Surely I left that Dambo village, I getting Mutelewa village ... My heart have been change the mind and I live in the village with the people of Nyasaland is very good peoples much willing the medicine not the Northern Rhodesian peoples and myself had been suffering from headache, and coughing and the pump of bicycle has been lost ...[32]

By the 1930s, however, the whole place of public health in the colonial medical system, and the theories of health which underlay it, were quite substantially changed from Stannus's time. A number of elements combined to produce this shift. Firstly, with advances in curative medicine, more of the (gradually increasing) colonial government resources for health were being spent on curative services.[33] Until the post-war period access to such state-run services remained largely limited to urban dwellers, but mission-sponsored medical services had created a demand amongst rural Africans. In particular the spectacular success of chemical treatments for yaws created a vocal demand for 'injections' of all sorts. This increasing use and popularity of the technical, curative end of western medicine was combined, however, with a shift in the colonial medical discourse away from the wide environmentalist public health theories of those like Stannus, towards a reification of the idea of cultural difference. This was, of course, part of a much wider shift in colonial discourse which incorporated a shift from emphasis on 'racial' difference to a 'liberal' cultural relativist position. Stannus's concern with physical 'types' and their relationship to environment was replaced with a concern with cultural difference. This focus displaced attention from the larger environmental and economic causes of disease and towards the idea that Africans were differentially susceptible to certain diseases on account of their cultural practices. It tended towards the attribution of blame. In Britain this shift in medical discourse had taken place at the beginning of the century and was largely focused on individual pathology and individual responsibility.[34] In colonial Africa it took a different form, focusing not on the individual but on the 'tribal' collectivity. Susceptibility to disease in Africans, then, was defined not through an analysis of the conditions under which they lived and worked, or through notions of individual lifestyle and responsibility (though missionary medicine stressed exactly this), but rather through the idea that the cultural practices of different ethnic groups disposed them to various disease patterns.

This was not a uniform process, nor was it a complete break with the early colonial period. An emphasis on cultural rather than 'racial' difference had, of course, been around in anthropology since early in the century: it did not suddenly appear in the 1930s.[35] There were continuities between the concern of someone like Stannus to document not only physical 'types' but differences in material culture, and the later concerns of cultural anthropology which found their way into medical discourse. But a shift is nevertheless clear, and it had an impact on medical practice in colonial Africa. This now became much more biologistic in orientation and began, at this period, to approximate to the picture of western medicine offered by critics such as Turshen. But the increasingly technical appearance of biomedicine went hand in hand with an elevation of the notion of cultural difference, replacing 'race' and environment as a central determinant of disease patterns. Colonial biomedicine was never without its cultural and social preoccupations and premises.

As part of this development public health, as many writers have noted, was downgraded and kicked to the side. Tropical medical research remained important, and medical campaigns continued, but these became more and more narrowly curative and less preventive in orientation. Preventive public health was not a fashionable area to be in for medics and in some cases was completely taken out of the hands of Medical Departments into separate Sanitary Departments.

Control of epidemic disease continued to demand the attention and resources of Medical Departments in East and Central Africa in the inter-war period, though the frequency and severity of epidemics was generally less than in the early colonial period. The gradual recession of epidemic disease was partly due to the advances in medicine. Smallpox remained a serious public health problem into the 1960s in many areas, but the provision of better lymph did aid its control. In some cases it was not medical advances but the slow improvement in the conditions of labour migration which gradually made a difference. Relapsing fever, for instance, had reached epidemic proportions in parts of early colonial Nyasaland as a result of the movement of labour migrants on foot and the appalling conditions under which they were housed travelling to and from their places of work.[36] As motorised transportation was introduced, so this became less of a problem and the epidemics receded.

In the case of epidemic disease, many medical officers retained a sense of the underlying causes and bemoaned the lack of resources to deal with these. When cerebro-spinal meningitis broke out in epidemic form amongst labourers in southern Nyasaland in the 1930s, the Director of Medical Services was emphatic that what was required was 'not additional legislation but improved social conditions'.[37]

In charge of measures against the epidemic in Mulanje district was W. T. C. Berry. His liberal position was marked by a wish to make public health measures more acceptable to ordinary people and therefore more effective. In practice this meant that he paid more attention to the idea that they had cultural practices and taboos which should not be offended or transgressed than he did to the question of living conditions. Like many others at this time, Berry feared that 'social disintegration' would increase susceptibility to disease, but was also certain that certain cultural practices which helped to maintain social cohesion were themselves bad for the health of the people. During the meningitis epidemic he campaigned against funeral practices whilst at the same time encouraging (for social rather than medical reasons) the maintenance of sexual taboos:

After one talk on the disease, a young man asked: 'When can we sleep with our wives?'. It was plain that this native taboo on sexual intercourse during an epidemic was a key issue between the 'senior citizens' ... and 'junior citizens' ... I answered smoothly, 'not for at least a fortnight', to the chagrin of the younger people and the gratification of their elders. Whether rightly or wrongly, I do not know, but it seemed probable to me that the authority of the old would not easily weather such a jolt if I did not uphold them.[38]

Comparing the careers and views of Stannus and Berry might help illuminate both the shifts and the continuities in colonial medical discourse between the early colonial period and the inter-war period.

Berry was born in 1909, trained as a doctor at Cambridge and, after a six-month course at the London School of Hygiene and Tropical Medicine, was posted to Nyasaland in 1936.[39] His first posting was to the African Hospital in Zomba, which Stannus had helped to set up. But the general shortage of medical personnel meant that doctors were transferred frequently from one district to another. After two and a half months at Zomba, Berry was posted to Mulanje for a six months period. Mulanje, in the south of the country, was in the heart of the tea plantation area and a place with formidable health problems. Berry was in charge of the hospital and the medical problems of the district. Working under him he had an African hospital assistant, an African anaesthetist, 'sundry African dressers, a store-keeper, a Sanitary Inspector and a labour gang'.[40] Amongst the major health problems in the area were hookworm (prevalent in the crowded and insanitary conditions of the estates and neighbouring villages), bilharzia, malaria, chest complaints, syphilis, gonorrhoea and conjunctivitis. Berry took a broad view of the production of ill-health and was unhappy with what he saw as the 'magical' belief in western medicine held by his patients. The 'injection syndrome' particularly worried him:

Many patients in Nyasaland, I discovered, were dissatisfied unless they were given some sort of injection. Among the hundreds of sick, partially sick and others with backs rheumaticky and aching from the heavy toil of breaking up the soil with hand tools, enquiry as to what might be wrong with them often elicited, not a direct reply, but the single word 'Jackson!'. Anthropologists of the future may report folk-lore telling of a wondrous healer, one Jack, whose skill was only surpassed by his sons! To spare their disillusion let it be said at once that this word is a relic of the reverence once paid to the dramatic response of yaws, which used to be very prevalent, to treatment by arsenicals, which had been given by injection. 'Jackson' was a corruption of the word 'injection'...[41]

Berry was an advocate of public health and clearly believed that the disease problems he encountered in Nyasaland were largely caused by poor living conditions. But he was also preoccupied with the idea that the people he was dealing with had very different ideas of disease causation. This was evident in his description of dealing with the cerebro-spinal meningitis epidemic, and also in his approach to the problems of sanitation. In both cases he attempted to provide cultural translations for the public health practices he was promoting. In the case of the meningitis epidemic this involved inventing a 'local' word for the disease and exploiting local categories of disease.[42]

Berry's approach to these problems was, of course, commendable in many respects. It could be a short step, however, from his position to the kind of cultural pathologization which was became common in this period. It would have been very alien to Stannus whose interest in African culture (including centrally African ideas of disease causation and their methods of treatment) did not include the idea that culture was greatly implicated in disease causation. Stannus was much more typical of the nineteenth century in viewing African culture as integral to 'nature'.

Continuities with the Stannus tradition are much easier to see in the field of medical research. Berry, like many of his contemporaries, was involved in carrying out local medical surveys in the 1930s.[43] These combined an environmental health approach with medical examination, and produced local profiles of disease incidence. Berry also took part in the Nyasaland Nutrition Survey, an immensely ambitious project, which reflected the rise of the new professional group of nutritionists and their influence on colonial research in the 1930s.[44] Though Berry complained that Platt, the nutritionist in charge, viewed nutrition as the panacea for all ills, the survey was in fact, remarkably inter-disciplinary, incorporating an anthropologist, doctors and agronomists as well as nutritionists, and designed to produce 'knowledge' of the African which was not purely biomedical.

The medical survey tradition continued into the 1950s with the institution of the East African Medical Survey.[45] The medical campaign, more curative than preventive now, also survived the entire period and continued to be conducted along military lines. There was, for instance, little hint of 'cultural accommodation' in the yaws eradication campaign carried out in eastern Nigeria in the 1950s.[46] Zahra described the procedures of this campaign in the *Bulletin of the World Health Organisation* in 1956. It is, I think, worth recounting its procedures at length.

The yaws eradication team would arrive in a village and, having won the support of the local chiefly authorities, would set to work. A palm frond shelter would be built in the middle of the village, and this shelter would be divided into an examination 'room', an injection 'room', and an out-patient section for dressings. The idea was

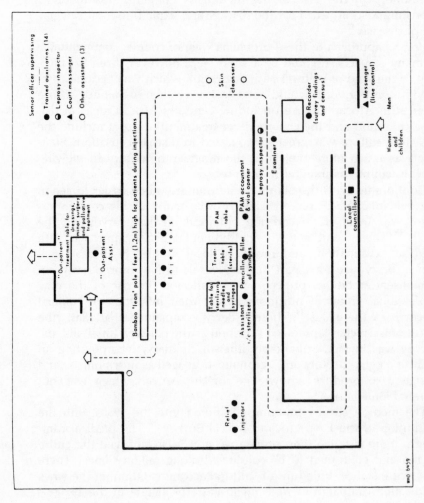

Figure 3 Layout of working place of yaws eradication team, Nigeria, 1956.

that there should be 'smooth work and traffic' throughout the makeshift building. It was a system which could be 'aptly described as the "sausage machine"'.[47]

The people (about 1,500 of them) would be called up by 'kindred' by local councillors and elders. These local notables, along with the court messengers, were present to identify the people. Two lines were formed facing the examination room – one for men and one for women and children. Then the procedure began:

> Young children are stripped of all clothing and adults retain only a loin cloth; the women retain only the usual short underskirt. They present themselves in turn before the examining doctor or assistant, who examines the patient systematically from head to foot, not forgetting the inspection of hands and fingers (both sides), armpits, soles of feet, genital region (for children), and the medial view of the tibiae . . . A pole is fixed in the ground next to the examiner to give support to the patient when the soles of the feet are inspected. The findings of the examiner are called out in a workable code with which the recorder is fully conversant, for example, 'female 17 years, "S", infectious, 4 ml'; 'S' denotes early skin lesion. The dose is chalked on the back of the patient over the right scapular region. Since a dry piece of chalk cannot be used for long because of the grease and dirt which quickly collect on it, it is previously soaked in water, and then used lightly. The chalked dosage may not at first show clearly, but the figure soon dries and becomes distinct. A leprosy inspector sits next to the yaws examiner, and recognizes and registers leprosy cases . . .
>
> The patient is then directed to the treatment 'room', where the right buttock is scrubbed vigorously with a nail brush and soap and water by a trained assistant; a second assistant washes the soap off with water and finally swabs the part lightly with a pad containing 1% Cetavlon solution.
>
> The patient then passes to a bamboo 'lean' pole with his face to the wall. An assistant administers the prescribed dosage, as chalked on his back, deeply and intramuscularly into the upper and outer quadrant of the right buttock. Babies and children under 5 years are lifted up and held by a trained assistant. The patient is then directed to the exit, unless he requires treatment for ulcers, abscesses, etc, in the 'out-patient room'.[48]

Medical campaigns such as this one inscribed, quite literally, biomedical practice on the bodies of their subjects. At the same time they inscribed, spatially, the practice of colonial rule through its unitizing and disciplining procedures. From the outside of the enclosure it was impossible to see what was going on behind its walls. As the men and women, in separate lines, entered the enclosure, they passed indigenous representatives of the colonial state – the court messenger, and local councillors, whose job it was to recognize them and to check that every member of the family was present. As they proceeded further into the enclosure (deprived now of most of their clothes), so the procedure became less 'administrative' and more directly 'medical'. While at the entrance to the enclosure they were identified by name, once inside the enclosure they were known only by the coded message chalked on the back. They became, quite literally, a prescription. Finally they were injected, and directed to an exit. Nobody went out the way they came in.

Quite how this procedure, and others like it, were 'read' by those subjected to it is not easy to know, just as it is not easy to know how the mass incineration of rats' tails during anti-plague campaigns was interpreted. On the one hand this appears to be a perfect example of the most repressive and objectifying of colonial medical procedures. Colonial subjects here are being codified and numbered, deprived of their clothing and of any individual choice, they are herded into an enclosure where various agents of the state make a direct assault on their bodies.

There are plenty of examples of direct and effective resistance to similar compulsory medical procedures. Mr Sichimata's sad account of his experience as a smallpox inspector makes it clear that African communities were not passive bodies upon which colonial medicine drew its designs. On the other hand, there is also evidence for the popularity of some mass treatments amongst African communities, and the celebration of the 'injection'. Unless we view 'the body' as having a universal and irreducible meaning, then we must be careful in drawing conclusions about how African colonial subjects interpreted such practices.

If we can say little about the subjective experience of the early colonial medical campaign, we can say rather more about how the medical discourses and practices of the early colonial period represented 'the African'.

Firstly, and most obviously, colonial medical practice, as it was applied to African communities in this period, was mass treatment. Africans were represented as an integral feature of a hazardous environment, they were, as a group, potential hosts for dangerous pathogens. In medical campaigns throughout the colonial period (and beyond) they were treated as inanimate objects of either research or treatment. Whilst they were 'unitized' as individual recipients of treatment (with their own individual dosage chalked on their backs), their identities, views and feelings were entirely irrelevant. In this sense the colonial medical campaign was very little different to medical campaigns in Britain and elsewhere, and conformed to the stereotype of biomedical practice as objectifying and alienating.

In the writings of colonial medical officers like Stannus and Berry, however, we can identify shifts in the biomedical discourse on

Africa which are not evident in the relatively unchanging history of the 'medical campagin'. Stannus was concerned to understand 'the African' as a product of a specific environment, and to represent differences in that product. Africans, in Stannus's research and photograph albums, were differentiated and labelled, like any other object of scientific enquiry. But in his work we can also identify the gradual emergence, in colonial medical discourse, of the idea of 'culture' as a separate and determining feature. Whilst Stannus saw 'the African' as straddling the worlds of 'nature' and 'culture', it was 'nature' which ultimately determined 'culture' in his model. Disease was produced through a complex interaction of all elements of the environment, including the organization of human societies as one of those elements. For Stannus's successors, however, 'culture' became an entity which could both produce and protect from disease, and therefore a subject of a distinct pathologising account.

But this is a very incomplete account of the medical discourse and practice of the early colonial period. Whilst colonial medical officers were elaborating the rituals of the mass treatment campaign, or engaged in the endless research pursuit of the pathogen, medical missionaries were elaborating quite different rituals, for quite different purposes.

NOTES

1 Hugh Stannus papers, Mss. Afr.s.476, Rhodes House, Oxford (hereafter Stannus papers). Stannus to Ethel, 18.9.1910.
2 Russett (1989).
3 Turshen (1984).
4 MacLeod and Lewis, eds (1988); Arnold, ed. (1988).
5 Worboys (1988a).
6 See, for example, the survival of climatic theories of health and disease in Australia in Helen Woolcock's account of attitudes to health in colonial Queensland: Woolcock (1988).
7 McKeown (1979); Curtin (1961).
8 Jordanova (1989), p. 46.
9 For the history of sleeping sickness research in colonial Africa see the work of Maryinez Lyons on northern Zaire: Lyons (1987); Ford (1979); McKelvey (1973).
10 J. B. Davey papers, Mss. Afr.s.97, Rhodes House, Oxford.
11 Davey papers, Diary entries, 1910–11.
12 For the significance of hunting in colonial ideology see John MacKenzie's work: Mackenzie (1988).
13 Ford (1971).
14 Worboys (1988a).
15 For India see Ramasubban (1988); Arnold (1988); Catanach (1988).
16 Curtin (1961).
17 MacKenzie (1988); Beinart (1989).

18 Iliffe (1987); Kjekshus (1977).

19 Feierman (1985).

20 Swanson (1977).

21 C. J. Baker papers, Mss. Afr.s.1091, Rhodes House, Oxford.

22 Baker papers, Box 3, File 2, 1921.

23 Brown (1978).
    The medical department in Lagos produced a health education film in
    1937 entitled *Anti-Plague Operations in Lagos*. This film shows European
    officials supervising the trapping of rats in a poor African housing area,
    and the subsequent redevelopment of the area into a 'model township'
    (National Film Archives, London). See Chapter 8.

24 Malawi National Archives (hereafter MNA): S1/326/19: Bubonic Plague,
    1919, Lambourn to Provincial Medical Officer, 1.2.19.

25 MNA: S1/326/19: John Abraham to Acting Chief Secretary, 31.8.20.

26 MNA: S1/1243/19: Smallpox, 1919–20.

27 MNA: S1/1243/19: Resident Chintechi to Chief Secretary, 21.11.21.

28 MNA: M2/5/16: Smallpox: General, 1929–32, Extract from Report of the
    District Commissioner, Mzimba, for quarter ended 30.9.30.

29 MNA: M2/5/16: Sub Assistant Surgeon, Chetan Dev, to Director of
    Medical and Sanitary Services, 12.12.29.

30 Marc Dawson has argued this in his study of smallpox epidemics in
    early colonial Kenya: Dawson (1979).

31 MNA: M2/5/49: Smallpox, 1946–8.

32 MNA: M2/5/15: Medical Orderly Thomas Sichimata: Report on smallpox
    at Mwenya village, 17.8.36.

33 This paragraph draws on a survey of the annual medical reports of Nyasa-
    land, Northern Rhodesia, Southern Rhodesia, Kenya and Tanganyika.

34 This is clear from the history of medical approaches to tuberculosis,
    for instance: Linda Bryder's work on the history of tuberculosis in
    twentieth-century Britain: Bryder (1988).

35 Harris (1968); Stocking (1969).

36 MNA: M2/5/15: Relapsing Fever, 1934–8.

37 MNA: M2/5/6: Cerebro-Spinal Meningitis: Acting Director of Medical
    Services to Chief Secretary, 6.5.38.

38 Berry (1984), p. 25.

39 Berry (1984), pp. xx–xxii.

40 Berry (1984), p. 15.

41 Berry (1984), p. 9.

42 MNA: M2/5/6: Berry to Director of Medical Services, 22.10.37.

43 MNA: M2/14/1: Medical Surveys, 1930–6; M2/14/2: Medical Surveys,
    1937–8.

44 Worboys (1988b); Berry (1984).

45 East Africa Medical Survey, *Annual Reports, 1949–53*. See also the
    memoirs of another participant in the East Africa Medical Survey: Dr
    Hope Trant: Trant (1970).

46 Zahra (1956).

47 Zahra (1956), p. 932.

48 Zahra (1956), pp. 933–4.

3 The Great Dispensary in the Sky: Missionary Medicine

On the Feast of the Epiphany 1936, after High Mass, the congregation of the Anglican cathedral at Masasi in southern Tanganyika took part in the consecration of a new hospital building. Singing a litany, they processed from the cathedral to the hospital, circling it a few times. They were then led by the clergy into the new hospital building, which was blessed and dedicated 'to the Glory of God and the honour of All Saints'. The congregation, still singing hymns, then returned up the hill to the old dispensary where each man, woman and child received an item of equipment – a bottle, stool, cupboard or box – which they then carried to the new building: 'Even the smallest children were seen toddling along each solemnly clutching a small bottle'.[1]

The opening of a mission hospital or dispensary was an occasion for elaborate ritual, expressing many fundamentals of the medical missionary endeavour in colonial Africa. Writing of these ceremonies for a British Christian audience the missionary doctor Leader Stirling was aware that they might seem unnecessary and 'old fashioned', as he put it, but insisted that they had a real significance for the African communities concerned. The people, he wrote, were in constant fear of evil spirits and witches so that for them 'to know that a house has been solemnly blessed in the name of Almighty God, and that therefore no evil spirit can enter in, is to give a great increase of confidence, and this is especially important in a hospital.'[2]

Much that has been written on the encounter between African communities and western medicine is strangely silent on the activities of mission doctors and nurses. Yet mission medicine cannot simply be subsumed under the heading of 'western medicine', itself a catch-all term. The Christian Church has, of course, a long history of healing, the significance of which has varied from time to time

and place to place. Modern western biomedical ideologies and practices have been heavily influenced by Christian teaching on healing,
so that to represent the encounter between western and African
concepts of healing as one between a scientific and pre-scientific
world view is oversimplistic on several counts. If this is true for
'secular' western medicine, it is clearly even more true for Christian
medical missionary practice of the late nineteenth and early twentieth centuries, which combined, sometimes uneasily, a belief in the
powers of biomedicine with a conviction that those 'called' to the
medical profession were mere servants of the 'Great Healer' of
souls.

Throughout most of the colonial period and throughout most of
Africa, Christian missions of one sort or another provided vastly
more medical care for African communities than did colonial states.
It was not until the 1930s, and in many places until the 1950s and
1960s, that secular medicine reached rural communities in any form
other than the 'great campaigns' against epidemic disease which I
have described in the last chapter. It was missionaries who in East
and Central Africa from the late nineteenth century pioneered the
setting up of rural hospitals and rural clinics, who trained African
medical personnel, who introduced 'western' midwifery and childcare practices, and who dealt with chronic and endemic disease. For
most Africans, then, any prolonged encounter with biomedicine was
likely to have been an encounter with an explicitly Christian version
of this. Though much has now been written on African 'medical
pluralism' and on the African healing Churches, little has been said
of the ideologies, practices and symbolisms of European medical
missionary practice, an important component of this 'pluralism'.[3]
    If it is true that, for most Africans before the Second World War,
any prolonged encounter with biomedicine came in the form of an
experience of mission medicine, it is also true that for church-going
Britons of this period one of the most popular representations of
Africa and of Africans came via the accounts in missionary journals
of the woes of the 'sick continent', and the trials, tribulations, and
triumphs of heroic medical missionaries.[4]
    This chapter cannot review the entire history of medical missions
in Africa, a large and rich area of research. It concentrates on East
and Central Africa, and draws primarily on sources produced by the
Church Missionary Society and by the Universities' Mission to Central Africa. Within the limitations of the material presented here, my
aim has been to describe the construction of both 'Africa' and 'the
African' in medical missionary discourse and in the rituals of mission medicine. In particular, I have tried to indicate where missionary and secular medicine differed in the diagnosis of the diseases

of Africa. Both relied heavily on social pathological models, but whereas secular medicine saw modernity and the disintegration of 'traditional' societies as fundamental causes of disease, missionary medicine, throughout most of this period, took the view that disease would only be conquered through the advancement of Christian morality, a sanitized modernity and 'family life'. Whilst secular medicine tended towards an ethnic model of collective pathology, mission medicine concentrated on individual Africans and individual responsibility for sin and disease. Missionary medicine, then, was involved in the attempt to create particular subjectivities through its practice.

The division between 'missionary' and 'secular' medicine in colonial Africa was never clear-cut, and this has to be borne in mind when reading this chapter. Neither, of course, were medical missions themselves a homogenous group. There were, for example, marked differences between the approaches to medical work adopted by Protestant and Catholic missions, but also between different Protestant Churches and Catholic orders. There were, and are, a very large number of independent African Churches for which healing was a central component of theology and practice, the history of which falls beyond the scope of this chapter.

David Livingstone was the great nineteenth-century hero of British missionary medicine in Africa. As an explorer-cum-healer, he had performed a dual role. In the familiar terminology of exploration, he had 'opened up' large parts of central Africa, and, finding Africa 'wounded' by the slave trade, had then called for the 'wound' to be healed. The basic difference between secular and missionary views of the problems of colonial Africa arises from their differing diagnoses of this 'wound'. By the 1920s official colonial discourse had it that the wound was primarily caused by the encounter with 'civilization', whilst the missionary discourse saw the wound as having been inflicted from within by the evils of pre-colonial African society.[5]

From Livingstone onwards, reports from Central and Eastern Africa insisted that the continent was 'sick' and suffering from the evils of the slave trade, from paganism and the creeping forces of Islam. Unlike many of those who came after him, however, Livingstone did not regard the African healers he encountered as intrinsic to this 'sickness' but rather insisted that they be shown the respect which one professional would accord another. It was desirable, he wrote, to keep on good terms with 'local medical men' at all times, and not to 'poach' patients from them. All slight cases should be referred to local doctors and 'severe cases before being undertaken should be enquired into of the doctor himself and no disparaging remark ever made on the previous treatment in the presence of the patient'.[6] Whilst advocating a kind of 'medical pluralism' and tolerance, Livingstone was nevertheless well aware of the evangelizing opportunities afforded by the prevalence of sickness in the parts of Africa he had visited. He advised other doctors never to neglect 'the opportunity which the bed of sickness presents by saying a few kind words in a natural respectful manner and imitate as far as you can the conduct of the Great Physician, whose followers we profess to be'.

How far the opportunities for evangelization afforded by the sickbed should be exploited was a question which occupied medical missionaries throughout this period, and was one over which there were many differences of opinion.

When Albert Cook, the famous missionary doctor, first set foot in Uganda in 1897, there was much suspicion and outright opposition to his work from fellow members of the Church Missionary Society who were already there.[7] Though Cook always claimed (and appeared consistent in his claim) that the conversion of souls was his priority, others felt that medical work would necessarily detract from evangelization. Above and beyond this was a feeling which lingered on throughout the period, that sickbed evangelization was bound to be superficial, and sickbed conversions consequently suspect.

Cook and his early colleagues trod a difficult path. On the one hand they wished to represent their work as being essentially the work of evangelization; on the other they had to take care not to represent it as too simple a route to the conversion of souls.[8] The very popularity of their medical skills was a constant source of embarrassment, as well as of pride, to these early doctors in Uganda. In the kingdom of Toro, for instance, where the early Church Missionary Society (CMS) missionaries were 'girding themselves to battle against the great darkness', there were already over two-hundred patients a day at the dispensary only a few months after it had opened.[9] Furthermore, the king of Toro seemed thoroughly won over by the missionaries when he witnessed an operation:

> At Toro the King begged to see an operation so, a suitable case appearing of a man with a large tumour on his back the size of two fists, we put him under chloroform and removed it. Fortunately for the credit of our medical work, it came out very nicely, and the wound healing quickly the man was soon all right. I think they were more astonished at the chloroform than the operation, the fact of the man suffering no pain being to them very extraordinary.

The removal of huge and disabling tumours remained occasions for the dramatic display of the powers of European surgery beyond this early phase of missionary medicine, and many medical memoirs are illustrated with photographs of such tumours. Given the popularity of this image, it is hard to avoid the conclusion that medical missionaries felt themselves to be excising a great deal more than the tumour.[10]

Cataract operations, sometimes performed *in situ*, were equally impressive. At the end of a long day in Busoga, Albert Cook and his wife were going for a walk when they were approached by a 'dignified looking' man, blind in one eye. Cook decided to perform an operation on the cataract there and then, since he was leaving the following day. So, as the light waned, he called for a mat, administered cocaine, and removed the cataract, to the amazement of lookers-on: 'We commenced the little operation by prayer, and by the time we had done a throng of uninvited spectators had gathered round, through whom ran a quiver of astonishment as they saw the little white object that had caused the friend's blindness'.[11] The 'magical' quality of certain aspects of western medicine was regarded, in these early days, as something of a difficulty. The people of Uganda were genuinely impressed by the skills of the missionary medics. But their very enthusiasm, and apparently unquestioning faith in the doctors' medicines, were hard to distinguish from their faith in other 'magical' devices. Sometimes this attitude could be seen by the missionaries as indicating a 'simple faith', but they were also inclined to interpret it as an indication of moral inadequacy. On leaving Toro at the end of a visit, Dr Howard Cook (Albert Cook's brother) was pursued along the road by the sick, pleading him for 'one more dose'. It was, he wrote, 'indescribably pathetic; even after we had started they ran along the road with us, and in vain we urged that the medicine had been packed and sent off'.[12]

If this enthusiasm was something of an embarrassment, so too was the tendency of many East African peoples to assimilate aspects of the medicine they had seen practised by the missionaries into their own healing and belief systems. At the CMS mission at Jilore, north of Mombasa, the missionaries had vaccinated around eight-hundred people against smallpox in 1898. In the following year when a man-eating lion was threatening the settlement, one man made a considerable sum by 'vaccinating' people against lion bites: '... when remonstrated with he showed the vaccination marks on himself, which had been done by us for smallpox, and could not see the difference between his work and ours'.[13]

A related source of frustration to medical missionaries in many parts of East and Central Africa was the all-encompassing meaning of the Swahili word *dawa*. This was used to denote medicine, of whatever origin, and was also the word for the mission dispensary itself. It could be employed for anything regarded as remedial or beneficial – shoe polish, for instance, was called *dawa*.[14]

In the early mission journals published in Britain, many an account was published of the frustrating tendency of African patients to misunderstand the status and function of the dose of medicine, and later of the injection. Readers were invited at times to regard such misunderstandings as amusing demonstrations of the African's 'ignorance' and 'simple faith', at other times as demonstrations of the dangers of superficial evangelization. Many people, it seemed, arrived at the dispenser's door demanding medicine, but with no complaint that could be identified. They simply asked for *dawa*, or *mankhwala* as it was called in some parts of central Africa. 'I want something to make me strong', demanded one man to the Anglican sister at Likoma in 1895. He had come to the island to visit a friend and thought that he would get a 'drink' of medicine before returning to his home where none was available.[15] African patients, it seemed, neither understood the operation of 'scientific' as opposed to 'superstitious' medicine, nor did they appreciate that there was more to this scientific medicine than the healing of the body. Mission medicine demanded a belief in both the scientific and the supernatural. For many African communities this was not a totally strange idea, as their own medical systems incorporated both the herbalist and the spirit medium, but early patients were more keen on the immediate benefits of mission medicine than they were on the theological theories of healing which went with them. To be sure, the situation which greeted medical missionaries in this part of Africa was preferable to the hostility which they encountered elsewhere,[16] but it did mean that the early mission doctors and nurses had constantly to reiterate that their medicine was different. In their reports to their subscribers at home, in the CMS journal *Mercy and Truth* for instance, this was continually emphasized. When medicine failed (and despite the success stories failure was extremely common in this early period of tropical medicine), souls had still been won. In the popular medical missionary terminology of the turn of the century, many an African left this world to meet the Great Physician, or ascended to the Great Dispensary in the Sky.[17]

Some of these early missionary fears about the uses and abuses of medicine were allayed once the medical missions became more firmly established and makeshift hospitals had been built to accommodate patients with chronic diseases. The 'great campaigns' against sleeping sickness, smallpox, and later against yaws and syphilis, continued to occupy mission doctors who, in many places, performed the role of a state public health service. However, this mass medicine was now supplemented by longer-term care within mission hospitals and dispensaries, opening up greater possibilities for evangelization.

The medical missionary pioneers in Uganda were amongst the first to recognize the opportunities for evangelization afforded by longer-term care of the sick. One of the early triumphs of mission medicine in East and Central Africa was in the treatment of ulcers. Many people suffered terribly from deep and infected ulcers on their limbs, caused by a variety of factors and exacerbated by malnutrition. Sometimes amputations had to be performed, but more often a cure could be effected through careful, and sometimes lengthy, nursing during which period the patient was often hospitalized. This afforded the opportunity for an intensive period of Christian instruction: 'Ulcers have one great recommendation from the Mission point of view – they take a long time to cure.'[18]

On the pages of the mission journals the routines and rituals of mission hospitals in the 'heart of Africa' were described. Regular readers were encouraged to keep track of their favourite patients, to pray for their souls, and to follow their medical and spiritual progress. This was particularly rewarding for those subscribers who had sponsored a hospital sleeping mat and who could keep track of each patient who slept on it. Through this process the African 'patient' was created. Each was accorded a personality and her or his idiosyncrasies were described in detail. There were 'good' and 'bad' patients – those for whom one was encouraged to feel largely unadulterated pity and compassion, and those who inspired a kind of awed fear, representing, through their 'gaping wounds' and 'suppurating ulcers', the evils of the society from which they had come, and the 'sickness' of Africa.

Many of the earliest patients treated in mission hospitals in East and Central Africa were victims of the disruptions and social disorder of the late nineteenth century – they were not only sick but often cut off from their kin. Having no kin to take responsibility for one's illness was indeed a sign of great social isolation, and many of these earliest patients lingered on in the hospitals long after they had recovered from their illnesses, becoming converts and, often, the first African medical assistants. The early mission doctors invariably chose their assistants from amongst former patients. In part this was because it was very difficult, initially, to recruit for work which was frequently regarded as lowly and demeaning but also because a mission medical assistant had also to be a believer, and most believers came from the ranks of former patients. A lengthy stay in hospital as a patient thus provided a medical and spiritual training for the job. It was a kind of rite of passage not unlike that experienced by many African healers whose status as former clients was central to their reputation.

Zamani was one such patient whose story was followed by readers of *Central Africa* in the early 1990s. Born in Zanzibar, he had apparently found his way, along the routes of the slave trade, to Kota Kota on the shores of Lake Nyasa, where he fell sick and was admitted to the UMCA hospital. During his long convalescence he became a catechumen, and generally helped out in the hospital. He had no relatives that he knew of, did not want to marry and had nowhere to go from the hospital. An appeal was made to readers to subsidize his continued stay in the hospital. 'Perhaps someone would like to adopt him?', suggested the sister-in-charge, by which she meant that a reader might like to pay the £2 a year which it cost to keep him, in return for a personal identification with, and partial 'ownership' of, his progress.[19]

There were many others like Zamani in these early years, for whom institutionalization in the mission hospital as either patient or worker was an attractive alternative which could at the same time be represented as a great triumph for Christianity. There were others who were, perhaps, rather less willingly institutionalized, being patients who represented a larger 'evil', and whose confinement therefore held another kind of symbolic importance. The Moslem patient at Mengo, in Uganda, in 1902, for instance, had undergone an operation and was cured, but had not been allowed home: 'We are keeping him in hospital, as we are very anxious to win his soul.' The patient himself was somewhat confused by this, arguing that he had come 'to the hospital for healing, and didn't see why he should change his religion'.[20]

There was no escape from a degree of evangelizing in the mission hospital. 'It is not our job, nor have we the power, to convert the souls of men', wrote Albert Cook in 1904, '. . . yet we do see again and again death beds irradiated by the smile of hope and peace given from on high.'[21] Prayers were said morning and night in the hospital, and lessons given on a Sunday. No opportunity was lost to arrange patients in such a way as a 'heathen' was placed next to a convert. The hospital building itself, it was often said, had a great influence on the 'absolute heathens'. Some, like that at Likoma in Nyasaland, were formed out of an old church; others were more modest, being nothing more than a 'larger, well-built native hut'. All had walls decorated with Biblical pictures which it was thought would be a source of great interest and enlightenment.

In Islamicized areas, the hope of winning converts was always present, and the Christian iconography which decorated the

Figure 4　'A Congo Child's Appeal'.

hospital walls was seen as a particularly useful tool. At the UMCA hospital at Kota-Kota in Nyasaland one Moslem patient, Chisni, was accommodated in an empty ward with both of his wives, who nursed him through a six-month period of convalescence. The discomfort felt by the missionaries at accommodating polygyny within the hospital walls was, however, made more bearable by the apparently powerful impact that Christian imagery had made on him. 'One day . . .', wrote the sister to subscribers of *Central Africa*, 'I found another Mohammedan man, Kapemba, with a picture they had taken down from the wall, explaining the "Raising of the Widow's Son at Nain" to him. He was teaching the story with the utmost reverence.'[22] It was said that great changes could come about in individuals as a result of a long stay in hospital – changes which could be measured in the transformation of features, the 'harsh, heathen lines' being gradually effaced as 'Christ seems to write his new signature across their faces'.[23] The physical transformation of patients was taken as a direct sign of the spiritual transformation which a stay in hospital could apparently bring about.

Belief in the efficacy and centrality of the hospital's religious rituals was reiterated well beyond the early colonial period. In 1950, for example, *Central Africa* reported a Whitsuntide ceremony which had taken place in a Nyasaland hospital, where Mass was said for four Anglican communicants in the fracture ward: 'To see that dull white wall lit with the glow of shining candles! To see the feast of the Holy Spirit brought to those four children of God . . . There was absolute silence in the wards – the Muhammedans watched with awe on their faces as the fair linens were laid reverently on the table – crucifix, candles, flowers, then the beautiful red vestments were laid out.'[24]

Mission hospitals in Africa were always short of doctors. Often there was only one doctor to cover a large diocese and much of the work of the hospital thus fell on the mission nurses and their African assistants. These latter were, up to the 1930s, almost entirely male, and known as *dawa* or dispensary 'boys'. Originally recruited from within the ranks of the patients, by the 1920s and 1930s, they were being drawn more often from the ranks of mission school boys. By the 1940s, when the job of 'Dispensary Boy' was well established in Nyasaland, it was possible to look back to a period in the 1900s when a schoolboy recruit to the job was taunted by his peers and came to be known as 'Touch Ulcers'.[25]

In fact it was these African assistants who were largely responsible for keeping up the hospital regime, performing many of the nursing and dispensing duties, interpreting, and sometimes inventing, the strange rituals of the hospital. In the Likoma hospital in

1902, a patient on being admitted to hospital would be put under the charge of a 'Dispensary Boy' who 'solemnly unlocks the big box and produces a blanket, a mat, an enamelled iron soup plate, and carefully explains that these luxuries are only lent and must be returned when the patient leaves'.[26] Asked to explain his work with hospital patients, one 'Dispensary Boy' wrote in 1926 that he first gave the 'orders of the hospital', as follows: 'Everyone who comes in this hospital must wash himself every day. Everyone must wash his bandage every day. Everyone must have his bed put in the sun every day.'[27] Medical missionary memoirs abound with stories of the early African dispensers, and the value of their work was readily recognized. In particular, they were at the vanguard of the 'battle against superstition and witchcraft', persuading recalcitrant patients and sceptics of the superiority of western medicine. They represented far more than the elementary training they had received would imply, and readers of the mission journals were continually called upon to pray for them, that 'they may never fail the Great Physician'.[28] On the island of Likoma, in Nyasaland, the elderly African 'dresser' was apparently honoured by all, despite the fact that he was not 'very highly educated, nor remarkably sanitary and antiseptic in his methods'. He was, however, 'honest and kind, gentle to the sick, encouraging to the timid, polite even to women'.[29]

It was continually stated that nursing and caring for the sick did not come 'naturally' to the African. The process of training was described as 'tedious and often disappointing', for 'the native does not naturally take to the work, and has a cordial dislike for anything nasty'.[30] Whilst the 'English babe' was said to imbibe the highest ideals of the medical profession with its mother's milk, this was the result of '1500 years of unbroken Christianity', and was not true of the African.[31] The sight of the *'dawa* boy' selflessly cleaning the sores of the leper was therefore a cause for rejoicing, for 'Here was practical Christianity, before our eyes, the spirit of One who "touched" the leper; two Christian boys, setting aside tribal custom and natural repulsion, were cleaning and binding up the wounds on the suffering fellow-men'.[32]

There is a consistency and continuity in this medical missionary discourse throughout the period up to the Second World War. Although the content of medical missionary work changed in this period, what changed very little was the representation of this work and of the African 'patient'. For medical missionaries the healing of the body had always to take second place to the winning of the soul and the fight against the 'evils' of African society. Of course, in practice, mission doctors and nurses were overworked and mission hospitals understaffed. It is clear from the many memoirs written by medical missionaries that their time was taken entirely in the day-to-day running of their hospitals and dispensaries. Mission doctors, like Leader Stirling in Tanzania in the 1930s, covered huge areas of rural Africa, attempting to bring health care to rural Africans where agents of the colonial state hardly ventured.[33] But even if medical missionaries had little time for direct evangelization, the practice of mission medicine remained one to which religious meaning was constantly attached. Suffering and sin were inseparable in the medical missionary discourse. This association, though also present in the 'secular' medical discourse on Africa, did not survive unchallenged in the thinking of colonial medical departments. For mission doctors and nurses, however, it remained a central tenet of their work. This was nowhere more apparent than in the field of midwifery and childcare, an area of medical intervention, like many others, where missionaries led the way.

Christian missionaries were quick to realize that African midwifery practices and associated ideas about fertility and childcare, were of more than practical significance for their own work. They were, they decided, the locus of the reproduction of many strongly-held beliefs. African 'midwives' it was thought, with some justification, exercised a large degree of social and moral control which had to be broken if Christianity was to succeed.

In Uganda, Albert Cook and his wife had focused their attention on midwifery and on the training of African midwives almost as soon as the Mengo hospital was founded in 1897. Their interest in reforming childbirth and childcare practices arose initially from their campaign against 'diseases of immorality' (examined in more detail in Chapter 6). It is clear from their reports that childbirth and childcare practices were regarded by the missionaries, as much as by African communities, as an area of great symbolic, as well as medical, significance. In these early accounts the 'darkness' of the African birthing hut was positioned against the candles and white sheets of the maternity ward. The elder women who assisted in childbirth came to symbolize for these missionaries the immensity of the 'evil' they were opposing in their work. There was no question who the 'enemy' was in these early accounts. Take, for instance, this report on the 'Dwellers in Darkness', published in Mercy and Truth in 1907, in which a Mrs Doulton describes her experience of assisting at midwifery cases in the villages:

Here opportunities have been given of speaking to many old women who never seem to leave the darkness of their dwellings ... I wish it were possible for you to see the faces of some of these old women as I have seen them – cruel, sin-disfigured faces ... These are the old women who keep up the horrible and cruel customs of the tribe, of which it is impossible for me to write.[34]

'The Last Fortress of Satan' was how the 'heathen grandmothers of Africa' were described. It was these grandmothers who apparently held mothers and babies in their power, leaving Christian husbands to stand by 'hopeless and despairing'.[35] But in Masalabani as elsewhere in East and Central Africa, medical missionaries (in this case Anglican sisters) had helped local Christians to build a 'House of Birth', which was consecrated on the feast on the Nativity of the Virgin Mary in 1931. Here was a place where women could give birth without the interference of the 'heathen grandmothers' and where 'peace and cleanliness' reigned. The very night of its opening a child was born of a 'heathen' mother in the House of Birth. 'The walls of the fortress of Satan have fallen', announced *Central Africa*.[36]

Babies born in the 'Houses of Birth' became known as 'mission babies'. The ideal 'mission baby' was one which was not only born in the mission hospital but whose mother attended the child welfare clinics, and perhaps joined a Mothers' Guild. At the Toro Baby Show of 1907, 'mission babies' (or rather their mothers) walked away with the great majority of the prizes.[37] The welfare clinic, it was said, helped rear contented, but disciplined, babies, its effects being as much moral as physical. Albert Cook wrote in 1932 that he had vivid recollections of 'fighting with untrained and absolutely undisciplined children in serious illness, when their very resistance was a menace to their recovery'.[38]

By the 1930s it was a commonplace to assert, as Cook did, that African child rearing practices, and infant feeding practices in particular, needed to be changed if the African was to develop a 'well-balanced' personality (see Chapter 5). Teaching the African mother to 'form habits of regularity' in the feeding and control of her children was thought to bring not only physical well-being but to assist 'baby in his first efforts at self-control, sowing the first seeds of character'.[39]

By the later 1930s and 1940s, and as a result of a new 'welfarism' in colonial policy, much of the missionary discourse on, and practice of, mother and child health had been secularized and more generally applied. The first two decades of colonial rule had in fact produced an alarming situation in many parts of East and Central Africa in which infant mortality rates and rates of infertility had probably risen. Even where this was not the case, there was enough alarm and anxiety on the part of colonial governments and African male elders, supplemented by increasing pressure from philanthropic lobbyists in the metropolis, to create a situation in which mission initiatives in mother and child care were eagerly supported by grants-in-aid from government.[40] The 'official' view of the health problems of this part of Africa in the inter-war period was not monolithic, but it is possible to draw its major lines. As in the case of the analysis of mental health in this period, the problems of high infant mortality, maternal mortality and child malnutrition, all of which were being increasingly recognized and documented, were seen as arising, in part at least, from the changes wrought by industrialization, and especially the development of a labour migrant system. There was a real fear in this period that the rural communities of this part of Africa could not continue to reproduce themselves, either biologically or socially. The very real problems faced by these communities, however, were more often described in terms of social decay and social disintegration than they were in terms of economic pressure and poverty. Medical evidence was increasingly cited to support this view. Low fertility rates and high infant mortality rates, along with the evidence of high rates of infection with sexually transmitted diseases (see Chapter 6) were seen as indicating what some termed 'racial degeneration' and others 'deculturation'.

Mission medicine shared in this 'social pathological' analysis of the inter-war period, but its diagnosis was very different. Christian medical missionaries could not share in the view that 'deculturation' was something to be feared, and could not agree that the solution to Africa's social and medical problems lay in the reinforcement of 'custom' and of 'tradition', for 'custom' and 'tradition' were the named enemies of health and progress in the missionary analysis. Many medical missionaries shared in the view that industrialization and the labour migrant system were causing increased hardship and misery for Africans, and indeed, some were outspoken in their criticisms of colonial economic policies. But, unlike most colonial officials at this time, they were not afraid of advocating policies of social engineering, of increased education and, crucially, of evangelization, to solve these problems. For medical missionaries, if there were high rates of infant mortality and malnutrition, this was indicative of the need to promote Christian notions of the family, rather than reinforcing 'traditional' kinship ideologies (including the medical missionary's arch enemy, the traditional midwife), as the system of indirect rule purported to do. The 'mission babies' of the welfare clinics, then, were symbolic of a much larger missionary programme – the battle against the evils of pagan society. As babies they were also a good selling point for British readers of mission journals, at a time when mother and child welfare was a growing concern in Britain itself.

There were 'good' babies and 'bad' babies, and although African babies and children were sometimes represented as innocent victims of disease, more often than not they bore the burden of much larger evils. From the 1890s through to the 1940s, the mission journals repeated this scene: a small welfare clinic or dispensary in the heart of Africa, full of mothers and their children waiting to see the nurse or doctor: 'What are the curious bits of wood hanging on that baby's hair, or those dirty pockets on that woman's neck ... They are heathen charms, worn to keep off the various diseases ...'[41] By the 1930s, though the evils of 'witchcraft' and 'superstition' were seen as ever present in the lives of African mothers and their babies, a rather more reassuring and domesticated picture could be painted of the clinic:

> These are the 'welfare' babies ... the beads are still there, but the majority wear little, simple coloured frocks, sent out by friends in England, all causing the mothers great joy. The babies, if they could speak, would probably tell you some of the strange rules and regulations laid down at the Welfare ... They would also, I am sure, wish to invite you to join them on the Holy Innocents' Day when, after the blessing of the children at Mass, there is the yearly party. The mothers drink many cups of the very weak tea which is such a treat for them, the gramophone is played, the Christmas tree stands in the middle of the dispensary, and St Nicholas distributes presents from it.[42]

Welfare clinics had indeed became part of a 'way of life' for some African families by this time. The missions had had a large measure of success in this field. Alternative midwifery practices and the opportunity to give birth in a clinic were eagerly taken up by many women, especially those who had been educated in mission schools. European midwifery had a great deal to recommend it for some, both in terms of its technical capacity to save lives and because it offered an alternative context in which to give birth. Giving birth in a mission hospital was a different, though no less symbolically loaded, experience to giving birth under the instruction of an elderly kinswoman. For some women the combination of technology and Christian ritual was preferable to the moral control of kin exercised through 'traditional' birth rituals.

If some women perceived advantages to mission midwifery, the benefits seemed all the more obvious to their husbands. Christian men attending the Baby Show at Toro in Uganda in 1907 were 'begged to exercise their authority in the home by putting a stop to the heathen practices which are carried on constantly by ignorant and wicked old nurses'. By the 1920s and 1930s many men did not need to be so urged, and were demanding from the colonial authorities more such facilities as were being provided by the missions. As many doctors and nurses remarked, delivery in a hospital and attendance at a welfare clinic had, by this time, become a status symbol of much wider significance, and a new area of struggle in the relations between husband and wife. In Nigeria 'infant welfare' had a longer history than it had in most parts of East and Central Africa, and baby shows were a central feature of an emerging middle-class culture. The 1937 film of Health Week in Lagos shows fathers, as well as mothers, proudly grooming the entrants (see Chapter 8). 'Modern' childcare practices were an important signifier of class position, and for this reason men could go to some lengths to persuade their wives to adopt the new practices. 'While I do not wish to bore the Doctor with my domestic affairs', wrote one Nigerian man to a missionary doctor in the 1940s, 'I must unwillingly remark that Mrs Onukwu [his wife] is ignorantly stubborn as far as the care of the babies is concerned.' There followed a list of instructions on the care of babies which he wished the doctor to convey to his wife.[43]

The Second World War was a turning point for the mother and child health movement in this part of Africa, and not only because, as one missionary in Northern Rhodesia wrote, it 'gave hundreds of African women and girls the opportunity to learn to knit with wool provided by the Government'.[44] More significantly, it marked the beginning of greater government expenditure on and intervention in this area of health care and its 'secularization' in the welfare movement. The relationship between colonial governments and missionary societies in the inter-war period had not always been an easy one. Whilst colonial governments recognized the value of the medical work provided by missionaries, government medical departments were frequently critical of their work, and especially the training of medical assistants, nurses and midwives, subsidized by government funds. The 'evangelistic' role of medical missionaries was seen, not infrequently, to conflict with their medical role.[45]

However, when in the post-war period the colonial state took it upon itself to fund directly an increasing number of mother and child clinics, to train midwives and so on, this presented something of a dilemma for the missions, whose 'baby' mother and child health had so clearly been. There was also the growing influence of psychological theories to be contended with. Some, like Dr Maclean of the Anglican Diocese of Nyasaland, believed that medical missionaries had somehow to come to terms with the new trends in secular medicine, though the way was not entirely clear. In his 1949 review of medical work of the Nyasaland Diocese he wrote that 'Laxity in marital relationships and in matters that affect community health are frequent' and that in combating these problems there was an important role to be played by the 'Christian psychologist and psychiatrist in the mission field'.[46] In 1950, however, he seemed somewhat less certain about how an accommodation between the missionary societies and the post-war colonial state would come about:

> the preservation of health and the relief of suffering are essential functions of the Christian missions. While this principle appears to receive increasing favour among many missionary societies, it is, at the same time, at variance with the present day tendency of state or local government departments to undertake the discharge of these functions. On the other hand religion and modern medicine – the trends in social and psychological medicine particularly – cannot, for long, go their independent ways.[47]

The Anglican mission in Nyasaland, wrote Maclean, would carve out an area of continuing influence in the field of 'family health', in which a combination of 'traditional' and modern medical missionary techniques would be employed. Medical missionaries would help to establish 'sound beliefs and practices regarding personal, family and community health by eliminating, as far as practicable, all communicable diseases and preventable psycho-neuroses ...'. Where present, a priest with training in 'psychology and psycho-pathology' would help to identify and treat the 'difficult child'.

In part the history of the Anglican and CMS medical missions is one of the gradual secularization of medical discourse and practice and their absorption into the state, culminating in the post-independence period. One of the points I have been making in this chapter, however, is that this secularization was a fractured process. The position of healing within the strategy and ideology of the Anglican mission in Central Africa was an area of ambivalence and contestation well into the twentieth century, just as it had been for the CMS missionaries in Uganda in the late nineteenth century. Terence Ranger has described in detail the dilemmas of the Anglican medical missionaries at Masasi, especially in relation to the discovery of the 'miracle' cure for yaws in the 1920s.[48] The very effectiveness of some areas of practice of biomedicine was, as I have pointed out, sometimes a source of great discomfort to medical missionaries, for whom the healing of the body was seen as a preliminary to the healing of the soul.

Part of this story is not a peculiarly 'African' or 'colonial' one, for in the 1920s there were heated debates within the Anglican church in England on the whole question of healing. This was a period when in Britain, as in Central and Eastern Africa, medical 'pluralism' of a sort was gaining in popularity, along with the increasing influence of psychological theories, and the continuing influence of spiritualism.[49] How far these developments in Britain fed on the medical missionary experience in Africa I have not been able to determine. Certainly there is evidence of a public interest in Indian healing systems at this time, and a general interest in the culture of 'primitivism'.[50] It is important to remember, therefore, that despite the hegemony of establishment biomedicine in Britain in the late nineteenth and twentieth centuries, healing remained something of a contested domain, especially within the Churches. Healing in Africa was also a contested domain, but one in which the lines were easily drawn for the medical missionaries, who continued throughout the period we have surveyed to represent African healing systems as not only ineffective and unscientific but as manifestations of evil. Though secular medicine in Africa had many of the same tendencies, it was the medical missionaries who, by and large, confronted alternative systems 'head-on' and on their own grounds – that is, not only in terms of 'science' but in terms of belief and ideology. At least this is how the medical missionary role was continuously represented to the British public. Take, for example, these 'Notes and Jottings' published in *Central Africa* as late as 1942, in which a mission doctor describes his confrontation with a 'witch doctor':

> I asked him if he had any medicine that would make a man live for ever. He fumbled in his basket, drew out one of the bundles and undid it with great deliberation. Inside he showed me some earth, scraped from the surface of a cliff on a river bank, and told me that it should be mixed with castor oil and used for anointing the body, so that the body may prosper. 'But even so', he added pathetically, 'we still die'. I told him the WE HAVE the Medicine of immortality and he asked me where and what it is. I told him that it was to be had in Church, but of course he did not know what I meant. Still, I don't think it would be very difficult to teach him. Perhaps I might begin by pointing out gently the inefficacy of his own medicines ...[51]

This encounter is a far cry from the careful regard for other members of the 'profession' advocated by Livingstone, but it is far more typical of medical missionary accounts of this period. Although, as others have pointed out, the domestic, British appeal of medical missionary work was found increasingly in its 'benevolent' rather than its evangelical role,[52] and although the internal missionary societies' rationale for medical work shifted accordingly, the two mission journals I have reviewed here – *Mercy and Truth* and *Central Africa* – continued to make much of the evangelizing possibilities of medicine. As Ranger has pointed out, there is no one history of healing in the mission Churches operating in Central and Eastern Africa, but several.[53] The debate over healing in the Anglican

Church, though still unresolved, did in twentieth-century Africa eventually result in a suspicion of 'miraculous' forms of healing and a resultant loss of converts to the many healing Churches which sprang up in this period. The UMCA missionaries, according to Ranger, were ever fearful of charges that they were leading African converts into a 'magical' view of Christianity, and hence the Anglican hierarchy maintained its commitment to modern scientific medicine as 'the only proper expression of Christian healing'.[54] Though I have no doubt that Ranger is right about the broad lines of UMCA thought on healing, the material in this chapter does pose a few questions for his analysis.

The discourse of missionary medicine in Central and Eastern Africa was one which, far from reiterating the post-Enlightenment soul/body division, constantly referred to their indivisibility. The diseases of Africa stood for larger spiritual ills, the sick bodies of Africans for the sickness of their souls. 'Certainly', wrote the medical missionary Tinsley in 1924, 'I am entitled by the facts to say of my parish that it is one uninterrupted running sore. And I cannot so much as wash it with potassium permanganate!'[55]

As many writers have pointed out, the cultural construction of illness through biomedical discourse is a powerful tool of social control. The discourse of mission medicine in Africa utilized this powerful biomedical discourse, but allied it to a rather different and very directly moral and religious one. It was, as one medical missionary put it, 'not merely a crude mechanical mixture of teaching and healing' but rather 'a chemical compound of the alchemy of faith and medical practice'.[56] This is not a subtle discourse, and there is no problem in identifying the 'enemy' in these accounts. The 'ignorance' of 'Africa' is what most powerfully struck the medical missionary. By this was meant that 'Africa' had not even reached the stage of recognizing 'her' needs:

> All down the slow centuries, right on to today, against the assaults of Knowledge the Ignorance of Ethiopia, garrisoned by Indolence, has remained inviolate. Refusing sturdy Truth, she has wived uxoriously with specious Error, and has borne him all the offspring of Confusion .... Far more terrible than the all the totality of horrific beliefs that the African holds to is his appalling ignorance of what he has not yet got at all. What an ignorance! What a spiritual darkness!
>
> Ignorance of nearly all that is high and noble and holy and beautiful. Ignorance of power to sublimate the passions, to which, in its absence, he gives hot unbridled licence ...[57]

Here, as often, 'Africa' is represented as feminine, her inhabitants as masculine. With her fertility 'Africa' continues to bear the 'offspring of Confusion', while with his 'unbridled licence' the African remains

ignorant of all that is 'high and noble'. God's diagnosis, wrote this
missionary, was 'CARELESSNESS': the African 'needs inoculating
with virulent fear'.

It is hard to measure the impact of these representations on the
audience to which they were largely directed – the British subscribers to mission journals, the Sunday School children with their
collection boxes (see Chapter 7) – but the medical–moral images are
powerful ones. In the late nineteenth and early twentieth centuries
thousands of Britons donated money regularly to the missionary
societies, sponsored mission hospital beds (or more accurately,
mats), or joined in mammoth bandage-making parties. The image of
the 'sick African' and of Africa as a 'sick continent' to be pitied and
despised is one which, though not entirely of the missionary
societies' making, was greatly influenced by the reports which they
sent home, and one which retains a strong hold even now.

If it is hard to measure the precise impact of the medical missionary discourse on British perceptions of the 'African', it is even more
difficult to say anything about the relationship such a discourse had
to medical practice and its impact on African peoples themselves. I
have cited the accounts of mission hospital ritual, perhaps naively,
both as representations of the medical missionary enterprise and as
records of medical missionary practice. There seems little doubt that
many of the rituals described did in fact take place, though how
they would have been 'read' by African patients is hard to tell. We
are told very often in these reports of the great impression which the
ritual of mission medicine made on the 'heathen' African, and the
most unlikely words are sometimes put in the mouths of grateful
patients, such as the man operated on by Dr Cook in 1904: '"I was
as a man walking in thick jungle grass, the sharp sticks wounded
my feet and I saw not the way, but now" (and a smile of joy lit up
his face) "I have found a straight road and I am walking in it".'[58]
Whether such words were uttered seems highly unlikely (though
not, of course, impossible). What is more significant for my argument is the consistent attempt by medical missionaries to effect
more than a physical transformation in their patients, and to create
new subjectivities. In theory, the mission hospital was a place where
the individual patient was 'created'. Each sick person was a potential convert, each had a 'soul' as well as a body to be attended to,
and the rituals of the missionary hospital reflected this. Healing, for
medical missionaries, was part of a programme of social and moral
engineering through which 'Africa' would be saved.

By the post-war period, however, the distinction between missionary and secular colonial medicine was being eroded. Mission
hospitals grew larger and more impersonal, and the medical treatment they offered more technical. Colonial medical departments

meanwhile became somewhat better funded and, in their new interventionist mood, colonial administrations began to intrude on areas of African life which had previously been regarded as missionary territory. One medical problem of Africa, however, remained a missionary 'baby' and retained its symbolic significance into the late twentieth century. This was leprosy.

NOTES

1 Stirling (1947), p. 41.
2 Stirling (1947), p. 73.
3 But see note 7 for work on medical missionaries in the history of Uganda. Also see Etherington (1987) on missionary medicine in nineteenth-century South Africa; Gelfand (1964) on mission medical pioneers in Nyasaland; Ranger (1981) on Anglican medical missionaries in south-east Tanzania, and Comaroff (1990) on southern Africa.
4 Recent work on the popular culture of imperialism in nineteenth- and early-twentieth-century Britain has had little to say about the specifically 'medical' aspect of the missionary 'collection-box' phenomenon, though this was clearly important in shaping the British public's image of Africa. MacKenzie (1984).
5 Jean Comaroff's analysis differs from mine. She sees an essential continuity between the ideas and practices of the early medical missionaries in southern Africa, and the state biomedicine which followed them. In the case of South Africa this seems far more apparent than in most of East and Central Africa. In other respects, our analyses of the biomedical discourse on Africa are very similar. Comaroff (1990).
6 Foskett, ed. (1964), p. 43.
7 For the story of Albert Cook's work in Uganda see Diane L. Zeller's thesis on the establishment of western medicine in Buganda: Zeller (1971); also O'Brien (1962); Cook (1945).
8 See also Ranger (1981).
9 *Mercy and Truth: a Record of the Church Missionary Society Medical Mission Work*, no. 26 (1899), p. 36.
10 See, for example, the photograph of the tumour removed by Dr Paul White (1977), facing page 136.
11 *Mercy and Truth*, no. 60 (1901), p. 281.
12 *Mercy and Truth*, no. 52 (1901), p. 88.
13 *Mercy and Truth*, no. 31 (1899), p. 166.
14 *Central Africa: a Monthly Record of the Work of the Universities' Mission*, no. 562 (1929), p. 215; *Central Africa*, no. 320 (1909), p. 213.
15 *African Tidings*, no. 73 (1895), p. 110.
16 See for example the reception given to CMS medical missionaries in Iboland: *Mercy and Truth*, no. 35 (1899), p. 270.
17 In the early period of medical missionary work in this part of Africa, a great many missionaries also ascended to the 'Great Dispensary in the Sky'. Mortality rates were high, and the deaths of missionaries filled many pages of the mission journals.

18 *Central Africa*, no. 454 (1920), p. 191.
19 *Central Africa*, no. 260 (1904), p. 173.
20 *Mercy and Truth*, no. 65 (1902), p. 6.
21 *Mercy and Truth*, no. 95 (1904), p. 338.
22 *Central Africa*, no. 388 (1915), p. 95.
23 *Mercy and Truth*, no. 146 (1909), p. 50.
24 *Central Africa*, no. 814 (1950), pp. 199–200.
25 *Central Africa*, no. 749 (1945), p. 62.
26 *Central Africa*, no. 240 (1902), p. 201.
27 *Central Africa*, no. 521 (1926), p. 113.
28 *Central Africa*, no. 532 (1927), p. 73.
29 *Central Africa*, no. 533 (1927), p. 87.
30 *Central Africa*, no. 311 (1908), p. 300.
31 *Central Africa*, no. 634 (1935), p. 212.
32 *Central Africa*, no. 497 (1924), p. 84.
33 Stirling (1977).
34 *Mercy and Truth*, no. 131 (1907), p. 365.
35 *Central Africa*, no. 577 (1931), p. 7.
36 *Central Africa*, no. 577 (1931), p. 8.
37 *Uganda Notes* (December 1907), p. 1.
38 Uganda Protectorate, *Annual Medical and Sanitary Report for 1932* (Entebbe, 1933): *Report of the Lady Coryndon Maternity Training School*, p. 47.
39 Uganda, *Annual Medical Report*, 1932, p. 47.
40 Vaughan (1988a).
41 *Central Africa*, no. 349 (1912), p. 15.
42 *Central Africa*, no. 576 (1930), p. 260.
43 Barbara Akinyemi, papers. Mss. Afr. s.1872 (2), Rhodes House, Oxford.
44 *Central Africa*, no. 729 (1943), p. 107.
45 Northern Rhodesia, Health Department: *Annual Report for 1946*: Northern Rhodesia (1949), p. 22.
46 *Central Africa*, no. 799 (1949), p. 92.
47 *Central Africa* no. 824 (1950), p. 190.
48 Ranger (1981).
49 Mews (1982).
50 Mews (1982), p. 316.
51 *Central Africa*, no. 717 (1942), pp. 94–5.
52 Walls (1982).
53 Ranger (1982).
54 Ranger (1982).
55 *Conquest by Healing* (Medical Missionary Association), New Series, vol. 1 (1924), p. 44.
56 *Mercy and Truth*, no. 213 (1914), p. 297.
57 *Conquest by Healing*, vol. 1 (1924), G. E. Tinsley, 'The Careless Ethiopian (Lake Mweru)', p. 45.
58 *Mercy and Truth*, no. 95 (1904), p. 338.

4 Without the Camp: Institutions and Identities in the Colonial History of Leprosy

I see on the road a caravan of horsemen and wanderers on foot, guided by a black policeman who bears a large official portfolio containing 'the papers' of the patients and the orders of segregation signed by their doctors. The lepers are tired, dusty, clothed with rags, but their companions remain unmoved. The stewards of the asylum do not say much, only 'Here the men, there the women'. They stand in a row – if they are able to stand – with their swollen features, their fingerless hands, their mutilated, ulcerating feet ... Besides food and sleep they have but one wish: to get medicine. As soon as they arrive, they want to take drugs which they hope will heal them, ignorant that, up to the present, science has not yet discovered the plant, the serum, or the chemical preparation which will conquer the terrible disease ...[1]

This is how the Rev. Dieterlen of the Paris Evangelical Mission described the arrival of a 'caravan' of lepers at the Botsabelo settlement in Basutoland in 1914. There is no mention in his account of the riot which took place there in May of that year, a riot which came about because of the bitter disappointment and anger the patients felt when their hopes of a cure were dashed.[2]

The story of what was always termed the 'fight against leprosy' in colonial Africa is not, however, primarily a story of incarceration and segregation. John Iliffe has argued that this is a history of the tenacity of hope and faith.[3] In this chapter I have placed a rather different emphasis on this history, seeing in it the projection on to Africa of a powerful Christian disease symbolism, and the attempt to engineer socially a 'leper identity' in the particular circumstances of colonialism.

Figure 5 Some of a group of fifteen hundred lepers waiting to be examined in the Sudan.

Basutoland was one of the few colonial African territories in which the segregation of lepers was made compulsory, and even here the policy was in practice short-lived. Elsewhere in Africa colonial governments lacked the resources to enforce segregation and left the treatment of lepers largely to mission societies. Fortunately for African sufferers of leprosy, by the time colonial medical departments were on a firmer footing and were more able to intervene to control the disease, 'expert' opinion was very firmly against compulsory segregation. Faith in the possibility of a cure, however, brought large numbers of leprosy sufferers into voluntary isolation in 'leper colonies' and 'leper villages' all over Africa.

The faith of the African patient was essentially a faith in the technical capacity of western medicine. Yaws, a similarly disfiguring disease, had been cured by 'injections' administered, in large part, by mission doctors; the belief that leprosy could be similarly cured was tenacious, despite numerous and bitter disappointments. Meanwhile the faith of the leprosy doctors and nurses in their ability to effect a cure was bound up with the enormous symbolic weight which leprosy carried in the Christian tradition. In Africa, as in India, this symbolism was not simply transferred but was partially transformed by the encounter with local societies and practices. But in some places it also played an important role in transforming African views of the disease and in defining the identity of 'the leper'.

In the course of creating institutions for the treatment of leprosy sufferers, mission societies had to make decisions regarding the relative weight of different African identities. Leprosy offered to the missionaries the possibility of engineering new African communities, isolated from, and expunged of, all those features of African society which they saw as impeding the development of Christianity. In such institutions leprosy patients were offered the leper identity as a 'liberation'. More often than not, however, this ambitious aim was compromised by the need, both to retain the co-operation of patients, and to maintain order. The model frequently resorted to was the recreation of the 'village' community within the leprosy asylum, and the reinforcement (and sometimes the invention of) ethnic identities and customs. The history of the 'leprosy colony', as a colony within a colony, points to many of the tensions within the wider colonial enterprise, between different forms of intervention, different degrees of social engineering, and between objectification and subjectification.

The power of Biblical imagery is manifest in the sources describing the plight of Africa's leprosy sufferers. Even in the post-war period, when technology and secular psychology make their mark in the treatment of the disease, African lepers are still depicted as they were in the Old Testament, ragged and dusty, simultaneously 'damned' and 'saved'.

The tenacity and appeal of the Christian discourse on leprosy is remarkable. In medieval Europe lepers occupied a strange ground as the 'living dead'. As the 'unclean' of Leviticus they were frequently placed 'without the camp'. In early medieval France a priest performed the ritual of separation in which the leper stood in a grave whilst the priest threw three spadefuls of earth on her or his head, announcing that they were 'dead to the world', but would be 're-born in God'. The New Testament, meanwhile, offered the hope of healing miracles in St Luke's Gospel, through which it was possible to interpret the leper as specially chosen by God for salvation – the leper's sufferings in this world would be compensated for in the next. But it was, as Foucault points out, a strange kind of salvation, accomplished through exclusion: 'in a strange reversibility that is the opposite of good works and prayer, they are saved by the hand that is not stretched out'.[4] Medieval views on leprosy were not without their contradictions. If leprosy was regarded as a sign of salvation, albeit a strange one, it was also seen as being closely associated with sin, and with sexual excess in particular.[5]

Though leprosy had receded in western Europe in the late Middle Ages (leaving a space, so Foucault tells us, for the madman to enter), when it was 'rediscovered' in the nineteenth century in Norway, the United States, India and South Africa, its medieval symbolism seemed to have remained intact.

African attitudes and beliefs about leprosy were far from uniform, as Iliffe has pointed out.[6] Early missionaries sometimes sought out the leprosy sufferers in their areas in a very self-conscious way. From amongst these sufferers, as amongst other socially marginal groups such as ex-slaves, many early converts to Christianity came. Yet the extent to which leprosy sufferers were socially marginalized varied enormously from one part of Africa to another. In the course of their encounter with this variability, the deep ambiguity of the Christian tradition on leprosy was revealed. For example, one of the oft-reiterated aims of the 'fight against leprosy' was to rescue leprosy sufferers from the terrible social isolation and stigmatization which they were presumed to endure. Where such a stigma existed, the missionary task was clear, but when societies were encountered in which leprosy was not stigmatized at all, a deep horror was expressed by European observers. Absence of fear of leprosy (as with absence of shame over syphilis – see Chapter 6) was seen as the mark not of humanity but of the extreme 'primitiveness' of such societies.

In one issue of *Leprosy Review* (the British Empire Leprosy Relief Association's journal) of 1931, two very different stories (and not incompatible ones) could be told. From Tanganyika, Janet Murray reported on the success of leprosy out-patient treatment which had encouraged sufferers to come forward at an early stage. The attitude of the African to the disease had changed radically in recent years, she claimed. While formerly the 'African leper' was an outcast, 'shunned by all and at death being given no decent burial', now this was no longer the case. In the same issue it was reported by R. Cochrane that leprosy was spreading in the Eastern Province of Uganda in large part because the people there were 'ignorant and dirty', and had no fear of the disease. This attitude he contrasted with that of the Baganda who were 'more developed' and 'more highly civilised' than any other group in Uganda. It was 'not surprising', therefore, that the Bagandan people had a 'great dread of the disease'.[7]

The fear of leprosy and stigmatization of its victims was to be combated with Christian compassion, but such a fear was always considered 'natural'. Acts of great individual heroism in the fight against the disease were performed against this background of 'natural' fear and abhorrence.

If collective fear of leprosy was seen as a sign of 'civilization', differential susceptibility was also regarded as highly significant in ways which reflected both the tenacity of the European Christian tradition on leprosy and the situation of colonial rule. As often in discussions of disease amongst Africans, differences in incidence were described initially in terms of ethnic or 'tribal' difference. As in the case of mental illness, the analysis of these 'tribal' differences in incidence was, by the 1920s and 1930s, allied to arguments about the disintegration of African societies and the resultant 'racial' or 'tribal' degeneration. The aetiology of the disease was, and is, highly complex and still incompletely understood. Our interest here is not to 'prove' that leprosy doctors 'got it wrong', for this was a period of advancement in the understanding of the disease, but rather to illuminate the specific ways in which they discussed these issues in the African context.

Leprosy was, as Iliffe has pointed out, a disease of poverty in a dual sense. Its incidence was higher in remote and backward areas, and infection was aggravated by malnutrition and poor hygiene. Where sufferers were isolated in remote areas and deprived of a livelihood, the disease was also a cause of their poverty. Though 'environmental' theories were put forward for the differential incidence of the disease, these almost always had a strong social component in which ethnic or 'tribal' difference was an explanatory factor.

For example, Dr Ross, who was Medical Superintendent of the notorious Robben Island Asylum in Cape Town in 1890, felt that 'racial degeneration' through 'cross-breeding' explained the differential incidence of leprosy in South Africa:

> The pure native races, like the Zulus and Kaffirs, are seldom effected with leprosy; but among the Korennes and cross-breeds between native women and the nomadic Boers of the coast districts are to be found a large number of cases with leonine countenances, sodden and leaden coloured features, and all the characteristic phenomena of true tubercular leprosy. The popular opinion here is that the descendants of the Chinese and Javanese (who are foul feeders and eaters of fish and grain, and not very particular as to what they consume) were the first to develop leprosy at the Cape ...[8]

In the 1930s and 1940s, when the British Empire Leprosy Relief Association (BELRA) campaign in Africa was well under way, ethnic difference was used to account for incidence in various ways. On the one hand, it was said by some that the more 'backward' the group, the higher the incidence of leprosy. This was connected, of course, with the idea that 'primitive' groups had no fear of leprosy and did not segregate leprosy sufferers. When the leprosy expert Dr E. Muir visited Northern Rhodesia and the White Fathers' leprosy settlement on Chilubi Island, he compared incidence between the Bisa and the Bemba. The Bisa, amongst whom leprosy was

common, had 'insanitary habits' and were 'promiscuous', while the
Bemba, amongst whom there was a much lower incidence, were
said to be more sanitary and to feed on millet and not cassava.[9]
Accounting for the high incidence of the disease amongst the Lala,
Muir also cited the 'fact' of the 'primitiveness' of this group, but
went on to say that because the totemic system was strong amongst
these people, it interfered with 'tribal discipline' Summing up, he
said that leprosy tended to spread where 'tribal discipline' was
bad.[10] Similarly, the difference in incidence of tubercular lesions
between Barotseland and Nyasaland was ascribed to some collective
attribute of the people in those areas: 'to use a metaphor', wrote
Muir,' the difference between the two regions . . . is not the bacillary
seed, nor yet the basic nature of the body soil, but the intensity with
which it is cultivated'. The people of Barotseland he understood to
be 'dirty and promiscuous'.[11]

Within the framework of an ethnic analysis, a complex set of
explanations was being put forward by Muir and others. Leprosy
was a disease of 'primitive' groups, with insanitary habits (a disease
of rural poverty, one might say). But it was also associated with
'promiscuity', with eating habits, and with the breakdown of 'tribal
discipline' through social change and modernization.

The association of leprosy with the 'breakdown of tribal authority'
was part of a familiar and much wider theme in colonial medical
discourse. Its association with 'promiscuity' was associated with this
theme, though it was also part of an older theme in the Christian
tradition. Dr Ross, on Robben Island, had explicitly connected leprosy with syphilis, and many other writers did the same. Leprosy,
when not seen as the direct result of sexual sin, was often regarded
by mission doctors and nurses as conducive to it. As one mission
nurse put it, leprosy was 'in itself a great perverter of moral sense'.[12]

When we move from an examination of the question of incidence
to that of treatment, however, the picture becomes rather more
complex. As has already been pointed out, this is not a story of
confinement and incarceration so much as one of faith and hope. On
the whole, leprosy patients who came to live in government or,
more often, mission-run settlements and colonies were there volun-
tarily. The ways in which these settlements were run and the degree
of institutionalization they brought about varied quite considerably.
What is evident, however, is that leprosy was often treated as a
thoroughly exceptional disease which broke through the usual colonial categorizations of difference.

Though colonial governments became more directly involved in
creation and running of leprosy settlements in the 1930s and 1940s,
the vast majority of such settlements remained in the hands of
mission organizations, with funding from those governments and

from the British Empire Leprosy Relief Association. The missionary medical discourse I have characterized in the previous chapter as standing apart from the secular discourse in a number of ways, the most important being its representation of 'traditional' society and the African collectivity as being the source of evil, and hence of disease. The way to health in the medical missionary ideology lay in part through rescuing the individual African soul from the influences of traditional society. When African medical problems were presented to the British mission journal subscribers this was frequently done through stories of individual patients – the African patient was 'created' through these accounts. When it came to leprosy, however, the missionary emphasis was on collectivity – not the collectivity of 'tribe', but the collectivity of fellow-sufferers: 'My lepers' was how many mission doctors and nurses referred to these patients. The leprosy settlement was a place where a new identity and new community could be forged. A countervailing tendency, however, was for leprosy settlements to be built along the lines of 'traditional' villages, and to divide sufferers according to their ethnicity. This was most common in government-run settlements where it was a direct reflection and reinforcement of rule through 'custom', but mission settlements frequently had to resort to such tactics simply to be able to keep their patients (who seemed genuinely to prefer living in 'villages', no matter how artificial these might be).

The leper settlement, like other colonial institutions, was a place of often complex social organization, on which a number of medical, religious and social ideas were brought to bear. Early settlements were miserable places of isolation, in which the Christian message, despite its ambiguities, must indeed have seemed like the only sign of hope. Visiting the appalling Lundu Island colony run by the German government of Tanganyika, the UMCA nurse recounted how she spoke to the sufferers 'of the life hereafter, and told them that though their bodies were decaying, and though this life did not give them all they had hoped for, yet each of them had a soul to be saved or lost'. They must try to look forward to the better life beyond the grave, she said, 'and not dwell too much on their present misfortunes'.[13] Lundu Island was indeed a 'place apart from the world', and sufferers there were only too happy to welcome the mission nurse, especially when she came with needles and medicine. On Funzi Island, off the coast of Tanganyika, things were not much better, even in the late 1920s, but leprosy sufferers were apparently cheered by the weekly visit of the UMCA missionary and nurses who came not only with bandages to dress their ulcers and doses of the new hydnocarpus treatment but also with a gramophone: 'All who are able turn up on the dispensary verandah

when that is played, and it is very pleasant to hear the roars of
laughter over Harry Lauder's songs ...'[14]

The arrival of the visitors every week was marked by an extraordinary little ritual: 'We landed at low tide, and were carried on the
shoulders of natives across a swamp. We then made our way to our
hut on one corner of the island, and partook of a meal of hard-boiled
eggs, cold plum pudding and tea. After this, the two nurses
changed into their 'leper dresses' which they keep in the hut and
only wear when in contact with the lepers ...'[15] After dispensing
treatment, a service was held in the small church, attended by
Christian patients: 'It was a moving sight to see them prostrating
themselves in prayer ...'

There is plenty of evidence for the real hope induced amongst
sufferers by the introduction of hydnocarpus oil injections after the
First World War. Leprosy doctors and nurses were often aware, in
fact, that these painful injections were nothing more than a 'confidence trick', as Iliffe has called the treatment, but they did keep
patients in the settlement or within the orbit of the mission clinic.
Such hopes of the treatment were partly accounted for by the effectiveness of the yaws cure by injection, and partly by other elements
of the care provided. By the 1920s and 1930s most, but not all,
leprosy settlements did provide patients with an improved diet,
sanitation and nursing – all of which tended towards an improvement of their health status, with or without the injections. Unlike
yaws sufferers, however, leprosy patients were expected, in the
words of one recent writer, to 'learn to be lepers'.[16]

The Annual Report of BELRA of 1935, under the heading 'Worse
Than Slavery', depicted this 'most terrible' of diseases in the following way: '... not killing, but mutilating by slow degrees, and
ultimately destroying even the semblance of a human being.
Men, women and children became moulded into that ghastly form,
in which personality, sex, and age, are blotted out, and the
victim becomes a mere caricature of humanity.'[17] According to this
horrific picture, leprosy destroyed the very identity of its victims.
An alternative identity as a 'leper' was what some missionaries
appeared to be advocating in their settlements. Here patients were
encouraged to identify as a group with the lepers of the Bible. They
were told that they were both damned and saved, that their
souls had to be cleansed along with their bodies, and that they
were special in the eyes of God. If they stayed and were successfully
treated (this became more likely with sulphone treatments after
the Second World War), they might be ceremoniously released as
'cleansed'.

In 1956, the Ven. A. S. Rice-Jones described one such 'cleansing'
ceremony at the Mngeke Leprosarium in south-west Tanganyika.

Figure 6 Leprosy patients applying hydnocarpus oil to each other at Itu settlement, Nigeria.

Held on St John the Evangelist's Day, its purpose was to present certificates of discharge to the Anglican patients who were being sent home cured to their villages: 'I gave a short talk', wrote the Ven. Rice-Jones, 'taking my text as was natural from the story of the healing of the lepers.'[18]

In the Qua Iboe Leprosy Mission in Nigeria, 'discharge days' were also memorable occasions:

> First came the selection of those symptom free, then the breathless anticipation as the list of names went up on the board, followed by jubilation – and the tears of the disappointed. Eventually the great day itself, with those discharged dressed in fine cloth, the ladies with bright headties and fancy jewellry. Their happiness was shared by visitors who joined in the simple service, as those receiving the prized certificate were committed to God with much thanksgiving.[19]

It is not easy to assess the degree to which African leprosy patients 'learned to be lepers' or indeed how they felt about ceasing to be 'lepers' when they were cured, 'cleansed' and sent home.

The earliest settlements were places in which all identities seemed to have been eroded. The Robben Island Asylum in the 1890s, for example, was a place into which lepers, lunatics, paupers and the chronic sick were herded, and which, in Iliffe's words, 'disturbed humanitarian opinion almost from its inception'.[20] 'Humanity' lay in appropriate classification and separation. The isolation of 'lepers' in separate institutions was seen as a humanitarian act as much as a public health measure. But many of these early settlements were little better than Robben Island. African patients at the Botsabelo settlement in Basutoland, for example, were cut off from their kin, and often from their husbands, wives and children – deprived, in fact of any social identity. The Rev. Dieterlen found the state of mind of inmates to be 'bitter, revolting and undisciplined', and somewhat resistant to his teaching of the virtues of 'submission and peace'. The walls of the building echoed with the cries of women separated from their children: 'Oh, those lamentations of the women, of the mothers', wrote Dieterlen, '. . . How many times do we hear them here? They are heart-rending.'[21] The real tragedy of the African leprosy patients in the early settlements, we are told in these accounts, was that they refused to relinquish their social identities as wives, mothers and husbands. Only when they had allowed the disease to take over would they find 'peace'.

Patients who arrived at the Asylum at Pretoria were also said to be confused and unhappy, finding themselves separated from their families (segregation was compulsory in South Africa), and in a totally strange environment. Sometimes they would find people from their own 'tribes' and villages, but more often they were 'perfect strangers'. But, wrote the Rev. Ernest Creux in 1918, they soon became receptive to the Christian sympathy offered by the missionary, and were comforted by the message he brought. They began to learn, in other words, to take on the identity of 'lepers'.[22]

When this happened, and a collective identity of some sort was forged amongst sufferers, it frequently brought the authorities nothing but problems. In Northern Rhodesia, Dr Wareham of the London Missionary Society met outright hostility amongst his patients at Mbereshi. In all his fifteen years in Africa, he wrote, he had not met with a more 'dissatisfied, grumbling and cantankerous group'. They broke all the rules, refused to do what they were told, shouted and raged.[23]

By the 1953, patients at the Chitokoloki Leprosy Settlement in Northern Rhodesia, identifying themselves as 'Deadbodies', complained about a change in the regime there under a new missionary doctor who made them work in neighbouring villages for their food: 'This is the new way which lepers help themselves to have enough food or to buy with their own money – to those who got fingers to work with, but some got no fingers to work with.'[24] Inmates of the Pemba Island settlement off Zanzibar had used the same terminology in their plea to the Government of Tanganyika in 1924: 'We are dead, you know we are dead ... the government has brought us to this place, let it now have the responsibility of us ...'[25] Patients at the Luapula Leprosy Settlement in 1954 wrote directly to the Principal Medical Officer in Lusaka with their complaints about a new regime which had been instituted there, depriving them of the blankets and 'leper uniforms': 'Think of us please we are poor and we get no blankets to cover our bodies. We haven't got any property to help us in this in good way, as we know that Government is our father, Why do Government let us suffuring [sic], why Government become our enemy nowadays instead of saving us, Government kill us. In many years we were in pity of Government why not today?'[26] The patients of Kabalenge also complained of the inadequate diet – they worked 'like slaves', they wrote, but were given an insufficient supply of meat and 'rotten fish'. Though they described themselves as powerless they knew, however, that as carriers of a contagious disease they held immense power. If pity failed to move the Government, perhaps this threat would: 'We hope many petient [sic] will leave this settlement and go to their villages without get well first but some if leprosy can be infected to many people.' And they ended with an appeal and a gesture of submission: 'Save us, our father and mother. There is no-one to save us except you.'

The formidable Electra Dory, who ran the UMCA leper colony at Likwenu in Nyasaland in the 1930s, recalled that patients there referred to themselves as 'The Dead'. They were, she wrote, apathetic figures 'with their blank expressionless faces these mutilated specimens already seemed part of the red earth, dust falling into dust'.[27]

There were, of course, both advantages and disadvantages to collective identification as 'The Dead'. In so far as leprosy patients wished to stay within the settlement (and many, according to Dory, were unwilling to leave even when better), then identifying oneself with the lepers of the Bible clearly carried advantages. Electra Dory, though she was highly critical of the morality and dependency of the patients in her settlement, was also frequently moved to compassion for them as 'lepers': 'These afflicted ones bore their burden with fortitude and courage, accepting their humiliations and disgusting sores with stoic heroism. They never rebelled against the fate that stigmatised them with a disease whose very name was used as a synonym for uncleanliness and corruption.'[28]

Pre-colonial African attitudes to leprosy had been variable within what became the Nyasaland Protectorate, with some groups recognizing the contagiousness of leprosy and others not. The colonial government and mission societies trod very carefully on the question of segregation. A Bill of 1921 which sought to 'Make Provision for the Isolation and Detention of Persons affected with Leprosy' contained fairly draconian restrictions on the movements of leprosy sufferers, but was never enforced.[29] But by the 1920s a generation of African medical assistants had been trained by the mission societies into a particular view of the disease. In 1927, Fred Nyirenda, a hospital assistant, addressed the North Nyasa Native Association on the subject of leprosy, telling them that the disease had receded from Britain in the Middle Ages because strict segregation of sufferers had been enforced. 'The Association discussed the subject with heartfelt awe and many members gave an account of much concern as regards the African Lepers' apathy toward their fellows. That the lepers have been found actually pleased to dine in the same dish and drink from the same cup with others; they carry other people's children in their arms, and have been angry when told not to do so.'[30]

The extent to which leprosy colonies were run with a view to creating a 'leper identity' should not, however, be exaggerated. There was, as I have already indicated, a tension between the tendency to define leprosy sufferers as a group beyond and outside of society, and the frequent recourse to an 'indirect rule' method of social control. By this I mean the practice of categorizing patients within the settlements along ethnic lines, as well as according to the severity and stage of their disease, of building the settlements along the lines of 'villages', and of instituting systems of control through 'chiefs' and 'headmen'. To this extent many leprosy settlements, including mission-run ones, reflected the larger colonial society and systems of control, and stood as microcosms of the 'British colony'.

Some missionaries felt unhappy with this, but most had to make concessions to any form of organization which would keep leprosy patients accessible to treatment and relatively isolated. Electra Dory complained that Likwenu settlement in Nyasaland, which allowed considerable freedom of movement, had aimed to recreate the village within its walls and was only too successful in this respect. Each patient built her or his own hut out of wattle and daub, and everyone was free to come and go as they wished. 'The colony', she wrote, 'resembled almost too closely the village life of the Africans which, with few exceptions, was squalid and insanitary.'[31] She was critical of the mission's policy which she characterized as always stepping 'right down into the squalor of African life', rather than 'lift[ing] it up'.[32]

On the other side of the continent and in the very different circumstances of Liberia, Dr Werner Junge set up a leper settlement on an uninhabited island in the 1930s. He was intent that 'my lepers', as he termed them, should find happiness on the island, and this was to be achieved in part through work. The theme of salvation through productive labour is a recurrent one in the history of leprosy treatment in Africa, and parallels contemporaneous practice for tuberculosis patients in Britain.[33] On Junge's island land was cleared and the lepers were 'planted out'.[34] In the first year they were given daily rations of rice, but after this it was intended that they should be self-provisioning. Gradually the colony grew. A 'palaver house' was built, a small hospital, a school and a church. Roads were made and bridges built, hens, dogs and goats were kept; patients engaged in fishing, and some opened a carpentry shop where they made doors and furniture. A 'chief' was appointed to be in charge of day-to-day affairs.

Junge divided inmates into three 'classes', not by ethnicity or by degrees of disablement (as happened elsewhere), but strictly 'according to the amount of work they actually did'. The first class, comprising the most industrious workers, were paid a wage which was approximately 80 per cent of that prevailing in the country at the time.

Perhaps the most innovative aspect of Junge's colony, however, was its 'family' system. With some difficulty he had persuaded his employers, an American Episcopalian order, to allow leprosy patients to 'marry' one another, even when they were already theoretically married to people outside the settlement in their 'other' life.[35] He also instituted a kind of child 'exchange', which enabled both infected and uninfected children to be cared for in families. When children suffering from leprosy were brought to the island they were allocated to a household, and 'adopted' by them. A married male leper was entitled to a third larger income than an unmarried man, and this was raised by a further third for each adopted child. Meanwhile, children born of these 'leper marriages' had to be isolated from their natural parents to avoid their being infected. Junge advertised for suitable foster mothers from the mainland, who were paid to look after the children, and provided with complete baby outfits by an American donor. At the end of a defined period they were given the option of returning the child or keeping it as their own. According to Junge, none of these foster-mothers elected to return the children, who were therefore successfully assimilated into uninfected households.[36]

Elsewhere different arrangements and different rules of conduct were enforced. Some missions were stricter than others when it came to relations between the sexes. Bishop Lucas of the UMCA in 1939 devised 'rules of conducts' for leprosy sufferers in Tanganyika, which included a clear prohibition against adultery. Those who abided by the rules, he said, deserved the sympathy and help of others, 'but a leper who does not keep these rules is in danger of being regarded as a menace'.[37] Presumably it was to avoid the problem of uncontrolled sexuality that all inmates of the UMCA Village of Mercy at Fiwila in Northern Rhodesia were expected to marry, if in a 'suitable state of health'.[38]

At the Ho leprosy settlement in the Gold Coast, founded in 1927, inmates settled in 'compounds', each of which was allocated farming land, and each of which was presided over by a headman, responsible for order and cleanliness. A chief headman and headwoman were elected by inmates to oversee the entire settlement, to judge cases and hear complaints.[39]

At Ngomahuru in Southern Rhodesia, the four-hundred or so patients were arranged in villages. All open cases were housed in one village, whilst in the remaining four consideration was given to 'tribe' and gender, resulting in the following arrangement. Village 1 housed the 'single, indigenous' (in fact male, single 'indigenous'); Village 2 housed the 'single foreign' (by which was presumably meant Africans from outside the territory); Village 3 housed 'married indigenous' and Village 4 'married foreign'. Unmarried girls were allocated to families in the 'married' villages. The Ngomahuru settlement expressed in its organization and classifications the practices and concerns of the Southern Rhodesian administration. It was, in fact, more like a mining 'compound' than a village, inmates being arranged in work gangs and employed for four mornings of the week on any work which was required.[40] This contrasted with the West African situation where the 'free market' seemed constantly to intrude, creating, for instance, the bustling activity at the Itu settlement in Nigeria. Here occupational classifications seemed as important as any in creating the identities of individual patients, and a balance was struck between individual and communal enterprise, reflecting the divisions of labour of the wider society:

> occupations followed by inmates include private store-keepers, who buy and sell produce at the evening markets in the settlement, canoe builders, a blacksmith, umbrella repairer and goldsmith. The tailors have their own sewing machines, but if employed by the settlement for making such things as uniforms for police, nurses, etc., they are paid 1/6*d* per day for work done ... the majority [of farms] are communal, producing yams, cassava, potatoes, corn, beans and groundnuts. The cassava is made into a flour called garri, and 20 women are employed at this work.[41]

Similarly, at another leper colony near Maiduguri, a variety of economic activities took place. The colony produced its own cotton, which was then spun to make bandages, though some of the 'more

Figure 7 Scenes from the Fiwila Village of Mercy, Northern Rhodesia.

wily patients' took to making their own trousers out of the bandage material. Inmates also made shoes out of old car tyre wheels, in part to protect their feet against ulcers. The women set up a weekly market, and the Saturday pay day ritual became a central feature of life in the colony.[42]

At the Dutch Reformed Church's settlement at Madzimoyo in Northern Rhodesia, an early attempt to house patients in a hospital-like brick building was abandoned due to what were described as their 'special tribal customs'. The patients asked to be allowed to stay in their small individual huts. The settlement was run as a 'native village', with a chief and his assistants to settle difficulties. This seemed to the superintendent, Dr Knobel, the best solution, for 'We will only drive them away if we put them in surroundings they are not used to.'[43] The Qua Iboe settlement in Nigeria was run along similar lines in the 1930s. At the head was a 'Chief' chosen by the missionaries as a reliable Christian. He was assisted by an Advisory Council of twelve 'senior patients', his own policemen, court messengers and magistrate.[44]

If the leprosy settlement run on the lines of a 'native village' had become the norm for both government and mission-sponsored institutions by the 1930s, there were some (and not only missionaries) who had lingering doubts about the wisdom of having taken this path and who looked back wistfully on the days when a greater degree of social engineering had seemed possible. Leprosy, wrote one medical officer in Nigeria in 1940, was a problem 'permeating native life' and would have to be addressed as such by Africans themselves. The control of leprosy could not be effected through a series of 'surgical operations performed on the body of the community': 'Leprosy cannot be excised from the people by means of the European-run settlement. The treatment is medical. As in the body of the individual, so it is in the body of the community – the body itself must isolate the foci of the disease.'[45]

If leprosy settlements had never done more than perform 'surgical operations' on the disease, then by the 1950s, with the advent of new sulphone treatments, they began to look almost redundant. As the proportion of arrested cases increased and more and more treatments were administered to out-patients, so the leprosy settlement became the home of those who had been chronically disabled by the disease – the true 'lepers' one could say. But as treatment became more generally available and more effective, so it became apparent how vast the proportions of the problem really were. Leprosy became a 'mass' disease.

In 1951, *Leprosy Review* (articles in which had become increasingly 'scientific' and technocratic in outlook) published an article which seemed to herald the end of leprosy as a 'special' disease. Entitled

'The Psychology of Leprosy', its author, G. A. Ryrie, was highly critical of what he called the 'irrational' factor in leprosy treatment. This 'irrational factor' he explained along Freudian lines as being 'attributable to the inheritance of our sense of guilt associated with an incest complex'. Leprosy work, he went on, attracted doctors and workers with a religious outlook,' and it is precisely such people who tend to have the guilt and punishment complex most deeply'. He criticized the running of leprosy settlements in which, he claimed, patients hardly ever received a proper medical examination, and were subject to unnecessary and elaborate precautions born of 'leprophobia'.[46]

If 'irrational' fears of leprosy could be explained away by an incest complex, such fears had always been, and remained, essential to the massive international leprosy relief campaigns orchestrated by BELRA and others. The essence of these campaigns was an appeal to the people of Europe and North America to show the depth of their compassion by helping the 'defiled'. By constantly restating the message that leprosy sufferers should be rescued from their isolation, these campaigns continued to entrench the idea of the 'leper' as a person apart. The oft-repeated aim of restoring the 'dignity' of the leprosy sufferer was offset by the images of the photographs used, and the captions placed under them. The BELRA annual reports of the 1930s and 1940s all had subtitles: 'The Empire's Open Sore', 'The Shadow of Leprosy', 'Dawn', and so on. In the 1935 report entitled 'Worse than Slavery', the dehumanizing effects of leprosy were discussed – the 'humanity' of the leper was to be recognized and restored. The picture published next to this, however, could have done nothing but reinforce the view that leprosy patients were, indeed, less than human. During the Second World War benefactors were reminded that the 'fight against leprosy' was still on: 'The war against bodily disease is far older than the war against Hitlerism and it will last far longer ... The daily work in a leper settlement may need as much pluck and patience as fighting in the trenches.'[47] After the war donors were encouraged to 'adopt' a child leper, and the cover of the 1947 Annual Report bore the picture of the Queen's 'adoptee'.

Through these means the figure of the 'leper' continued to encourage unrivalled acts of charity on the part of western Europeans and North Americans. The extraordinary campaigns organized in the 1950s and 1960s by Raoul Follereau were aimed at encouraging mass, worldwide support to bring an end to leprosy. They depended for their appeal on the idea of the 'leper' the world over being peculiarly worthy of acts of charity. Whether the 'leper' concerned was Indian, Chinese or African was hardly relevant in the context of this campaign, the attraction of which was partly its

appeal to internationalism. World Leprosy Day, instituted by Follereau in 1954, was conceived as a universal and simultaneous
demonstration of Christian charity towards leprosy sufferers.
Follereau's appeal on the radio on the Seventh World Leprosy Day
went like this:

> Stop fiddling with the knobs of your radio, Sir.
> And Madam, leave off your housework.
> Come and sit down beside each other.
> And listen to me.
> Do you want to save 15 million men?
> Do you want 15 million men to have the right to live and be happy like
> you?
> It's in your power,
> I'm referring to the most wretched , saddest and abandoned of all
> mankind: the lepers.[48]

So it was that Follereau's highly successful mass campaigns rested
on the perpetuation of the figure of the 'leper', reinforced rather
than undermined by Follereau's ostentatious personal displays of
kissing leprosy sufferers wherever he found them.

Contracting the disease was what every leprosy worker dreaded,
but such a misfortune was also construed as perhaps the greatest act
of medical heroism possible. The heroism was, in part, a function of
the real hardship of isolation which had to be prescribed. It was not
so much isolation itself as isolation with African lepers which seemed
to inspire the real dread and awe, implying, as it did, the capacity of
the disease to make uncertain the boundaries of race and the hierarchies of colonial power. Edith Shelley, a UMCA nurse in Tanganyika
in the 1920s, contracted leprosy and isolated herself amongst her
'fellow lepers' until she felt that she was cured. Her experience led
her to be an outspoken opponent of segregation and an advocate of
'humane' methods of treatment. In 1939, A. D. Power suggested, in
an article in the *Journal of the African Society*, that the problem of
European contraction of leprosy in the Empire might be a much
larger one. He argued that there were 'at least half a hundred (and
probably more) lepers at large in this country', by which he meant
England.[49] In Southern Rhodesia, at the Ngomahuru leprosy settlement, there was, according to Power, one self-exiled Englishman
suffering from leprosy. This seemed to Power to be an excellent
place to locate a European leprosarium which might serve the entire
Empire. It was 3,000 feet above sea-level, 'in beautiful surroundings,
with fishing, riding, shooting, lawn tennis and many other amenities available'. Indeed, the Ngomahuru gardens had even featured
in *Country Life* magazine.[50] The question of transporting potential

patients from India and elsewhere would, he suggested, require some thought. Ultimately the leprosarium might have to acquire its own areoplane, but in the meantime he suggested getting 'some sort of cloth bag made, with a respirator, in which the patient could be placed and then carried in an ordinary chartered areoplane without fear of spreading infection'.[51]

These extraordinary arrangements were never, as far as I can tell, put into practice, but, as in the history of the European insane in the Empire, they indicate the deep concern with boundaries felt by Europeans in the Empire. Whilst missionaries saw leprosy as a unique disease through which the identity of the sufferer became completely synonymous with the illness, in practice the classification of leprosy patients became a highly complex matter, reflecting the larger colonial society. Theories of leprosy causation also came to reflect not only Christian concerns but wider colonial concerns over social change and social order. But in two important ways leprosy was unique. It was unique in the amount of attention it attracted from medical missionaries, medical departments, and international charitable organizations, and unique in the degree of intervention and institutionalization it inspired. No other disease called forth the resources required for institutionalization on a large scale.

Whilst the leprosy settlements were taking their various shapes in colonial Africa, in Britain it was tuberculosis which was receiving the equivalent kind of attention and carrying the same kind of symbolic weight. A brief comparison between these two histories helps to illuminate the extent to which the medical approach to leprosy in Africa was distinctly 'colonial', and how far it reflected a wider trend in biomedicine's social constructionist tendencies.

A national campaign against tuberculosis was launched in Britain in the early part of the twentieth century, and is described by Linda Bryder in her book *Below the Magic Mountain* (1988). Bryder examines reasons why tuberculosis became such a focus of state concern in this period, and discusses the measures devised to combat the disease. In particular, she examines ideas about causation, the treatments devised, and the social construction of the tuberculous patient. Whilst consumption had been a 'romantic' disease of the upper classes in the nineteenth century, in the twentieth century tuberculosis became conceptualized more as a mass disease of the working classes, and the focus of a discussion on the habits of the poor. Though poor housing, workplace conditions and malnutrition were seen, at various times, to be associated with a high incidence of the disease, the medical profession saw the solution to the problem not in a direct improvement in social and economic conditions but in reform of what came to be known as 'lifestyle'. Tuberculosis threatened the nation, but its defeat would only come about through individual responsibility and education. The discovery of the tubercle bacillus in 1882 had been one element in bringing about a new social pathology of the disease which played down the factor of heredity in favour of the idea of personal responsibility. In a statement very similar to many made about leprosy, one TB expert is quoted as saying, in 1917, that 'Those ... who obey the dictates of their physical conscience may feel well assured that in them the tubercle bacillus will fall on stony soil'.[52]

Much emphasis was laid on hygiene and social habits. The stresses and strains of 'modern life' were seen as contributory factors. The focus of this discourse, however, was the individual and individual responsibility. Medical discussions on tuberculosis amongst the British working classes in the first half of this century created a social distance apparently almost as great as that between colonial doctors and their African leprosy patients. The difference between the two lay in the conception of the individual in each case. In Africa, despite medical missionary emphasis on the individual soul, the collecltivity was seen to define both the African and African disease patterns, including that of leprosy.

It is to the 'Celtic fringe' that one has to turn for a similar discussion of tuberculosis in Britain. High rates of the disease in Wales, for instance, were explained in ways which emphasized 'Welshness' itself as a predisposing factor. There was some suggestion of a racial predisposition to contract the disease, but greater emphasis was given to peculiarly Welsh social habits – including over-indulgence in tea, but also 'the intense conservatism of their social habits, the closeness and tenacity of their family relationships, and their fatalistic outlook ...'.[53]

Isolation was the major prescription for combating tuberculosis as it was for combating leprosy. The practices of twentieth-century sanitoria in Britain make some of the African leper colonies look like holiday camps. The social and geographical distance created between patients in sanitoria and the outside world seems to have been comparable to that created by the earliest colonial attempts to isolate leprosy patients. Interestingly, many tuberculosis patients explicitly compared their fate to that of lepers.[54] The sanitorium was a 'total institution', a place where patients were consciously socialized into a particular sick role. Sex and alcohol were strictly controlled, and patients were frequently warned that their fate depended on their obeying the myriad rules of the institution. Some sanitoria were organized, like leprosy colonies, into 'villages', but this did not imply any kind of patient-run democracy – the organization of sanitoria was strictly hierarchical, usually with a medical superintendent at the top behaving like a patriarchal head of household. Patients were frequently shunned by the local communities in which the sanitoria were situated (that is when they were not completely geographically remote, as many were), and many suffered the stigma of tuberculosis even after they had been sent home cured. Like leprosy patients, many inmates of sanitoria complained about conditions, and discharged themselves. Isolation could never be compulsory but, as with leprosy, the idea that it was the social duty of an infected person to go into isolation was continually stressed. In colonial Africa, meanwhile, no attempt was made to institutionalize tuberculosis sufferers, despite the alarming pace at which the disease took a hold on rural as well as urban populations.[55]

A comparison between tuberculosis in Britain and leprosy in colonial Africa helps to illuminate the limitations of colonial 'bio-power'. Whilst in both cases sufferers were stigmatized and objectified by medical discourse and by the practice of institutionalization, in the colonial case the classification of the 'leper' was always complicated (and often overridden) by other imposed identities. The African leper could never be 'just' a leper – she or he was, first and foremost, an 'African', and, beyond that, the member of a 'tribe'. Even the most ardent of medical missionaries, who at times had tried to make leprosy sufferers into blank pages on which to inscribe their ideas about new African identities, had generally found themselves reinventing the village and African 'traditional' structures of control in their leprosy colonies. Where African patients did self-consciously take on the identity of the 'leper' they could, like the inmates of 'Kabalenge Leprosy', exploit all the ambiguities of the European Christian tradition in an attempt to improve their unhappy situation. An apparent compliance could, we are reminded, facilitate resistance at another level.

NOTES

1 *Leprosy Review*, no. 72 (1914), pp. 118–9.
2 Iliffe (1987), p. 217.
3 Iliffe (1987), p. 219.
4 Foucault (1989), p. 7.
5 Palmer (1982), p. 82.
6 Iliffe (1987), chapter 12. Numerous articles were published in *Leprosy Review* on this subject.
7 Cochrane (1931).
8 *Journal of the Leprosy Investigation Committee* (National Leprosy Fund), no. 2 (1898), p. 78.
9 'Visit of Dr Muir to Nyasaland, Northern Rhodesia, Belgian Congo, Southern Rhodesia, Union of South Africa, Basutoland and Nigeria', *Leprosy Review*, vol. 11 (1940), p. 22.
10 'Visit of Dr Muir', p. 37.
11 'Visit of Dr Muir', p. 13.

12 'Funzi Island Leper Settlement' by 'E. B', *Central Africa*, no. 544 (1928), p. 122.
13 'Lundu the Leper Isle', *Central Africa*, no. 320 (1909), pp. 213–4.
14 'Funzi Island Leper Settlement', *Central Africa*, no. 544 (1928), p. 122.
15 G. M. Dawson, 'A Visit to the Lepers', *Central Africa*, no. 531 (1927), p. 43.
16 Waxler (1981).
17 'Worse that Slavery', *Annual Report of the British Empire Leprosy Relief Association* (1935), p. 4.
18 *Central Africa*, no. 880 (1956), p. 81.
19 A *Symbol of Love and Sacrifice: The Story of the Qua Iboe Church Leprosy Hospital* as told by Dr O. J. Gbadamosi and Dr E. M. Davis (1982), p. 22.
20 Iliffe (1987), p. 103.
21 'At the Leper Settlement of Basutoland' by Rev. H. Dieterlen, *Without the Camp (Quarterly Magazine of the Mission to Lepers)*, no. 72 (1914), p. 118.
22 'Interesting News from Pretoria', by Rev. Ernest Creux, *Without the Camp*, no. 86 (1918), p. 28.
23 'Pioneer Problems at Mbereshi' by Dr H. E. Wareham, *Without the Camp*, no. 85 (1918), p. 4.
24 Zambia National Archives (ZNA): NR 7/187: Chitokoloki Leprosy Settlement, 1952–8: Letter from 'Deadbodies' to Director of Medical Services, 19.1.53.
25 W. A. Young papers, Rhodes House Library: Mss. Afr.s.1519: Box 3: *Annual Medical and Sanitary Report for Weti District and Funzi and Nduni Leper Settlements*, 1926.
26 Zambia National Archives, NR 7/89: Luapula Leprosy Settlement, vol. VI (1953–5): Letter from 'Patients at Kabalenge Leprosy' to PMO, Lusaka (n.d. April 1954).
27 Dory (1963), p. 40.
28 Dory (1963), p. 68.
29 Malawi National Archives (MNA): S1/470/20: Leprosy, 1914–22; M2/5/12: Leprosy, 1922–8.
30 MNA: S1/512 (1)/24: The British Empire Leprosy Relief Association, 1924–37: Extract from meeting of the North Nyasa Native Association, July 1927.
31 Dory (1963), p. 46.
32 Dory (1963), p. 55.
33 Bryder (1988).
34 Junge (1952), p. 163.
35 Junge (1952), p. 165.
36 Junge (1952), p. 167.
37 'Rules of Right Conduct for a Leper', devised by Bishop Lucas, *Leprosy Review*, vol. 10 (1939), p. 80.
38 'Fiwila Village of Mercy', *Leprosy Review*, vol. 8 (1937), p. 186.
39 'History of the Ho Leper Settlement' by F. H. Cooke, *Leprosy Review*, vol. 2 (1931), p. 9.
40 'A Description of the Work at the Leprosy Hospital at Ngomahuru' by B. Moiser, *Leprosy Review*, vol. 4, pp. 13–14.

41 'Account of Visit to Leprosy Institutions in Nigeria' by H. C. Armstrong, *Leprosy Review*, vol. 6 (1935), p. 155.
42 A. Brincklow papers, Rhodes House Library, Mss. Afr.s.1872 (16).
43 'Worse than Slavery', *Annual Report of BELRA for 1935*, p. 26.
44 *A Symbol of Love and Sacrifice*, p. 9.
45 'Enugu Leprosy Conference', Report by T. D. F. Money, *Leprosy Review*, vol. 11 (1940), p. 81.
46 'The Psychology of Leprosy' by G. A. Ryrie, *Leprosy Review*, vol. 22 (1951), pp. 14–19.
47 'The Fight Against Leprosy', 16th *Annual Report of BELRA* (1939).
48 Follereau (1968), p. 119.
49 A. D. Power, 'A British Empire Leprosarium', *Journal of the African Society*, vol. 38 (1939) pp. 465–8.
50 Power (1939), p. 467.
51 Power (1939), p. 466.
52 Bryder (1988), p. 21.
53 Bryder (1988), p. 127. It may be relevant that Prof. Lyle Cummins, professor of tuberculosis at the Welsh National School of Medicine in the 1920s, was also the author of a number of reports and articles on tuberculosis in the Empire. It is possible that 'tribal' theories of tuberculosis, elaborated in the course of this experience in Africa, were then applied to the Welsh!
54 Bryder (1988), p. 201.
55 For the history of tuberculosis in South Africa see Packard (1989). Iliffe refers to the theory that leprosy recedes in areas such as South Africa where tuberculosis takes a hold: Iliffe (1987), p. 217.

5 The Madman and the Medicine Men: Colonial Psychiatry and the Theory of Deculturation

In 1935 Drs Shelley and Watson, two Nyasaland Government medical officers, appointed to investigate 'mental disorder in Nyasaland natives', reported on their findings.[1] In the territory's one lunatic asylum they found a high percentage of inmates suffering from 'schizophrenic delusions' which, they wrote, could be divided into two categories – the 'European type' and the 'Native type'. Examples of the 'European' type of delusion were given as follows:

> Very rich man and built asylum at his own expense.
> Heaven and earth are separated and he wants to join them.
> Owns Port Herald and is married to a white girl.
> Owns a silver mine, is son of a king, an Englishman.
> Thinks himself God and Principal Headman of the sky.
> Thinks himself very wealthy.
> Lives at Government House, which a previous governor gave him.
> Is commander of a great army.

'Native type' schizophrenic delusions were apparently less common, but Shelley and Watson gave the following as examples:

> Is a lion, wants to kill people and eat them.
> Thought he was a barking dog and tried to bite people.
> His wife is always committing adultery.

As is the case with many other colonial documents on African insanity, Shelley and Watson's report reveals a great deal more about colonial categories than it does about madness. In order to define the mad, it was necessary first to define the 'normal' African. This exercise, as we shall see, preoccupied many a colonial psycho-

logist. Having defined the 'normal' workings of the African mind, it
was then possible to identify a 'normal' African delusion ('I am a
lion and I want to eat people' or 'My wife is always committing
adultery'), as against those apparently very unAfrican delusions of
power and control ('I am wealthy'; 'I am God'; 'I am married to a
white girl').

The history of madness in colonial Africa is not a simple one.
Though there are many parallels with the now well documented
history of the defining and the confining of the mad in modern
Europe, there are times when the specificities of a colonial situation
seem to stand out in relief. To put it simply, whilst the history of
insanity in Europe is the history of the definition of the mad as
'Other', in colonial Africa the 'Other' already existed in the form
of the colonial subject, the African.[2] The category of the mad
African, then, more often included the colonial subject who was
insufficiently 'Other' – who spoke of being rich, of hearing voices
through radio sets, of being powerful, who imitated the white man
in dress and behaviour and who therefore threatened to disrupt the
ordered non-communication between ruler and ruled. I should
make it clear, however, that the history of the creation of these
colonial categories and their articulation is not synonymous with the
history of psychiatry in colonial Africa. Theory and practice, colonial
thought and colonial policy, only rarely meshed. There was no
'great confinement' in colonial Africa to match that of nineteenth-
century Europe, and colonial psychiatric institutions, as we shall
see, have their own, rather separate history.

Michel Foucault could describe the creation of mental illness in
European society as having by the end of the eighteenth century,
destroyed the 'stammered dialogue' which had previously existed
between madness and reason.[3] Where the voices of the mad had
once been heard for their apparent wisdom (the more so since this
wisdom was not easily interpreted), for the visions of other worlds
which they described – now, though never completely silenced,
they went mostly unheard, muffled by the walls of institutions
where loquacity itself was seen as a sure sign of madness. Recent
historians have tried to rescue the words of the mad from the
'babble' of the madhouse, and to hear what they had to say about
their lives and times. For, as Roy Porter puts it, insanity is not 'an
individual atom, a biological accident, but forms an element in the
history of sub-cultures in their own right'.[4] If the voices of the mad
are strange and alien, they are nevertheless the voices of their
specific cultural and historical settings.

If madness, in Porter's words, is 'a foreign country',[5] what of
madness in a colony? If 'normal' communication between ruler and

ruled was no more than a 'stammered dialogue', and one which was, for most of the colonial period, purposively so, how were the utterances of the mad interpreted? For the most part, of course, the voices of the mad cannot be heard by us at all. Historians of Africa search constantly for the authentic 'African voice' in the colonial archives, and find it hard to uncover. Hearing the authentic voice of the mad African in written documentation really does involve straining the ears. However, many colonial governments adopted some form of legislation for the control and care of 'lunatics', and this legislation produced its own historical record, notably in the form of enquiries and court cases.

In Nyasaland, the first such piece of legislation was the Native Lunatics Ordinance of 1913 which stated that 'Any District Magistrate upon the information of any informant to the effect that such informant has good cause to suspect and believe, and does suspect and believe that any native within the District of which he is magistrate is a lunatic and a proper subject for restraint may in any place which he deems convenient examine such suspected native and may hold an enquiry as to the state of mind of such suspected native.'[6]

Such enquiries were relatively rare, and their recording marked more by the silence of the 'suspects' than by their voices. As with all early colonial court records, what we are left with are usually a few utterances, often already filtered through a colonial court assessor, who was often eagerly acting as cultural broker for the baffled white magistrate. If the voices of the 'alleged lunatics' are unclear, the records nevertheless often tell an interesting story. In particular, they reflect on the process by which the magistrate sought to define 'mad' behaviour in a group of subjects whose normal behaviour he usually regarded as 'alien', to say the least.

The colonial magistrate and district officer were, for most of the colonial period, enjoined to rule through 'custom', except where 'custom' was deemed 'repugnant'. For this to be done, 'custom' had constantly to be defined and deviations from it identified. Logically this would result in a highly relativistic view of madness – the mad could only be so defined by close reference to the particular norms and customs of a 'tribal' group. But in practice the system constantly strained at the seams. 'Custom' frequently proved an inadequate instrument of colonial rule, leaving the magistrate to work with his own, quite different, legal and cultural categories.[7] The African participants in these courtroom dramas meanwhile attempted to provide their own interpretations of 'customary' behaviour, and to understand the implicit working categories of the magistrate's mind.

In 1912, for instance, a man named Kacheni came before the District Resident in the small town of Ncheu, charged with the murder of a small boy, who had been in the bush cutting grass. No motive was apparent, so the Resident asked the headman of Kacheni's village if the suspect had ever, to his knowledge, been mad. The headman replied that:

Last dry season Kacheni disappeared from our village and the same day was brought back by some strangers. They said they met him running very fast on the road and going on like a mad person and they brought him back to our village to find out if he belonged to us. When they brought him back he was put in a 'gori' [slave-stick] and remained in it for three weeks when he got better and was released. This rainy season he went to work and we thought he was alright again, but when he killed the child we wondered.[8]

Asked for his own account of events, Kacheni's words were:

Always when I fall sick in my village the people say I am mad and although they are asked to come and see me when I am sick they do not come because they say I am mad. Then I ask them how is it that you say I am mad, when you did not know me at the time of my birth, and some of my friends always interrupt me when talking and then always I am angry.

Having collected this evidence, the Resident charged him with murder and transferred him to the Lunatic Asylum in Zomba for further investigation of his mental condition. When the case reopened, however, and all the evidence had been heard, the court assessors, who were both local chiefs, gave their opinions, as follows:

Chief Kamwendo: 'I am of the opinion that the accused killed the boy Chikalusa, that he is not mad now and was not mad when he killed the boy. He certainly had no reason for killing the boy that we know of. He had not been mad enough to kill people on account of his madness'.

Chief Nchize: 'I do not think that the accused was mad when he killed the boy because he had not been mad long enough. It takes some time for insanity to develop into homicidal mania'.

Almost audibly exasperated, the District Resident disagreed: 'There is no doubt', he said, 'that the accused was insane when he committed this crime. He was mad last year and since then his behaviour has been strange on two or more occasions.' Finding Kacheni guilty but insane, he further found that Kacheni's father and cousin were responsible for 'this terrible affair' in that they had known that he was insane but had taken no steps to keep him under control. He fined them the large sum of £3 each.

In this case there seemed no doubt in anyone's mind but Kacheni's that he was mad. He had behaved in a way widely acknowledged by his own community to be abnormal. He had run away and he had assaulted people for no reason. He had even had to be forcibly confined in a *gori*, or slave-stick, by the village headman. But there are many opaque and unfathomable aspects to this case as recorded. Firstly, and most obviously, it is all in translation. 'Has this man ever been mad?', may have appeared to the District Resident to have been a straightforward question, but how was it translated into the local language (probably either chiYao or chiChewa), and which word meaning 'mad' was used in the translation? The languages of central and southern Malawi, in common with other African languages, are rich in words to describe different forms and degrees of 'madness'. One early dictionary of the Mang'anja language, for instance, listed a number of words with quite specific meanings: *misala ina ya ku-chita ndeo, misala ina yo lowa m'tengo* (one kind of madness is quarrelsome, another kind retreats into the bush). There was a word for the madness that caused one not to obey 'but not from disobedience'; a word for a mad person who was subject to visions; another for foolishness and folly, and another for those who suffered fits. Similarly, in chiYao it was possible to distinguish 'early' madness from 'periodic' madness; degrees of eccentricity could be defined in language, and there was a separate word for those who experienced visions.

But the record of the Kacheni case indicates that there might be many levels of linguistic and conceptual translation and mistranslation involved. When Chief Nchize said that 'it takes some time for insanity to develop into homicidal mania', we do not know how this was translated from the original, or if the chief had actually used the English phrase. Possibly he had in mind a local distinction between short-term and long-term insanity. Certainly he and his fellow-assessor, Chief Kamwendo, seem to have understood that in the British legal system there existed the concept of diminished responsibility. It seems likely that this had been explained to them, or that they had witnessed other cases in which this had been brought into play. At all events they seem to have been anxious that Kacheni's act of murder should not be regarded as the act of a 'fully' mad person. They were overruled, for in the Resident's view the case was clear – Kacheni had been mad when he murdered the boy, and therefore the asylum, rather than the prison, was the appropriate place in which to confine him.

Many a case heard in the early colonial courts of Central Africa involved the murder of a wife by her husband, and the subsequent suicide, or attempted suicide, of the murderer. In 1924 one Njoromola was sentenced to death in the Dedza district of Nyasaland for the murder of one of his wives and her child.[9] The magistrate (and later the High Court judge) was faced as always with the problem of defining whether the man had been legally insane at the time of the crime. Arriving at a view on this involved a prior understanding of many things, including the nature and meaning of relationships between husbands and wives, their emotional and symbolic significance. This was not easy. No evidence was provided for a motive, except that provided by Njoromola himself: 'People believed me impotent and wanted to kill me so that my wife could marry someone else. So I decided to kill my wife and child and then be hanged myself.'

The magistrate will have known, through his hearing of the hundreds of marriage cases which came to his court at this time, that impotence and infertility were frequently the cause of great anguish, of much friction between spouses and their families, and of divorce.[10] With this in mind, he had asserted that there was a distinction between insanity and what he described as a 'fit of passion due to perverted imagination', and had sentenced the accused to death. But when the case reopened other evidence was brought forward to indicate that Njoromola had been suffering from more than a 'perverted imagination'. People in his village, it was said, looked upon him as mad. In 1923 he had attacked his other wife with a knife, for no apparent reason, and on the way to the Boma (the local colonial government headquarters) he had fallen over a cliff ('though that may have been an accident'). For two years he had not visited friends 'as is the native custom', and after the murder he went to the house of his aunt and 'sat naked inside the fence, and attempted to kill himself'.

As a result of such evidence, Njoromola's sentence was commuted to life imprisonment with hard labour, and he was confined in the Central Prison at Zomba. By late 1926 his mental condition had begun to deteriorate. He assaulted other prisoners and warders, believing that the warders wanted to kill him. He was found 'digging up the ground near B-block, and when asked why he was digging he replied "I am digging for tobacco", and when told there was none there he replied "I am making a Boma".' Njoromola, who by now was recognized by all as 'very far from normal', was transferred from prison to asylum to live out the rest of his life.

If colonial officials had problems interpreting the rationality or otherwise of murder in this cultural context, things were further complicated by witchcraft beliefs and the legislation designed to eradicate these. With both a Witchcraft Ordinance[11] and a Lunacy Ordinance on the statute books in Nyasaland by the First World War, it was essential to distinguish not only between the mad and the bad but between the mad person and the person who thought himself or herself bewitched. The confusing part of this was that whilst insanity was held to be a real and definable condition (despite all the problems of understanding local behavioural norms), bewitchment was held not to exist in reality but to be evidence of malice. Denial was the basic approach of colonial authorities to the phenomenon of witchcraft, and if you believed yourself to be bewitched you were just as culpable as the person who purported to have bewitched you. But if insanity was real and witchcraft not, what was to be done with the woman whose children had died in quick succession, who went 'berserk' and assaulted her mother-in-law in the belief that she had caused these deaths? Was she mad, and therefore ill and to be pitied, or was to be charged under the Witchcraft Ordinance for accusing another of being a witch? It was 'normal'(if punishable) for an African to believe in witchcraft – it was not 'normal', however, to suffer from paranoid delusions. Unsurprisingly, the distinctions were very often blurred, and magistrates relied heavily on the opinions of 'native court assessors' in such cases. Certainly in the Nyasaland asylum, as in other colonial African asylums, a fair proportion of inmates suffered from the peculiarly 'native' delusion that they were bewitched, or that they had offended against some 'custom'. Any attempt to classify and distinguish 'witchcraft' and 'insanity', then, largely broke down under the pressure of African realities, reminding us that colonial categories were not all-powerful.

However, African communities could sometimes pick up these categories and run with them. The idea that insanity was a condition sometimes calling for confinement in a distant institution, at no charge to the insane or their relatives, held some attractions. On occasions, individuals exhibiting slightly abnormal behaviour might be presented as 'insane' to the magistrate because there existed other grudges against them. In one Nyasaland case of 1934, headmen Mwamadi claimed that Chipendo was mad and should be confined.[12] The case was suspicious from the beginning, Mwamadi making the following statement (presumably in response to the magistrate's prodding): 'I myself owe no money to Chipendo, nor have had any trouble with his women. His wife, Ellesi, cannot come in as she only gave birth to a child yesterday and is not in a fit state to attend. I am certainly not the father of the child.' Other evidence pointed rather conclusively to the fact that Chipendo was not insane at all but had differences with his headman. He was released into the custody of his brother, Kettle, who took him off to live in another village, and the case was closed.

Ben-Tovim cites an exchange in colonial Botswana between Chief Tshekedi and the Resident Commissioner in 1944, in which Tshekedi describes the problems caused by 'lunatics' for whom there was no government provision.[13] They set houses on fire and were a danger to others. There were some women lunatics 'who go about naked, with not a rag on their bodies':

> We understand from Government that cases of insanity require specialists to deal with them, and that these doctors are difficult to find. My request therefore is merely to ask whether it is not possible for the Government to find some place where such people can be detained without being put in gaol, and have a doctor to visit them occasionally and people to look after them perhaps some nurses, male and female nurses, some place outside a village to prevent these people coming into the village.[14]

Though the colonial government in Botswana eventually responded to Tshekedi's request, for the most part colonial officials were, for a variety of reasons, inclined to the view that African communities could care for their own 'lunatics'. Those disturbed people who wandered into towns, hung around Boma offices, or who were repatriated from labour migrant contracts on the grounds that they were insane, were usually sent 'home' to their villages rather than confined.

The 'labelling' of the mad African as carried out in the colonial court room, then, was often a confused and hesitant business. It would be hard to read this record, incomplete as it is, as the process whereby, in Thomas Szasz's words, society creates the mad person, so that by invalidating her or him as evil, it may be confirmed as good.[15] The colonial authorities had no need for such a scapegoat, such was the colonizers' belief in their innate superiority – the social distance between the European and the colonized African was sufficient to create the objectification described by Szasz and others, there was no need for the mad person to be invented for this role.

But the history of the colonial classification of insanity amongst Africans can be read in other ways. The writings of colonial psychiatrists and psychologists provided one language, and perhaps a potent one, in which to describe and define the 'African' in general and not just the 'mad African'. The changing nature of African insanity itself could stand for the more general problems of colonial rule – the social and economic upheavals of industrialization and the problems of social order. But the languages of psychology and psychiatry, as we shall see, described these problems largely in terms of cultural and 'racial' difference. 'The African' in the twentieth century, like the European woman in the nineteenth century, was simply not equipped to cope with 'civilization'.[16]

We might begin to explore these aspects of the colonial history of African madness by returning to Shelley and Watson's report on insanity in Nyasaland. The two doctors had individually examined each of the eighty-six inmates of the Lunatic Asylum and had divided them into what were the current categories of psychiatric disorder. 'Schizophrenia' accounted for 35.7 per cent of the total, and 'affective psychoses' for another 21.4 per cent.[17]

The doctors believed that the incidence of insanity was rising, especially amongst the educated, but the evidence they used to support this view was already determined by the theory that 'civilization' was sending Africans mad. Finding that 24 per cent of inmates of the asylum were from the Yao 'tribe' (whose representation in the population as a whole was only 14.5 per cent), they argued that this might be expected as 'the Yao form the intelligentsia of the indigenous peoples and have been in more intimate contact with European civilization than the members of other tribes'. Only 15 per cent of the inmates were female, and this could be easily explained because 'women do not come into intimate contact with Europeans and their minds lack the stimulation which the male mind encounters by such contact'.

Their argument would have been a familiar one to those with an interest in African psychiatry in the 1930s – the central cause of insanity was 'acculturation', brought about, in the main, by education. Just as the late nineteenth-century Social Darwinians warned European women of the profound dangers of education and self-fulfilment,[18] so psychiatrists of the 1930s to 1950s warned that Africans would face similar consequences.

Shelley and Watson provided further evidence to support their thesis that 'deculturation' was the cause of rising insanity. It appeared to them that inmates of the asylum fell into two main categories – firstly, those whose illnesses could be explained by reference to the strains and injuries of 'traditional' society (in particular those driven mad by the fear of witchcraft) and secondly, the more numerous category of those driven mad by 'acculturation' and the strains of 'modern' society. These two groups could be distinguished not only by their educational backgrounds but, as we saw at the beginning of this chapter, by the content of their delusions, which were either 'European' or 'Native' in character. Their argument appeared to be that not only had contact with the colonizer's culture affected the content of the delusions (producing images of bicycles, radios, telephones and so on) but that such contact had actually caused the illness to come about in the first place. Shelley and Watson focused their attention on the group they had defined as schizophrenics. 'Native schizophrenics', they wrote 'with their sexual disturbances and European type of delusions, and their fondness for offence against property, seem to manifest a more European attitude of mind than the members of other groups.'

A preoccupation with sexual matters, along with visions of bi-cycles and 'motors', defined the 'native schizophrenic'. Missionaries were largely to blame for destroying the 'primitive innocence' of so many Africans, for they had 'encouraged the natives to clothe them-selves and at the same time stimulate[d] the sex consciousness by causing to be hidden the natural functions of the body'. It seemed to the doctors that education and Christianity had had 'an obscure influence on the powers of copulation', for many of the 'Christian natives' in the asylum complained of impotence.

What was behind these theories of Shelley and Watson? The methods and reasoning of their investigation are of dubious 'scien-tific' value, yet there seems to be a real concern behind the pseudo-scientific language. Though the Chief Secretary drew his red pen through large sections of this report (more especially the discussion of African sexuality), there is no doubt that Shelley and Watson's ideas had many familiar resonances for colonial administrators of the 1930s. This was the decade in which social and scientific re-search on the problems of African colonies really took off. In the Central African colonies there were investigations undertaken on many aspects of African life, which particularly focused on the changes which had been wrought by over thirty years of British rule. There were reports on nutrition, on health, on the fertility of the population, on the status of women, on education. There were anthropological studies of the effects of education and economic change on rural societies, on ritual and beliefs, and studies of 'tradi-tional' political systems. Underlying all of this research was a deeply felt colonial fear, expressed more and more anxiously in the 1930s, that the 'disintegration' of the 'traditional' structures of African societies was endangering social control, that industrialization, education and urbanization contained within them the seeds of disaffection. The political solution devised to address this problem was the system of indirect rule. The disruptive changes wrought by colonialism and capitalism could, so it was argued, be contained if only people obeyed their 'traditional' leaders and followed 'tradi-tional' norms. Africans would be ruled through 'custom' – one had only to identify such customs and to give them the new force of law. Of course some customs were unacceptable and would have to be discarded (it could not be denied that 'civilization' held some advan-tages), but in general customs were a good thing. It was especially important that Africans experiencing the upheavals of industrializa-tion should know who they were, that they should retain a cultural identity (expressed in terms of belonging to a specific 'tribe' with its distinctive customs). Only by this means would the alienation and disorder of the nineteenth-century European experience of indus-trialization be avoided.

This is necessarily a very schematized account of colonial philosophy of the period. There were many ambiguities, strains and fractures in the system of rule through custom, as Martin Chanock has shown.[19] In particular, the idea of colonialism as a 'civilizing' mission was never entirely eradicated, and was, indeed, revived somewhat in the post-war period. Education, more than anything else, came to represent the essential dilemma. Education was a 'benefit' to be bestowed on colonial peoples, but it was also a danger to colonial social order. Educated Africans were known to be prone to acts of subordination. They forgot their customs, they forgot who they were, and they 'aped' the colonizer's dress and manner in a thoroughly alarming way.

It is in this context that we must read Shelley and Watson's report and the many other writings on African psychology and psychiatry of this period. Their report expressed, in the powerful language of science, many of the fears already felt by colonial administrators. It was now possible to say, on the basis of such a study, that education and acculturation were not only dangerous but were bad for the health of Africans. Of more general significance, however, the writings of psychology and psychiatry, along with other (and often related) discourses of anthropology, actually helped to determine, define and 'create' the colonial African subject for their European audience. *Knowing the African* was the title of one mission-produced manual in the 1940s describing the customs, psychology and sexuality of Africans,[20] but it could be taken as the title for the whole corpus of African 'pop psychology' which drew on the writings of the professional psychiatrists and psychologists working in colonial Africa.

The most famous of these psychiatrists, whose work would undoubtedly have been familiar to Shelley and Watson, was J. C. Carothers, around whom grew something of an East African 'school' of psychiatry.[21] The early writings of this group of psychiatrists working in the East African territories were overtly racially deterministic. They claimed to have established scientifically that there was a link between the organic brain structure of the African, African psychology, and African psycho-pathology.[22] Dr H. L. Gordon, the Superintendent of the Mathari Mental Hospital in Nairobi in the early 1930s, worked alongside F. W. Vint, a Government Bacteriologist, to provide the scientific 'proof' for what was essentially an argument about the racial inferiority of the African. Vint carried out post-mortem examinations in the African hospitals of Nairobi which were to establish the 'stage of cerebral development reached by the East African native'. He concluded, from weighing the brains and measuring the pre-frontal cortex, that 'the stage of development reached by the average native is that of the European boy aged between 7 and 8 years'.[23]

The 'scientific vigour' of this theory held much appeal, judging by the record of the discussion which followed Vint's presentation of his findings. One Dr Anderson asserted that 'he had been out here 32 years, all of which he had spent in close contact with the native, and in all that time he had not met one local African who had achieved normal European intelligence'.

The East African 'findings' were clearly read and discussed elsewhere in Africa. An editorial, with a strong eugenicist bent, in the *South African Medical Journal* drew on the work of Gordon and Vint to conclude that 'the best of natives are biologically inferior to the average European', and that this fact had far-reaching consequences for 'our whole policy with regard to the natives under our guardianship'.[24]

A number of 'biological facts' were cited to attest to the supposedly innate psychological inferiority of Africans. J. C. Carothers used the data for the 'underdevelopment of frontal lobes' collected by him and his colleagues to construct his theory of the 'natural lobotomy'. He argued that 'the resemblance of the leucotomised European patient to the primitive African is, in many ways, complete': 'The African, with his total lack of synthesis, must use his frontal lobes but little, and all the peculiarities of African psychiatry can be envisaged in terms of frontal idleness.'[25] 'Frontal lobe defect' became a catch-phrase, and was widely discussed in the, albeit limited, literature on African psychiatry well into the 1950s.[26]

The East African school was not without its critics, however. The South African Jack Simons launched a swingeing attack on their writings in a paper published in the international *Journal of Mental Science* in 1958.[27] As Professor Simons pointed out, Carothers and his colleagues had never relied entirely on anthropometry to 'prove' their theories of African inferiority. Though the biological arguments were never jettisoned (and were still strongly represented in Carothers's writings of the 1950s), over the years there had been something of a shift towards the use of what we might call social anthropological data in their arguments. Their model of the psychopathology of the African became increasingly dependent on a representation of something called 'African culture'. This was conceived of as simple and static: 'During an estimated 10,000 years', wrote Dr Smartt, a psychiatrist working in Tanganyika, 'the rural African has remained almost unchanged'.[28]

In *The African Mind*, published in 1953 and a culmination (and compilation) of his life's work, Carothers discussed the 'ancient cultural modes' of the African. Generalizing across the continent and over long historical periods, he outlined the features of the 'essential African culture'. This was said to be typified, first and foremost, by the importance of magic, by the lack of a clear distinction between 'subject and object', and a resulting lack of 'personal integration' in individual Africans. In the childhood of Africans,

Carothers asserted, logic was distorted and curiosity stifled. But, furthermore, the African never emerged from this state for the psychology of the African was 'essentially the psychology of the African child'. The pattern of mental development was defined by the time adolescence was reached 'and little new remains to be said' on adulthood.[29]

Carothers maintained that the incidence of mental illness amongst 'traditional' Africans was very low indeed. Depressive states, he wrote, were almost unknown, and this fact could be explained by reference to his theory of African culture and its construction of the individual. Depression was said only to occur when there existed a high degree of personal integration, 'a sense of responsibility for one's past and of a retribution that must follow for one's sins'. Given that African ritual and religion relieved individuals of responsibility, and that Africans never achieved full 'personal integration', it followed that they did not feel guilt or the depression attendant on it. It also followed that 'deculturation' must provide the major explanation for what Carothers and others believed to be a rising rate of mental illness in colonial Africa. He could offer no direct evidence for such an increase, given that baseline data for what he called the 'untouched African' was unavailable. Instead he drew on the evidence for high rates of schizophrenia amongst American blacks (the ultimate 'decultured' Africans in Carothers's view) to make his point.

There was a very large measure of agreement on the 'deculturation' theory amongst writers on psychology and psychiatry from the 1930s to the 1950s, for some of the reasons I have already outlined.[30] It resonated well with larger colonial concerns of this period, and it could be represented as a 'liberal', paternalist position. It did not go entirely unchallenged, however. Work in West Africa in the 1940s and 1950s took a rather more complex view of African culture and the effects of the changes brought about by colonialism. One such example was the work of Geoffrey Tooth, who had been commissioned by the Colonial Office in the 1940s to undertake a study of the effects of trypanosomiasis on mental health.[31] As well as concluding that trypanosomiasis was probably the commonest cause of mental derangement in large parts of West Africa, Tooth also challenged the view that there was little mental disorder in rural Africa, arguing that much rural mental disorder was 'hidden' by the effectiveness of local community care. Literate, urban schizophrenics however, were much more clearly recognized by Europeans since their delusional content made them more noticeable and their psychoses took a more antisocial form. According to Tooth, then, circumstances combined to make the literate lunatic both more prominent and less socially acceptable and to suggest to the casual observer that literacy itself was the causal factor. Tooth concluded that his own survey 'provided no evidence in support of the hypothesis that psychosis is commoner amongst the westernised group than in the rest of the population'.[32]

Margaret Field, the psychologist turned anthropologist who worked in the Gold Coast in the 1930s and again in the 1950s, agreed that literacy and 'culture contact' could not be simply assumed to be the causes of mental disorder. She thought it true that 'literates' had more serious mental troubles than 'illiterates', but she thought this not due to 'culture contact and conflict' but to the fact that 'they have heavier demands made on their diligence, adaptability, endurance, judgement and integrity'.[33] Though she did not believe in the 'culture conflict' theory, she did think that there was a growing sense of insecurity, especially in the cocoa-growing areas of the Gold Coast, which imposed severe strains on individuals. She also asserted that 'depression' (which Carothers and his followers believed not to exist in rural Africans) was in fact extremely common, especially amongst women, but that this depression was expressed through the idiom of witchcraft and its sufferers found relief through the innumerable new religious shrines which had sprung up in Ashanti since the 1930s.[34]

Field's work both attacked the 'deculturation' or 'culture conflict' theory and pointed to the particular cultural expression which could be given to depression in an African community. Without an understanding of the whole culture and its symbolism, 'depression' could not be detected and the myth of the carefree African was prolonged.

Despite the work of sensitive observers like Field, the 'deculturation' theory remained virtually hegemonic in both professional and popular writings on African psychology. While Field's view of the cultural expression of mental illness allowed for a dynamic view of cultural difference, that of Carothers and his colleagues did not.

In their work the authority of the language of psychiatry was employed, above all, to assert that the 'African' could be known, and could be known to be fundamentally different from the European. The theoretical status accorded to this 'difference' varied. Carothers himself believed that, despite the overwhelming problem of 'deculturation', Africans remained strongly influenced by 'ancient cultural modes' which affected the structure as well as the content of their mental disorders. It was the educated, urbanized (and by definition, male) African who was most likely to go mad, and he would have been driven mad by the strains of 'deculturation'. He would, nevertheless, go mad in a definably 'African' way.

As we have seen from the discussion of the Shelley and Watson report on Nyasaland, there were variations on this theme. Shelley and Watson's confident categorization of 'European' and 'African' delusions implied a theory rather different from that of Carothers. They made no distinction, as Carothers did, between the structure of the mental illness and the content of delusions, and implied thereby that a 'European' type of delusion was indicative of a 'European' type of mental disorder.

As early as 1933, the South African psychiatrist and psychoanalyst Wulf Sachs had attempted to refute the orthodoxy that there were deep structural differences between the mental disorders of Africans and those of Europeans. From his work amongst both black and white patients in South Africa he had concluded that in the form of mental derangement 'the native did not differ appreciably from the white'. Further, if this were the case in abnormal states, then 'the working principle of the mind in the normal state must be identical in both cases'.[35] This was a controversial conclusion, as Sachs was well aware: 'I realise that to people who still cherish a privileged position in the universe, my statement will sound exaggerated and based on false deductions from the abnormal to the normal. Whoever is acquainted with the essence of the psychotic symptom and with its similarity to other unconscious manifestations of normal people, will not be deterred from such conclusions.' But Sachs's view did not have the currency of that of Carothers, whose work was cited widely in the region. In a debate on racial equality in the Federal Parliament in Salisbury in 1954, for example, Prime Minister Huggins recommended than all should read Carothers's work for in it 'they will find a description of almost every race in the world emerging from the pre-literate stage'. The lesson drawn by Huggins from this work was clear: emerging from the 'pre-literate' stage would take a very long time, and meanwhile equality of treatment was inappropriate.[36]

With the growth of nationalist movements in the 1950s, the work of Carothers and others was being read for its direct political lessons. Carothers himself was employed by the colonial government of Kenya to 're-educate' Mau Mau detainees.[37] Meanwhile, O. Mannoni had produced an extraordinary book entitled *Prospero and Caliban*, which employed psychological theories of the African to explain the Malagasy revolt of 1947.[38] He argued for Malagasy society, as Carothers had for the whole of Africa, that in such a society individualism was underdeveloped. Indeed, the individual was held together only by his 'collective shell' and his 'social mask'. It followed that when there was rapid economic and social change in which the dependence of the individual on the collectivity was broken, so there would be a great deal of fear and insecurity. In particular a 'threatening inferiority complex', which Mannoni thought was 'probably a Freudian castration complex', would come to the fore. In such a situation individuals and societies would actively seek colonization. Such people needed dependence, he said, and anti-colonial revolts were to be explained not by the 'Firm Hand' of colonial rule but by the 'invitation to walk without it'. Frantz Fanon was to write a biting critique of Mannoni's work in his *Black Skin, White Masks* (first published 1952), though there were elements of Mannoni's analysis of the psychology of colonialism which were very similar to his own.

Though it would be wrong to imply that colonial psychologists and psychiatrists were in any way a homogenous group, they were all grappling, in one way or another, with the question of who 'the African' really was. In this discussion, however, they were locked into a discourse of difference. It seemed that either one had to argue that the construction of African subjectivity was in no way different from that of the European subject or one had to argue that 'the African' was fundamentally different. Evidence for such 'fundamental difference' had initially been drawn from physical anthropological studies but, by the 1930s, it was increasingly drawn from social anthropological ideas. One very central piece of evidence for difference was that 'the African' was no individual at all but was inextricably tied to the collectivity. African psychological development was held, by many, to be 'arrested' at adolescence. The African never reached adulthood at all.

Of course it is very likely that the construction of the individual differs across cultures and across time. It would be very strange if the development of subjectivity was the same in a rural African society as it was in an early twentieth-century industrialized nation.[39] But the discourse of colonial psychology and psychiatry was unable to contain any notion of difference that was not directly tied to the question of inferiority and the necessity of subordination.

Freudian ideas, more or less loosely applied, offered another distinct psychological language in which to express the puzzles of cultural difference and colonial rule, and with which to describe the African subject. Some writers, like Wulf Sachs, saw Freudianism as a universalistic and therefore conclusively non-racist theory. But others demonstrated that supposedly universalistic categories could be manipulated in such a way as to enable them to present the African as clearly inferior. Freud's own comparisons between 'primitive' and 'schizophrenic' thought were a direct invitation to those like Laubscher (writing in South Africa in the 1920s) who saw Africans as collectively stuck in a Freudian 'stage' of individual development.[40] The distinction between such ideas and those of Carothers is therefore often blurred, although the routes taken are different. Laubscher's study of Tembu ritual, for instance, was the forerunner of many discussions on the existence of the Oedipus complex in Africa.[41] Witchcraft beliefs and the centrality of the ancestors to Tembu religion were proof that the African's cultural status was 'phylogenetically on a par with the Oedipus complex phase in ontogenetic development'.[42] In other words, Africans as a 'race' were stuck at a stage of development from which the normal European individual would have emerged. The theory of 'recapitulation' survived well beyond the nineteenth century in its application to Africa.[43]

The language of Freud could thus be employed alongside older Social Darwinian theories throughout the 1930s and 1940s, without any marked conficts. But the language of Freudianism was also used to discuss another long-standing concern of the European in Africa – that was African sexuality. African sexuality was so pathologized as to make the point, once again, that the African was 'normally abnormal'. Of course some, like Shelley and Watson, regarded the 'primitive' African as somehow sexually innocent, with real problems arising through the destruction of this 'innocence' and the introduction of Christian morality. Others, however, were more shocked by 'primitive African' sexuality, and saw a direct association between sexuality and madness. Davidson's analysis of the Bemba of Northern Rhodesia was typical of this genre.[44] Davidson began his analysis of Bemba psychiatric problems with a description of the apparent eroticism of Bemba dance and its public display of sexuality. It seemed to him that there was a great deal of gratification of desire in Bemba culture and very little sublimation. This detracted from the establishment of a stable culture and inhibited the development of a scientific, enquiring mind 'which is in part dependent on unsatisfied curiosity about sexual factors'. The Bemba, unlike the European, had not learned to 'renounce his pleasure for cultural gain'. The supposedly high incidence of schizophrenia amongst 'Europeanized' Bemba could therefore be accounted for as a 'strong attack of the Id on the Ego', from which they could only recover through psychoanalysis, supplemented by electric shock and insulin coma therapies.[45]

Since the popularization of Carothers's work it had become essential for anyone writing on African psychology or psychiatry to state where they stood in the 'same' or 'different' argument. J. F. Ritchie, an amateur psychoanalyst and a headmaster in Northern Rhodesia in the 1940s, declared in an article published by the Rhodes–Livingstone Institute that he saw no *essential* difference between the African mind and that of the European, but went on to describe how nursing and weaning practices in African societies, together with an overindulgence in sex at adolescence, combined to create a situation in which 'hardly any Africans are emotionally balanced'.[46] Though starting from different theoretical premises, Ritchie reached similar conclusions to those of Carothers regarding the African personality which, he said, was 'never liberated and brought under conscious rational control, and self-realisation is thus unknown to him'. Ritchie contrasted the African's upbringing with that of the 'normally nurtured' European baby of the 1940s, who all along is subjected to the discipline of a feeding regime which lays the foundations of a 'moderate attitude to good or ill fortune'. Unlike all those other colonial writers who were worried about the effects of European influence on the African psyche, Ritchie was, like many Christian missionaries, able to see it as fundamentally beneficial. He went as far as to suggest that the spread of European childcare practices could solve the major social and political problems of Africa.[47] Wulf Sachs was apparently of the same opinion.[48]

Later work in West Africa by Paul Parin and his colleagues started from Freud's belief that schizophrenic behaviour and the contents of dreams were regressions to the 'archaic', and worked on the hypothesis that psychoanalysis might therefore be the best way of understanding normal 'primitive' behaviour. They set out, therefore, to psychoanalyse an entire 'tribe'.[49] This view of the African as 'archaic' of course had a history which pre-dated Freud.

The work of Ritchie and others like him did not go uncriticized. The anthropologist Max Marwick published a critical review of Ritchie's work[50] and there were doubtless many who regarded him as something of a crank. But his work was given the respectability of print by the leading institute of African anthropology. It is doubtful if many colonial officials or policy-makers viewed whole African 'tribes' as suffering from 'Obsessional Neurosis' (as Davidson had claimed the Bemba were), or that many seriously thought that the problems of Africa could be solved through a stricter feeding regime for babies.

The post-war period was, however, one in which colonial governments in Africa involved themselves more and more in such matters. This was, as I have already mentioned, the period of welfare interventions, of the extension of childcare and maternity services; a period in which intervention and social engineering once more became acceptable, and in which the credibility of indirect rule through 'custom' was beginning to be challenged. Watered-down and unorthodox as they were, the Freudian views of Ritchie and others could provide a rationale for such interventions, and could co-exist quite comfortably with the still current 'deculturation' thesis.

The universalistic, 'liberal' and Freudian-influenced theories of African psychology and psychopathology shared with the overtly racially deterministic theories a characterization of the African individual and collectivity as immature, childlike, and inadequately differentiated from 'the group'. Whether the scientific language used was that of evolutionary theory and anthropometry or that of psychotherapy seems less important when one considers the assertions made regarding African culture by both groups. African society was portrayed as encouraging gratification and sexual promiscuity. At the same time it was said that the emphasis on social conformity in African culture led to the excessive dependence of the individual on the collectivity. There was both too much and too little restraint in African society, the end result being that the African lacked a clearly defined personality, was emotionally unstable and might easily become insane if subjected to the stress which accompanied 'deculturation'.

We have now moved a long distance from the colonial courtroom and from the utterances of the 'alleged lunatic'. We have also moved a long distance from the practice of colonial psychiatry which for the most part, as I will show, consisted of no more than confinement. Though the theories I have been outlining all began with an expressed concern over mental disturbance amongst Africans, they all work backwards from psychopathology to 'normal' psychology. The effect was, as we have seen, to pathologize the 'normal' African. This is why, as I hinted at the beginning of this chapter, the social history of madness in colonial Africa does not directly parallel its modern European history. The madman and madwoman emerge in the colonial historical record not as standing for the 'Other' but more often as being insufficiently 'Other'. The madness of colonial subjects is to be feared, for it is indicative of 'deculturation' and the breaking of barriers of difference and silence. But the central concern of the writings I have been reviewing is not so much with the construction of the mad African but with the construction of 'the African', and a constant re-stating of their 'Otherness'. So much of the discussion of African psychology and psychiatry then revolves around how far the African can be said to be fundamentally 'different', the literature and its authors locked into the discourse of 'difference'. Of course there were some, like Margaret Field, who were able to write about cultural difference in psychopathology in a more subtle, less polarizing way, but for many liberal white writers of the 1930s to 1960s, the only possible position to take in the political climate of colonialism was one which denied the existence of cultural difference in the structure of insanity. It remained for African psychiatrists and philosophers of the post-Independence period to reclaim and reappropriate cultural difference for other ends.[51] An essential part of this process had been the recognition that all forms of psychotherapy, whether European or African in origin, are themselves born of a particular culture and historical period. But as Leith Mullings has shown in her sensitive study of mental healing in urban Ghana, such a recognition is only the first step in a new analysis.[52] In comparing 'traditional healers' of Accra with the 'spiritualist healers' of the new Churches, Mullings shows that there are African healers who stress the responsibility of the individual in a way which would have been interpreted by colonial writers as being peculiarly 'western'. As to the causes of mental illness, Mullings shows that it is not 'westernization' or even urbanization which has produced an increase in mental disorder in urban Ghana but rather the economic insecurity of life for many urban Ghanaians, and the social consequences of this.

There are ways, then, around the discourse of difference and 'deculturation' which so dominated discussions of the colonial period. In their time, researchers like Tooth, Field and Sachs had negotiated some of these paths. Field had pointed to the very real stresses and strains experienced by rural Ghanaians entering a system of commodity production; Tooth had also discussed the effects of economic insecurity on mental health, as well as pointing to the central role taken by organic disease in creating mental disturbance. Wulf Sachs, in his extended psychoanalysis of one African published as *Black Hamlet*, had recognized that his whole project was coloured by the political system of South Africa, in which his subject could be arbitrarily arrested and removed from his land. The idealized relationship between analyst and subject was clearly an impossible goal in this context and the notion of 'free association' had an ironic ring.[53]

The discourse on 'blackness and madness' is a powerful one in western culture. Gilman has sketched some of its contours for late-nineteenth-century America.[54] The discourse on 'Africanness' and madness in colonial Africa has many of the same features, though I have tried to argue that it was given a particular shape by the circumstances of British colonial rule. I have also argued that the literature on madness in colonial Africa was more concerned with a definition of 'Africanness' than with a definition of madness. As I have argued in the Introduction, it is of course insufficient to describe a discourse: its effects must also be traced. The discourse on Africanness and madness was not monolithic but was fractured at many points. Its main effects were seen in its contribution to a wider colonial discourse on the 'African'. The history of this discourse is, however, but a small component of the social history of madness in Africa, and a small component of the history of the changing construction of African subjectivities and definitions of madness. For a small minority of Africans, however, British notions

of insanity were of less relevance than their practices of institutionalization and confinement. These were the unfortunate few who
found themselves confined in colonial asylums.

The history of colonial ideas about the nature and causes of mental
disorder amongst Africans has only an indirect bearing on the history of the institutionalization of the insane. Colonial asylums were
primarily places of restraint. In this respect they were little different
from equivalent institutions in Britain, except that they were more
primitive, more understaffed and more generally inadequate. They
were also relatively few and small, only ever housing a tiny proportion of those who would have been defined in twentieth-century
Britain as requiring institutionalization. There was no 'Great Confinement' of the insane in colonial Africa as described by Foucault
for nineteenth-century Europe. The lunatic asylum cannot then be
regarded as a major instrument of colonial social or political control.

The history of the institutionalization of the mentally disturbed
and mentally subnormal in twentieth-century Britain, is one
couched in terms of reason, humanity and rationality. While the
nineteenth century had seen incarceration on a massive scale of the
'debris' of a newly industrialized society, the twentieth century
architects of institutionalization prided themselves on the refine-
ment of their classifications. It was seen as a tribute to science and to
humanity that a society should be able to classify and segregate
groups with differently defined 'problems' – the 'mad' were to be
distinguished from the 'mentally subnormal', the 'problem child'
was identified, as was the 'problem family'. The science of psychology extended itself to define and prescribe a solution to almost any
'social problem'. Emphasis was given to the development of
'appropriate' subjectivities, through the application of the idea of
'social adjustment' and individuals' responsibility for the development of a suitable 'attitude' to the modern society in which they
lived. Those who didn't 'adjust', however, were thought to be best
removed from society to an appropriate institution.

In colonial Africa, as in post-war Britain, the chief constraint on
institutionalization was lack of resources. The labelling of the insane
in colonial Africa was, as I have outlined, a complex and often
hesitant business. Most colonial officials were only too happy to the
allow the majority of those ultimately defined as insane to remain in
their families and communities, where the state would not have to
take any direct responsibility for their care. The criminally insane,
however, were a difficult group to deal with, and their definition as
a separate category of 'the mad' eventually brought about the provision of lunatic asylums.

In Nyasaland, this development took place early in the colonial period. In 1910 the Zomba Lunatic Asylum was established as a wing of the Central Prison, specifically for the purpose of segregating the criminally insane from other prisoners. This segregation was couched in humanitarian terms, just as it had been in Europe in the eighteenth century.[55] Unremarkable in every other way, what was remarkable about the Zomba asylum was its early foundation. This was a time when government expenditure on medical and educational services for African was virtually non-existent.[56] The majority of such educational and medical facilities as there were for Africans at this time were run by mission societies, and perhaps it is because the missionaries so consistently refused to deal with the mentally disturbed that the government stepped in. Early mission settlements, it seemed, had acted as something of a magnet for the mentally disturbed, and missionaries found their presence profoundly threatening.[57]

Though the debate leading to the enactment of the Native Lunatics Ordinance of 1913 gave rise to much humanitarian expression of concern for the 'early treatment' and care of 'native lunatics', in reality there was no 'treatment' available in the asylum, which was almost entirely populated by the 'criminally insane'. In 1912 there were just eighteen inmates, one of whom was a woman. Classifications were elementary: seven were classed as 'maniacal and dangerous', nine as 'quiet and chronic', and one as 'idiotic, paralytical and epileptic'. The woman meanwhile was described as 'melancholy and suicidal'.[58]

The majority of inmates had commited crimes, the most common being murder and arson. Reflecting this, life inside the asylum was little different from that in the Central Prison. All inmates were kept in separate cells, and if violent they were locked in special rooms or restrained with handcuffs fastened to leg irons. The diet was the same as that of the prison and, despite the recognition that many of the inmates were physically debilitated, no attempt was made to improve the diet until after the First World War. Indeed, the 1912 rations of one and a half pounds of rice or maize meal and half an ounce of salt a day, plus 'beans and fish frequently during the month' was clearly inadequate and produced pellagra in some inmates – a disease with its own serious consequences for mental health.[59]

Elsewhere in Africa early asylums were much the same. In South Africa, where the institutionalization of the insane had begun in the mid nineteenth century, conditions were little different to those in Britain at the same period.[60] Patients were originally classified into two just two groups – those suffering from 'mania' and those suffering from 'dementia', with the former far outnumbering the latter. By the 1890s, T. Duncan Greenless, in charge of the

Grahamstown Asylum, was classifying inmates with rather more complexity.[61] 'Mania' was sub-divided into 'acute mania', 'chronic mania', 'recurrent mania' and 'puerperal mania'. Other classifications included 'melancholia', 'dementia', 'general paralysis', 'epilepsy', 'idiocy' and 'imbecility'. But classification within the asylum was not only according to type of insanity. Inmates were also divided into nine categories of what Greenless called 'nationality', including one category 'other' which contained nine sub-groups. Whether classification by disorder or by 'nationality' took precedence in the running of the asylum is not clear, but Greenless implied that the relationship between the two classifications was significant.

As in the leprosy asylums of colonial Africa, so to a lesser extent in the lunatic asylums attempts were made to create self-sustaining institutions. The early Mathari asylum in Nairobi, for instance, aimed to be self-supporting through coffee production in 1917–19.[62]

Production was one thing, reproduction quite another. Asylums threw a number of difficult issues into relief. It was said of the insane in Kenya that 'no case which can procreate its species should be considered as harmless',[63] and reference was made to the report of a commission appointed in South Africa in 1913 to investigate the treatment of lunatics. This report, heavily influenced by eugenicist ideas current at the time, drew attention to the large number of 'feeble-minded' persons who were at large and who constituted 'a serious danger to future generations'. Listing the categories of 'harmless and incurable' cases in the South African asylums, the report went on to point out that it was from among these people that most of the asylum workers were drawn, and that 'staffs would have to be greatly augmented if those were withdrawn'. The solution proposed in South Africa was that these 'harmless and incurable' cases should be 'put in big areas of ground, that they should be encouraged to work as much as they can, to grow their own mealies, raise cattle and to make these institutions as far as possible self-supporting'.[64]

The 'degeneration of the races', both white and black, was a concern in East Africa at this time too. Cases of European insanity and dementia were profoundly threatening to the culture of colonialism. Leprosy cases amongst Europeans, whilst they caused embarrassment, could also be represented as cases of extreme heroism. European cases of insanity or dementia could not be anything but an acute embarrassment. In Nairobi a long and complicated case arose over a white 'demented' woman inmate of the Mathari asylum who, in 1917 gave birth to a child. Identified as 'European' initially, the child was placed in the care of a white foster-mother, but this arrangement did not last long 'owing ... to certain opinions having been expressed regarding the ancestry of the child'. The child was sent back to the asylum where she lived until a convent school for 'half-caste' children in Mombasa was persuaded to accept her.[65]

The case caused a minor uproar within the settler community of Kenya. The East African Women's League demanded that more 'suitable' accommodation be made available for women patients in the asylum. A commission was appointed to inquire into the case and recommended that European female attendants should be provided who would be able to attend European female patients at all times. A large measure of blame was attached by the commissioners to the African female attendants of the asylum. 'We think', they wrote, 'the occurrence into which we are asked to enquire is most likely due to the venality, incapacity and want of morality of the native female attendants ...' Clearly concerns over race, sex, and madness all came together in this case, in which a number of social boundaries appeared to have been breached.[66]

It was only when a scandal of this order occurred that the silence of asylum life was broken. For the most part colonial lunatic asylums leave only skeletal records of their internal organization and functioning. Annual reports of the Nyasaland asylum from 1913 to 1930 indicate numbers of admissions, discharges and deaths. Discharges were few, but physical illness was frequent. Apart from the occurrence of pellagra, there was also a high incidence of chest complaints and neuralgia, both attributed to the fact that patients had to sleep on concrete floors which were 'apt to be damp'. Seclusion and restraint were frequently resorted to. In 1927, out of a total of fifty-seven inmates, twenty-one had been kept in seclusion for some periods, and twenty-one had been subject to physical restraint.

In 1928 a new Lunacy Ordinance and an Asylum Ordinance were enacted in the Protectorate. The former made clearer the procedure for dealing with the non-criminal insane who were coming to the attention of the authorities in increasing numbers, and the latter regularized the establishment of the asylum by providing rules for the conduct of both asylum officers and inmates.[67] Schedule B of the new Ordinance defined a list of 'Offences by staff of the lunatic asylum' which included using violence against a superior, disobeying orders, being drunk, sleeping while on duty, allowing a lunatic to escape, theft, soliciting, quarrelling, selling equipment, malingering and incurring debt. Schedule C set out 'Offences by Lunatics' which included insubordination, damaging the premises, immoral or indecent behaviour, depriving other inmates of food, theft, and breaking out.

Despite obvious differences in the content of Schedules B and C, the striking impression given by these rules is that 'insubordination' and 'mutiny' were as likely to come from the asylum staff as from

the inmates, underlining many of the ambiguities of institutionalization in a situation in which all colonial subjects, and not just the
insane, were potentially dangerous.

Asylum attendants came, in fact, from the older ranks of prison
warders. This was felt to be somewhat inappropriate, since the
asylum was supposed to be a humanitarian institution. In 1930 an
attempt was made to differentiate asylum attendants from prison
warders by providing them with khaki field service caps in place of
blue ones.[68] It is doubtful if this change made much difference to the
atmosphere within the asylum. In 1951, when some reforms had
taken place, it was possible for the medical officer in charge of the
asylum to look back on these 'bad old days' and on the conduct of
the attendants. They had few ways, he wrote, of dealing with
refractory patients: 'At the first sign of trouble, and trouble was
frequent, the nearest attendant blew a whistle, other attendants
converged on the patient, overpowered him, and heaved him into a
cell where he was left to his own devices. The attendants could then
sit down and relax until the next whistle blew.'[69]

In the 1930s and 1940s physical conditions inside the Nyasaland
asylum gradually improved. In 1943 an annexe was built for the
'quieter' patients, permitting them greater physical freedom. Also in
the 1940s greater attention was paid to the problem of malnutrition
within the asylum. But the real 'revolution' in treatment came after
the Second World War with the greater availability of hypnotic and
sedative drugs. The asylum became a 'mental hospital' in 1951,
under the direct control of the Medical Department. The liberal use
of drugs and of electro-convulsive therapy made the task of control
easier for the attendants, who were now increasingly drawn from
the ranks of ex-King's African Rifles soldiers. Occupational therapy
was introduced, and a system of payment for work was instituted.
To provide incentives an Indian trader was invited to the hospital to
display a range of his goods which patients might buy with their
earnings. One patient set himself up as an unofficial money-lender.
According to the medical officer in charge these changes to the
environment meant that the 'inherently cheerful, sunny temper of
the African reasserted itself'.[70]

There was still no psychiatrist, and in fact no staff with any
training in psychiatry or psychiatric nursing. The complexities of the
debate over the nature of African madness in medical journals and
colonial reports had little bearing on life within the institution in this
period. The only real change which had taken place as the asylum
became a mental hospital was that an eerie, drug-induced silence
had descended on the place.

Elsewhere in late colonial Africa asylums remained more
nineteenth- than twentieth-century in appearance and practice. In

1958 a group of psychiatrists was commissioned to tour mental institutions in Africa and report on conditions in them. One of these psychiatrists, Paul Sivadon, produced a grim account of his four-week tour. Though he had encountered some liberal regimes and the imaginative use of out-patient therapy in Nigeria and the Sudan, elsewhere conditions were uniformly terrible, and African institutions resembled 'les plus mauvaises réalisations occidentales de la fin du siècle dernier'.[71]

Though conditions within many African mental institutions remain just as shocking as this in the 1990s, there were some significant if isolated changes of practice in the 1960s and 1970s. These changes in part reflected trends within European psychiatric practice, but they were also the result of pressure from western-trained African professionals for a more 'culturally appropriate' psychiatric service. The Nigerian psychiatrist Adeoye Lambo led the way in the 1960s by establishing 'villages' within mental hospitals, and by allowing patients access to 'traditional' therapies and healers.[72] Similar practices have been adopted elsewhere,[73] in a recognition both that western psychiatry has relatively little to offer the majority of African patients and that the controlled use of 'traditional' therapies is cheaper than institutionalization on a large scale. This is a late-twentieth-century and post-colonial version of the arguments about 'difference' which so preoccupied colonial psychologists and psychiatrists. Though much effort was expended in defining the problem of madness in colonial Africa, relatively little was expended on the practice of psychiatry or the institutionalization of the insane. In part this was due to the poverty of colonial administrations, in part to the ambiguities surrounding the definition of 'madness' in a colonial situation. Those defined as mad were those who, in some sense, were insufficiently 'Other'. It was these individuals who had 'forgotten' who they were, and had ceased to conform to the notion of the African subject, who most often found themselves behind the walls of the asylum. Once there, little effort was made to 'rehabilitate' them, except through the culturally neutral devices of drugs and convulsive therapy. The process of subjectification through the 'talking therapy' of psychoanalysis, which Foucault sees as a component of twentieth-century power regimes, was hardly a feature of colonial psychiatry, since talking was itself a problem between the ruler and ruled.

NOTES

1   Malawi National Archives (MNA): M3/4/3: Report on an Investigation Concerning Mental Disorder in Nyasaland natives, 1935.

126　　　*The madman and the medicine man*

A shortened version of this report was published in the *Journal of Mental Science*, vol. LXXXII (1936).

2　I owe this point to Ann Whitehead.

3　Foucault (1989).

4　Porter (1987).

5　Porter (1987), p. 9.

6　Nyasaland Protectorate, Native Lunatics Ordinance (no. 5 of 1913). This Ordinance was replaced in 1928 by An Ordinance to provide for the detention and care of lunatics (no. 17 of 1928).

7　Chanock (1987).

8　MNA: BS1/2/5: Native Criminal Cases, Ncheu, 1912–13: case 81.

9　MNA: S1/1191/24: Rex *v*. Njoromola, 1924.

10　Vaughan (forthcoming, 1991). Many similar cases can be found in the court records for Northern Rhodesia in the same period: see Chanock (1987).

11　Nyasaland Government, Ordinance no. 67 of 1911 (Witchcraft Ordinance).

12　MNA: BA3/9/1: Lunacy Cases, Blantyre, 1929–34.

13　Ben-Tovim (1987).

14　Ben-Tovim (1987), p. 77.

15　Szasz (1971).

16　Showalter (1987).

17　The full categorisation went as follows: psychopathic constitution 8.3%; epileptic psychoses 13%; dementia 7.16%; oligophrenia 2.3%; psychoses related to organic brain disease 3.77%; affective pscyhoses 21.4%; schizophrenia 35.7%; general paralysis 4.7%; confusional states 2.4%; undetermined 1.1%.

18　Showalter (1987), chapter 5; see also Russett (1989), and Dijkstra (1986).

19　Chanock (1987).

20　Smith (1946).

21　The work of Carothers and his colleagues is also discussed by Littlewood and Lipsedge in their study of psychiatry and ethnic minorities in Britain: Littlewood and Lipsedge (1989).

22　For example, Gordon (1935–6).

23　Vint (1932).

24　Editorial, *South African Medical Journal*, vol. 3, no. 8 (1934), p. 2.

25　Carothers (1953), p. 177.

26　For example, Smartt (1956).

27　Simons (1958).

28　Smartt (1956), p. 443.

29　Carothers (1953), p. 106.

30　A note of scepticism was, however, sounded by F. C. Bartlett: Bartlett (1937).

31　Tooth (1950).

32　Tooth (1950), p. 62.

33　Field (1960), p. 53.

34　See the discussion over the function and meaning of these shrines in Fortes and Fortes (1966).

35 Sachs (1933).
36 Federal Assembly Debates: Federation of Rhodesia and Nyasaland (1955).
37 Carothers (1954).
38 Mannoni (1956).
39 On the construction of African subjectivities see Sow (1977); Piault, ed. (1975); Reismann (1985); Dieterlen, ed. (1973).
40 Laubscher (1937).
41 Fortes (1983); Ortigues and Ortigues (1966); Deleuze and Guattari (1984).
42 Laubscher (1937), p. 50.
43 See Chapter 1 for a discussion of this theory, and Russett (1989).
44 Davidson (1949).
45 Davidson (1949), p. 83.
46 Ritchie (1943).
47 Ritchie (1943), p. 49.
48 Sachs (1933); see also Albino and Thompson (1956).
49 Parin, Morgenthaler and Parin-Matthey (1980).
50 Marwick (1944).
51 Fanon (1986); Sow (1977); Orley (1970). See also the influential writings of T. A. Lambo who, whilst critical of western psychiatry as applied to Africa, has nevertheless worked largely within its categories: Lambo (1955); Lambo (1957).
52 Mullings (1984).
53 Sachs (1937).
54 Gilman (1985), chapter 5.
55 Foucault (1989).
56 In 1909–10, total expenditure on (European and African) medical services was just over £8000, a large proportion of which was absorbed by the salaries of European doctors and nurses working in hospitals for European patients. Government expenditure on African education consisted of a £1000 grant-in-aid to mission schools. Nyasaland Protectorate, *Blue Book*, 1910: Nyasaland Protectorate (1910).
57 See statements by Rev. Laws in Nyasaland Legislative Council Proceedings, 11th Session, 13–15 May 1913. In 1912 the death of an epileptic in custody in Ncheu gaol provoked some discussion of missionary attitudes to mental illness. MNA: BS1/2/5: Native Criminal Cases, Ncheu 1912–13, Case no. 37: Inquest on the body of criminal lunatic, Gwedi.
58 Nyasaland Protectorate, *Blue Book*, 1912: Lunatic Asylum: Nyasaland Protectorate (1912).
59 Dr Hugh Stannus had been the first to identify this problem. See Chapter 2.
60 Minde (1956).
61 Greenless (1895).
62 The information in the following paragraph comes from notes made by Dr Luise White of material in the National Archives of Kenya. I am very grateful for Dr White for having generously allowed me to use this material.

63 Kenya National Archives (KNA): MD 47/252: Native Lunatics (Harmless), confinement of J. Newman, Native Civil Hospital, Nairobi, to Principal Medical Officer, 28.3.19.
64 Quoted in KNA: MD 47/252: J. Newman to PMO, 28.3.19.
65 KNA: MD 47/195: Birth of a Child by a Female Lunatic, 1917–21.
66 For similar concerns in British India see Ernst (1988).
67 MNA: M2/11/1: Amendment of Lunatics Ordinance of 1913 to provide for discipline of native staff of the Central Lunatic Asylum.
68 MNA: M3/1/12: Central Asylum Report, 1930, p. 3.
69 Nyasaland Protectorate, *Annual Report of the Medical Department for 1951*: Annual report of the Mental Hospital: Nyasaland Protectorate (1951), p. 29.
70 Nyasaland Protectorate (1951), p. 31.
71 Sivadon (1958).
72 Lambo (1960).
73 Ben-Tovim (1987).

6 Syphilis and Sexuality: the Limits of Colonial Medical Power

'Uncultured Africans are not familiar with the name of Freud, but sometimes they appear to act as if they were Freudians.'
                                    Edwin Smith (missionary) in *Knowing the African*.

Freud is hard to avoid in any discussion of the 'colonial encounter' in Africa, not because colonial Africans were closet Freudians but because colonialist discourse is so thoroughly sexualized itself. As we have seen in the last chapter, the languages of psychology and psychiatry played an important role in defining the 'normal' African, and in pathologizing that 'normality'. Central to the concerns of colonial psychology and psychiatry was the construction of African sexuality. There were two variations on this theme of African sexuality, which mirrored more general representations of African society. For some, including many missionaries, African sexuality was, and always had been, 'primitive', uncontrolled and excessive, and as such it represented the darkness and dangers of the continent. For others, the supposed 'primitiveness' of pre-colonial African sexuality was reassuringly 'innocent'; the danger lay rather in the degeneration of this sexuality which was seen to have come about through the social and economic changes of colonialism. Shelley and Watson, for example, had voiced this view in their study of insanity in Nyasaland.

Psychologists and psychiatrists did not have a monopoly on the discussion of colonial African sexuality, however. Changing African views of sexuality are generally not perceivable from the kind of material I am dealing with here, but from time to time the problem of sexually transmitted diseases in colonial Africa created a direct, biomedical interest in African sexuality and a discourse on that sexuality which was produced not only 'about', but in dialogue with, certain groups of Africans.

This chapter explores part of the history of sexually transmitted disease in colonial East and Central Africa, and the discussions of African sexuality which arose out of attempts to deal with this biomedical problem. There were moments, as I indicate in this chapter, when female sexuality became the focus of a shared attention from colonial medics, administrators and African male elders. These were moments when, as Gilman and others have argued, the black woman came to symbolize and stand for the fear of uncontrolled sexuality more generally. In late-nineteenth-century Europe, Gilman argues, the perception of the prostitute merged with that of the 'black'. Loss of control over female sexuality in particular implied degeneration into primitivism: 'the primitive is the black, and the qualities of blackness, or at least of the black female, are those of the prostitute'.[1] The influence of Freud in the twentieth century represented, according to Gilman, a continuity with, rather than a change to, these nineteenth-century images, a continuity clearly demonstrated in Freud's *Three Essays on Sexuality* (1905).

But if we move from a generalized discussion of images of 'blackness' and sexuality in European culture to an examination of the specific circumstances of colonialism in East and Central Africa, African sexuality, even when not explicitly gendered, is more often 'male' than 'female' in its representation.[2] This, like any other generalization, must always be qualified. The colonial discourse on African sexuality was not uniform, and the extent to which it appeared 'male' or 'female' varied according to particular circumstances. Female sexuality *was* a concern of colonial administrations for its control, and containment was one measure of the effectiveness of an indirect rule policy in shoring up existing systems of social control. But male sexuality was a more immediate problem because men appeared to be more autonomous in the conduct of their sexual relations, and because it was men, more than women, who peopled the colonial cities and constituted the labour force. As this chapter demonstrates, however, colonial administrations and medical departments showed a marked reluctance to intervene directly in the conduct of African sexual relations, and in this colonial policies and laws were much less directly repressive than were their metropolitan equivalents. Rather the issue was deflected back on to women through the elaboration of a discourse on mother and child welfare and the construction of the ideal African family. Women as mothers, it seemed, ceased to have any sexuality at all, but they had a potentially important role in controlling the development of the sexuality of their children. It was, as Ritchie and others had argued, only through the introduction of 'proper' feeding methods that Africans would learn the importance of deferred gratification.

In *Black Skin, White Masks*, Fanon described the colonial objectification of the black as a sexualized 'Other'. The experience of sexual objectification, argued Fanon, was central to the experience of being black in a racist society. The myth of black sexuality was a myth of excessive sexuality: it held that 'with the Negro, everything takes place at the genital level'.[3]

The 'myth' of black sexuality was, however, one which defined the reality of the colonial situation, according to Fanon. Whilst the myth could be challenged at one level, there was no escaping its reality at another. Fanon was, after all, engaged in a psychoanalytic analysis, the very terms of which were highly sexualized: 'If one wants to understand the racial situation psychoanalytically, not from the universal viewpoint but as it is experienced by individual consciousnesses, considerable importance must be given to sexual phenomena. In the case of the Jew one thinks of money and its cognates. In that of the Negro, one thinks of sex.'[4] Whatever analytical status one would want to accord the preoccupation with sex in European writings on the 'black' and on the 'African', its presence is inescapable and, as Gilman argues, pre-dates Freud. But representations of African sexuality in the nineteenth and twentieth centuries need also to be seen in the context of a more general history of ideas about sexuality in Britain.

Both Frank Mort and Jeffrey Weeks have pointed to some of the discontinuities of this nineteenth- and twentieth-century history, to the sometimes strange and strained alliances of social forces which campaigned on issues related to sexuality, to the debates about the propriety of state intervention, and to the often ambiguous position of the medical profession over questions of control.[5] To point to the fractures in this history does not, in itself, imply a denial of the power of the medicalized discourse on sexuality. Foucault's contention, after all, was that the modern European history of sexuality is not one of repression so much as of the power of description and production.

The problem of 'racial degeneration' was a focus of much national and imperial concern in Britain in the first decades of the twentieth century.[6] This concern was partly born of the continuing medical and social problems of industrialization and the creation of a working class but it was also closely tied to imperialism and the colonial encounter. Though Social Darwinian theories of superiority still served the British well in their imperial encounters with other 'races', there were moments, it seems, of national self-doubt in the early twentieth century. In particular, the poor performance of British troops in the Boer War fed fears of 'racial' degeneration and brought about pressure on the state to intervene in the health of certain key groups in British society – children, mothers and soldiers.[7]

The sexuality of the working classes, and of women in particular, had of course been a major concern in nineteenth-century Britain. The debates over the Contagious Diseases Acts, in particular, had brought forth a new medico-moral language in which the 'dangers' of female sexuality were now described, and pathologized.[8] The eugenics movement of the early twentieth century continued to emphasize the need for control over what Mort calls 'dangerous sexualities', but with a new emphasis on genetic or 'racial' theories as opposed to environmentalist ones. The eugenist strategy, according to Mort, incorporated a sustained attack on nineteenth-century environmentalism, which was viewed as flabby and unscientific. Eugenists redefined the terrain of social intervention, refocusing attention on the individual and defining more closely the realm of sex and sexuality.[9] Only through closer intervention in sexuality could 'degenerate' elements of the population be eliminated and a healthy and moral nation produced. Women as reproducers of the 'race' became a focus of new concern – Havelock Ellis paid much attention to the question of the 'liberation of women' as part of his larger programme of Social Hygiene.

The early-twentieth-century medico-moral discourse on African sexuality should be seen in the light of these contemporaneous developments in Britain, for it was not only in the colonies that 'race' and sexuality were explicitly linked. As always, however, the medical discourse on sexuality in Britain was not merely transferred but also transformed by colonial circumstances.

We can begin this story with a debate which unfolded on the pages of *The Lancet* and of the *British Medical Journal* in 1908. This debate concerned the causes of an apparent 'epidemic' of syphilis which had broken out amongst the Baganda people of Buganda in the Uganda Protectorate. The attention of the British medical journals had been drawn to this problem through a paper presented by an officer of the Royal Army Medical Corps, Colonel Lambkin. The paper was entitled 'An Outbreak of Syphilis on Virgin Soil'.[10] In this paper Lambkin (who was held in high regard for his work on sleeping sickness in Uganda) described to his medical audience a catastrophic situation. He estimated that 80 per cent of the Baganda people were infected with syphilis, that the disease was producing an infant mortality rate of 50–60 per cent and consequently threatening the very existence of what he called the Baganda 'race'. Lambkin laid great stress, in his analysis, on the notion of Buganda as a 'virgin soil' in which an unsuspecting population had been exposed to a new and devastating disease. But the vulnerability of the people of Buganda to this disease had been created by the disintegration of their traditional social and political system brought about, according to Lambkin, primarily by the introduction of Christianity.

It was Lambkin's insistence on the role of Christianity in creating the syphilis 'epidemic' which gave rise to the debate on the pages of the medical journals. In many respects, his paper constituted one of the first articulations of an idea which, as we have seen, was later to become widely accepted in colonial East and Central Africa. This was the idea that disease was largely brought about by social disintegration and moral degeneration produced by the changes of colonial rule, and it came to be applied to a number of disease problems, from leprosy to tuberculosis. When applied to the analysis of a sexually transmitted disease, the relationship between morality and disease was, of course, seen as a peculiarly direct one. In the case of the Baganda, whose pre-colonial political system the British much admired, the moral problem was seen to stem from the disintegration of 'traditional' patriarchal authority, unleashing an uncontrolled female sexuality as Lambkin made very clear:

> The freedom enjoyed by women in civilised countries has gradually been won by them as one of the results of centuries of civilisation, during which they have been educated ... Women whose female ancestors had been kept under surveillance were not fit to be treated in a similar manner. They were, in effect, merely female animals with strong passions, to whom unrestricted opportunities for gratifying these passions were suddenly afforded.[11]

Female sexuality was everywhere a danger, it seemed, but the enlightened early-twentieth-century male medic saw that female sexuality in 'civilized' countries had been successfully tamed. Only when female passions had been brought under control was it possible to grant women greater freedom without endangering the entire society. In Buganda, Lambkin seemed to be saying, there was a long way to go before women could be safely let loose, for they were merely 'female animals with strong passions'.

At least under traditional rule these dangerous 'passions' had been kept under 'surveillance' – now, with the coming of Christianity, the abolition of severe penalties for adultery, and the opening up of the country to traders from the East coast, there were no longer any effective controls over 'female passions'.

Although there was a general consensus amongst commentators that female sexuality was responsible for the syphilis problem in

Buganda, the underlying causes of the 'unleashing' of this sexuality were disputed in missionary and medical circles. The missionary lobby was understandably unhappy with an analysis which placed the blame firmly at the door of Christianity, and produced an alternative analysis. In a letter to the editor of the *British Medical Journal*, Robert Elliott, Secretary of the Church Missionary Society's Medical Committee and Charles Harford, Physician to the Church Missionary Society, protested at the *BMJ*'s account of Lambkin's findings and of events in Uganda and asserted that many missionaries working in the country held a rather different theory of the causes of the spread of syphilis.[12] At the instigation of the CMS, the Bishop of Uganda, Albert Tucker, who was visiting Britain at this time, produced a missionary account of events which was published in *The Lancet*. It was, he wrote, the 'sweeping away of the feudal system' in Buganda which had brought about 'not liberty merely but licence'. The introduction of Christianity had, in his view, 'nothing to do with these lamentable consequences'. Quoting Sir Harry Johnston, he argued that, far from Christianity bringing about a decline in moral standards, the religion was, in fact, bound to have the opposite effect. Only through the introduction of a Christian morality and its 'appreciation of female chastity' would the Baganda be saved from dying out as a 'race'.[13] Albert Cook, the famous CMS medical missionary in Uganda who had been the first to draw attention to the problem of syphilis, was also urged by CMS headquarters in London to produce a defence of the moral influence of Christianity. Cook disputed Lambkin's figures for the incidence of the disease (though he was later to quote them approvingly), and also disputed Lambkin's analysis. In a letter to the *BMJ* he wrote:

> I must give an emphatic denial to the assumption that Christianity has been the chief cause of this epidemic. It has been all the other way. Read 'Civilization' for 'Christianity' and there may be a certain amount of truth in it ... I venture to assert, Sir, that Christianity from the beginning has acted as a deterring and restraining force and is, indeed, when intelligently accepted, the only true prophylaxis to this terrible scourge.[14]

The differences of opinion over the social causes of disease in African society between lay and missionary medical opinion have been outlined in Chapter 3. Here these views were crystallized around a debate over the sexuality of the Baganda. Two views of 'traditional' Buganda were being represented here, along with their respective analyses of the process of 'westernization'. On the one hand, Lambkin represented the views of many British officials when he expressed his admiration for pre-colonial Buganda and its sophisticated, hierarchical system of social and political control. This view was continually reinforced by the elite male Baganda with whom he held discussions and who gave evidence at his commission on syphilis. They told him that in the past such an epidemic would have been unthinkable, because in traditional society women were firmly controlled by men.[15] The Prime Minister of Buganda, Sir Apolo Kagwa, whom Lambkin much admired, expressed this view straightforwardly: 'The probable immediate cause of the outbreak', he told Lambkin, 'is the emancipation of Baganda women from the surveillance to which they have been hitherto subjected.'[16]

There was a powerful consensus of male opinion, both British and Bagandan, around the view that the 'epidemic' could have come about only through the breakdown of chiefly authority occasioned by the introduction of Christianity and 'civilization'. For the male Baganda elite control over women and their sexuality was central to their control over marriage and kinship, and hence over the society as a whole. For the British, loss of control over female sexuality stood for and symbolized the problem of control over African society in general.

Lambkin was greatly impressed by the way in which the Baganda chiefly aristocracy received his account of the syphilis 'epidemic'. In January 1908 he had given an address on the subject before the King and a group of senior chiefs. Not only had they listened 'with great interest and attention', but they had also delivered their own speeches 'showing the most complete and intelligent grasp of the subject under discussion, as well as a thorough knowledge of the ravages which syphilis had already perpetrated'. Lambkin found it difficult to believe that he was learning these thoughts 'from the lips of negroes in the centre of Africa'.

Given that Lambkin's whole analysis of the problem centred on the disintegration of traditional authority, and that his prescription was the bolstering of this authority, it is perhaps not surprising that his speech was well received by this particular audience.

The medical missionary view of syphilis, as of many other medical problems was bound to be rather different, however. In the first decade of the twentieth century medical missionaries like Albert Cook were still under considerable pressure to justify their work to their evangelist colleagues (see Chapter 3). Suspicion of medical work ran deep, and Cook had constantly to emphasize the moral and evangelical contribution of his medical work. An 'epidemic' of syphilis provided a good opportunity to make such a justification, and it was irksome that so much publicity damaging to the missionary cause had been given by Lambkin and others. In response the medical missionaries stressed the essential and 'innate' sinfulness of traditional African society and the connection between this essential sinfulness and disease. Cook and his colleagues, though they also held a certain admiration for the Baganda people, found it necessary to place more emphasis on the 'immoral' features of that society, singling out polygyny in particular. Polygyny, they claimed, was responsible for the rapid transmission of syphilis through the population. The problem of syphilis represented the enduring evils of traditional society and could not be tackled other than through a deeper extension of Christian morality. Syphilis, in the medical missionary discourse, was rarely named, or named only in hushed tones. The connection between sin and suffering was made all the more clear by these silences, however: 'I cannot, dare not, speak of the fruits of these diseases', said J. H. Cook (Albert Cook's brother) at a Medical Missionary Association meeting in London in 1915. He could say, however, that 'these diseases' were 'ruining that country and sapping the strength of manhood of the natives'.[17]

The belief that the Baganda were a 'dying race' was one apparently shared by many Baganda chiefs who in 1913 promulgated laws which would compel infected individuals to attend for treatment. The Baganda regents also diverted the tribute labour of their peasant clients to the building of the CMS Mulago Hospital, which was to include two isolation wards for 'males and females of the better classes' suffering from what were now termed in official reports 'contagious venereal diseases'.[18]

There is some evidence that, in this period, syphilis became a rather 'fashionable' disease amongst the Baganda. Certainly, although it was prevalent elsewhere in Uganda, British attention continued to focus on the plight of the aristocratic Baganda and the projected depopulation of their rich country.[19] In Bunyoro meanwhile, chiefs were also very anxious about the 'ravages of venereal disease' and were 'prepared to offer every inducement within their power to Government to commence an anti-venereal scheme'.[20]

When and where treatment was available (at this time in the form of Salvarsan, an arsphenamine), the men of both Buganda and Bunyoro came forward readily. Women were, it seems, less inclined to offer themselves for treatment. British officials, sensitive to accusations of coercion, were always keen to point out that enthusiasm for various forms of compulsory examination and treatment came directly from the chiefs, not from the medical profession. In 1921 an English woman doctor appointed to Uganda to examine and treat women with venereal diseases had caused something of a stir by resigning in protest against the compulsory examination of women.[21] This prompted a defensive reaction from Major Keane, by now the Principal Medical Officer, who pointed out that such examinations were 'not a major feature of this work', and argued that it was the chiefs who were responsible for them:

Examinations are undertaken at the request of the chiefs. The examinees set great store by the examination certificates, which are handed to each person found free of infection ... No great importance can be attached to these examinations because of the uncertainty of the procedure followed by chiefs for gathering persons for examination, that is whether any favouritism exists and whether any exemptions are permitted.[22]

By this time, missionaries and colonial officials had submerged differences in their analyses of the syphilis problem in a joint campaign against the disease. Most treatment continued to be carried out in mission hospitals, but much was funded by government. In 1921 Albert Cook was commissioned by the government to tour remoter parts of Uganda giving lectures on the dangers of sexually transmitted disease and devising propaganda material in local languages. He continued in these tours, to press home the missionary message on sin and disease. At Boa he addressed a group of two hundred chiefs who 'listened with close attention while I unfolded the grave danger their country was facing from the prevalence of venereal disease'. Dwelling, in particular, on the effects of these diseases in causing sterility, abortion and infant mortality, he predicted the ultimate 'extinction' of the 'nation' and emphasized that these diseases differed from all others in 'affecting the soul as well as the body'.[23]

As the geographical focus of the 'venereal disease' campaign in Uganda widened, and as, after 1923, it was progressively integrated into the rest of the medical policy, so it lost some of its impetus and much of its appeal, at least to the Baganda who, it was said, resented the fact that Mulago Hospital now treated all diseases and all social groups.[24]

There were other reasons, however, for the loss of direction which afflicted the Uganda Venereal Diseases Campaign in the mid to late 1920s. One was the increasing recognition of the difficulties of diagnosing syphilis, and, in particular, of distinguishing it from yaws, a disease primarily of childhood and poverty. There had been a great many misleading diagnoses, remarked the Medical Officer for Gulu in 1927: 'Yaws is commonly known in this district as "Native Syphilis", and every case of yaws sent down to be treated from the Missions is described as "native syphilis" by the missionaries.'[25] When correctly diagnosed, the two diseases appeared to be quite geographically specific in their occurrence, a fact attributed sometimes to supposed 'racial' differences:

in the Buganda Province, where the inhabitants are almost pure
Bantu, syphilis accounts for about 95% of the total incidence. In ...
Northern province, where the inhabitants are mostly Nilotic, yaws
accounts for a larger percentage of the incidence. In the rest of the
Protectorate, where the tribes are made up of varying proportions of
Bantu, Nilotic and Hamitic elements, neither disease predominates to
the same extent.[26]

Even Albert Cook, who was still campaigning against the 'diseases
of immorality', began to sound a cautious note on the question of
diagnosis. 'Ten years ago', he wrote, 'I should have replied with the
utmost confidence that two out of every three Baganda mothers
have had syphilis at one time or another in their lives and that the
percentage of abortions or premature births in women showing
active signs of syphilis is in the neighbourhood of 65% ...' Experience, he said, had now made him much more cautious about
diagnosing syphilis.[27]

By 1938 there were more reported cases of yaws than of syphilis in
the Protectorate, a reversal of previous patterns and one thought to
be due not to an epidemiological shift but to the fact that 'many
conditions previously considered to be syphilis are now being diagnosed as yaws'.[28]

Much later it transpired that the epidemiological picture regarding
syphilis in early colonial Uganda was more complicated than that
suggested by a confusion of yaws and syphilis. In 1956, Professor
J. N. P. Davies, who had himself practised as a doctor in Uganda, was
able to suggest that the entire history of syphilis in Uganda had
been misinterpreted. Not only had a confusion with yaws existed,
he wrote, but there was also the question of endemic, non-
venereally transmitted syphilis. This disease, caused by the same
spirochetes as caused yaws and venereal syphilis, was a non-
sexually-transmitted form. There was some evidence to suppose,
from a re-reading of the accounts of Cook, Lambkin and others, that
what these doctors had found so widespread amongst the Baganda
at the beginning of the century was yaws, endemic syphilis, and an
admixture of the more recently introduced sexually transmitted
disease.[29] Endemic syphilis, like yaws, was more easily treated than
the venereal variety. With treatment, with changes in the environment and clothing, and with new standards of hygiene, endemic
syphilis had declined rapidly in the first half of the century to be
replaced by the more severe, intractable and resistant disease of
venereal syphilis. A similar picture is now emerging for many other
parts of Africa.[30]

The correct identification of the disease under question is,
perhaps, less important here than the examination of the discourse

on sexuality which the diagnosis of syphilis brought forth. This discourse has less in common with that described by Fanon, with its emphasis on the danger and potency of the black male, than it does with the nineteenth-century European discourse on female sexuality. Doctors in early colonial Buganda, both military and missionary, would have been immersed in this discourse, and there were many resonances of it in discussions of the 'venereal diseases' problem in colonial Africa. Lambkin's account of syphilis in Buganda did more than resonate with European discussions on female sexuality and its control, it drew on them directly. Female sexuality was a danger that took centuries of 'civilization' to tame. African female sexuality was doubly dangerous, being both African and wild and female and wild.

But it is also clear that the particular representation of the problem of syphilis in early colonial Buganda was not simply transposed from Britain and imposed on this 'virgin soil'. The Baganda male elite made a substantial contribution to it. For them, as for many colonial administrators, the medicalized discourse on syphilis provided a ready and malleable language in which to express many problems of power and control. Female sexuality was one of these problems, but it also stood for a larger range of problems. Turn of the century Buganda was, after all, experiencing rapid social and political change. Nineteenth-century Bagandan society was a highly stratified one, in which gender relations, as crucial social relations, were governed by a complex set of rules and customs. This was a sophisticated system in which, as Nakanyike Musisi has shown, the sexuality of Bagandan women was defined in relation to their class position, and was not a simple function of gender.[31] The events of the late nineteenth century may have led to a weakening of chiefly male control over some sections of the female population, and some junior men, though this was not a universal or general process. In these circumstances, the chiefly elite of Buganda were enthusiastic in their reception of the idea that what their country was experiencing was an 'epidemic' of a sexually transmitted disease, caused by the 'promiscuity' of uncontrolled women. Whilst there is no doubt that syphilis, both endemic and sexually transmitted, was a serious problem in Buganda at this time, it was only one contributory factor making for a crisis in social and biological reproduction. This 'crisis' certainly did have much to do with gender relations and control over women, but the nature of this control could not be adequately described by the medical model employed by Lambkin and others. Control over gender relations, especially over marriage alliances, was, indeed, crucial to chiefly political control, but did not consist merely, or even centrally, of control over sexual relations. The western medical model, however, did just this – it reduced a larger crisis to one of control over the sexual activities of women. In this, it reflected a very European preoccupation with sexuality, and particularly the sexualized nature of power. For the British in Buganda, as elsewhere, a perceived crisis of control over female sexuality stood for the much larger problem of control over the sexualized African, both male and female.

In Uganda the panic over syphilis had receded by the late 1930s and efforts to combat the disease were largely subsumed under maternalist policies. Albert Cook and his wife spearheaded the creation of a policy towards mother and child health, and the training of midwives. The emphasis in these policies was less on the direct control of female sexuality through the bolstering of chiefly authority and more on the moral education of mothers, reflecting the concerns of inter-war Britain as well as Ugandan conditions. It is in this inter-war period that concern over syphilis, and increasingly over gonorrhoea, becomes heightened in other parts of East and Central Africa, and in this period that the medicalized language of social crisis again finds a focus in the problem of sexually transmitted diseases.

The language of degeneration and sterility dominates official discussions of the economic and social problems of East and Central Africa in the inter-war period. In a circular to the governors of African territories of 1930, the Secretary of State for the Colonies expressed his fears for the future in these terms:

> It has recently been represented to me that the numbers of the native population in many parts of the Empire is stationary, if not actually on the decrease, and that the general level of their physique is considerably below standard ... It has been suggested to me that, in many places, low health standards and slow increase in population may in large measure be attributed to the prevalence of certain native customs which are directly repugnant to European ideas of hygiene and medical knowledge ... It has further been represented to me that the status of native women is in some places scarcely distinguishable from that of slavery.[32]

Before considering the substance of the Secretary of State's circular it is important to ask who was responsible for 'representing' to him the problems of colonial Africa in this way. This was a period in which a number of pressure groups and professional groups took an increasing interest in the problems of colonial Africa. Partly as a result of League of Nations deliberations, there was philanthropic and missionary pressure on colonial governments to document, and if need be, legislate against, such practices as child marriage and polygyny, which came to represent, for western humanitarian opinion, 'Other', less 'civilized' societies. Amongst these groups, as amongst many missionaries in Africa, there was a certain frustration with the perceived reluctance of colonial governments to intervene directly in African societies. In order to make the case for intervention a finer specification of such customs was required. This is, in effect, what happened in the inter-war period, though by no means all of those involved in researching on and describing African societies were in favour of greater intervention. The policy of indirect rule, which came to be more thoroughly applied in most territories in this period, was, as we have already seen, itself predicated on the production of knowledge about African societies and especially their 'customs'. Knowledge of custom included centrally a knowledge of marriage customs and of relationships between the genders. The 1930s were also distinguished, however, by the rise of another professional group with an interest in Africa – the nutritionists.[33] Despite all its shortcomings, the 'science of nutrition' did, at least, provide something of a materialist analysis of the social crisis which many African societies were perceived to be undergoing in this period. There was, in the inter-war research on Central Africa, for instance, an attempt to provide an economic dimension to an essentially social pathological analysis. The problems created by industrialization, and especially by the labour migratory system were, for example, addressed in very direct economic terms by the anthropologist Godfrey Wilson,[34] while another anthropologist, Audrey Richards, attempted to provide both a materialist and a cultural analysis of food and nutrition in a labour migrant economy.[35]

Though much of this work certainly did not aim at pathologizing African society, it is clear that there was a tendency for it to be read in this way during the inter-war period. The overriding concern of colonial administrators in this period was that the populations under their control were undergoing a crisis of biological reproduction – they were simply not reproducing themselves at a sufficient rate to ensure the economic viability of the colonies. This was a far cry from the excessive fertility of the 'black' which Fanon saw as a central feature of the European discourse on black sexuality.

There were two dominant views of this problem of underpopulation. The first, reflected in the Secretary of State's cricular, was that certain 'native customs', vestiges of a 'primitive' society, were responsible for low birth rates. These 'customs' included postpartum taboos, practices surrounding childbirth, marriage practices (especially polygyny), and the servility of women. The other view was less concerned with the supposed evils of customary practices and more concerned with a perceived 'degeneration' of African societies brought about as a result of contact with western 'civilization'. As we have seen, disease was a dominant metaphor in this representation of the problems of industrialization and colonial rule, and sexually transmitted disease became perhaps the most powerful vehicle for conveying this idea.

There are no easy generalizations to be made over the question of which of these views was dominant in inter-war East and Central Africa. There was a kind of push and pull between them, and in any case the two do sometimes look more like part of the same line of thought rather than two distinct ones. The second view, dominated by the idea of 'degeneration', relied heavily on the documentation provided by the first, for an account of 'primitive' customs needed to be provided if one was going to argue that they were functional.[36]

In Nyasaland official concern over birth rates and fertility went back to the 1920s, and was shared, as in Uganda, by at least some chiefs and headmen. In 1925 medical officers in Nyasaland were asked to report on 'any causes which are operating to affect the native birth rate', and to do so under the predetermined headings of: '(a) natural causes; (b) habits and customs, and (c) diseases'.[37] Reports varied from one part of the country to another, and there was as yet no clear medical consensus as to the causes of the problem. Indeed, it is apparent from these reports that some medical officers had not perceived a problem until asked to document it. The most coherent representation of the issues came from the predominantly labour-migrant areas of the north and centre of the country, where rural populations were sparse. Here it was said that the 'absence of better males' contributed to a low birth rate, as did the increasing incidence of 'venereal diseases' (which were unspecified) which caused sterility and spontaneous abortion. Labour migration was also said to contribute to the lowering of the birth rate in another way – women, it was asserted, committed adultery in the absence of their husbands and resorted to abortificants when they became pregnant. The absence of 'better males', these reports implied, led to a loss of control over the sexuality of women, and this had serious health consequences. There were one or two dissenting voices, however, and it is important to note their presence. The Sub-Assistant Surgeon in Fort Manning district (another labour-migrant area) was one of the Indian doctors imported by the colonial administration to work in the Nyasaland medical service. In his view, the chief cause of low birth rates was clearly the 'agricultural distress and poverty of the masses'. His solution was an economic rather than a medical one: the introduction of new cotton varieties and the spinning wheel to stimulate rural industries.[38]

In Northern Rhodesia around the same time, similar fears were being expressed about underpopulation and low birth rates, especially in labour-migrant areas. Reports of the late 1920s purported to show the variation in birth rates between 'labour exporting' and 'pastoral and peasant farming' areas and produced evidence linking labour migration with low birth rates. Some officials, however, felt that the role of labour migration in producing these low birth rates in some areas was liable to be exaggerated, and emphasized instead the supposed benefits to the health status and physique of men which a period at the mines was said to produce.[39]

Infant and child mortality rates were also a source of administrative concern in this period, and again focused attention on African women, this time as mothers. African child rearing, and especially feeding, practices were documented, and their supposed deficiencies noted. These deficiencies were seen to have both physical and psychological effects resulting in the stunting of growth and a lack of self-control. As I have already indicated in Chapter 5, some commentators attributed virtually every social evil found in Africa to infant feeding practices.

In the inter-war period then, African female sexuality was associated with infertility and degeneration. The mother and child welfare movement, which got under way in many parts of colonial Africa at this time, sought to redirect this female sexuality into more 'wholesome' directions, stressing the sanctity of family life and of the mothering role. Midwifery and childcare services remained very largely in the hands of missionary societies (see Chapter 3) until after the Second World War, though they were often subsidized by colonial governments.

There were few direct attempts on the part of colonial governments to control female sexuality. In labour-migrant economies such as that of Southern Rhodesia, the growing incidence of prostitution brought some attempts at direct control, as it did on the Northern Rhodesian Copperbelt.[40] Though women in urban areas were frequently represented as 'health hazards' their presence was tolerated, and sometimes encouraged, as being essential to the well-being of male labour. African male sexuality, unlike female sexuality, was thought to require expression if its dangers to a white population were to be contained. Furthermore, as Luise White and others have shown, African women defined as 'prostitutes' by colonial authorities performed a set of social reproductive services for male labour, of which sex was but one.[41] If some stability in the labour force was required, as it was by the inter-war period on the Copperbelt, then women, it appeared, were essential.

Though indirect rule mechanisms were manifestly incapable of addressing the massive social dislocations which industrialization brought about, colonial governments in this period generally tried to operate through them. In Nyasaland and Northern Rhodesia, for instance, the dislocation of family and kinship systems brought about by the labour-migrant system was largely addressed through an attempt to bolster marriage 'custom' through the customary courts set up in the 1930s.[42] Once again, a complex set of social changes could be subsumed under the 'problem' of women, for it was women who symbolized 'tradition', control and stability in a situation of rapid change. Any reading of the court records of this period, however, makes it clear that 'the problem of women' was shorthand for a number of related problems including changes in property rights, in rights to labour, and relations between generations. The autonomy and sexuality of younger men was often as much of a concern as was the behaviour of women. The real issue, of course, was that with far-reaching changes taking place in economic relations, so enormous strains were placed on both gender and generational relations. In the social pathological models of the inter-war period, however, these complex changes were described in terms of degeneration, of uncontrolled sexuality, and of disease.

It was the Second World War and the increasing incidence of sexually transmitted diseases which focused attention on the question of direct control over African sexuality. Within the medical discourse on sexuality of the 1940s, there was an ongoing tussle between the language of 'custom', representing African sexuality as fundamentally 'different', and an increasingly confident, technical and apparently universalizing strand. The social pathology of the inter-war period receded, along with indirect rule, before post-war technocracy, but not without a fight. The arguments over intervention which the problem of sexually transmitted diseases called forth rested on further definitions of the 'African' and of 'African sexuality'.

The Second World War brought an increase in the reported incidence of both syphilis and gonorrhoea throughout East and Central Africa. The recruitment of large numbers of African men into the army, the movement of these troops over very wide areas, and the general disruption to 'normal' life which the war occasioned, were anticipated by most medical departments to give rise to an increase in the incidence of sexually transmitted diseases, following the experience of the First World War.

In Kenya, the anticipated 'epidemic' was slow in materializing. In 1942, the Medical department could offer no evidence for any notable increase in the incidence of sexually transmitted diseases, and reported instead that the 'East African labourer and soldier are much more continent and less promiscuous than they were thought to be'.[43] By 1944, however, there was a significant rise in reported cases and a flourishing black market in the new drug therapy – penicillin.[44] In Uganda, Southern Rhodesia, Northern Rhodesia,

Tanganyika and Nyasaland, a war-time surge in the incidence of both syphilis and gonorrhoea was reported and throughout the region a tension was evident between the approaches of the military authorities and civilian government medical departments over ways of dealing with the problem. In general terms, the military authorities were in favour of greater control, intervention and legislation than was acceptable to most medical departments, and by targeting the 'native prostitute' as the source of the problem, they also defended what was seen as the legitimate (and necessary) expression of male sexuality.

In Nyasaland, as elsewhere, the military authorities defended the moral reputation of their soldiers and blamed the spread of sexually transmitted diseases directly on African prostitutes. The civil authorities, meanwhile, objected to the coercive methods used by the military to check the spread of these diseases, in particular, the enforced examination of women.[45]

The question of how far the colonial state could intervene to control African sexual relations directly was one which had been in the background of discussions over sexually transmitted diseases since the early colonial period, but which became heightened in war conditions. The discussion involved the articulation of ideas about African sexuality but also a notion of an African 'private life' and what the role of the state should be in relation to this. This was the kind of discussion which Christian missionaries had been having since their arrival in Africa, but it was one which, in the official administrative discourse, had been subsumed under the notion of 'custom' and 'tradition'.

The career of Dr W. A. Young, a medical officer in Tanganyika who became Venereologist to the East African Command during the war, illustrates some of the new dilemmas faced by the administration in this period in which 'custom' very manifestly could not contain the perceived dangers of African sexuality. Young had in his earlier years articulated a non-interventionist position on the issue of African sexual relations. This was not a peculiarly 'colonial' position, but reflected a wider shift in Britain from criminalization to education on matters of sex.[46] During the Second World War, however, he became 'converted' to what he called the 'military hygienist' position. Public health, he argued, must take priority over individual liberties. In 1943 he argued that sexually transmitted diseases were already 'epidemic' in the army and that a 'free exchange of varieties' of these diseases was taking place. He feared that a widespread and intractable epidemic would occur after the war. 'We are preparing to the full a cornucopia for distribution among the homes of Africa ... and are even now spilling ripe seeds as men go home on leave.'[47]

The interesting point about the position taken by Young and

others was not so much that they were prepared to override individual liberties in the name of public health but that they articulated a notion of African individual liberties, and implicitly of African 'private life' at all. This was a relatively new development in the secular discourse on African sexuality, and one in which it is possible to see the beginnings of a shift from an 'objectifying' to a 'subjectifying' position. Though prepared to sanction many interventions, Young, like many of his medical colleagues, remained suspicious of others. In particular he and others were against the forced examination of women, such as had taken place in Uganda earlier in the century. When asked by the Chief Secretary of Tanganyika Territory to comment on emergency powers which would allow such examinations, he had several criticisms to make. He doubted the effectiveness of such measures given the difficulty of identifying carriers and he was 'loath that this Government should interfere with the dignity of the individual until it has a fair appreciation of the probable measure of effectiveness'. He was greatly worried by the compulsory examination of women, and pointed out that it was not likely that the War Office, which had recently objected to measures taken to control an epidemic of cerebro-spinal meningitis, would agree to it anyway: 'The swabbing of the vagina of any large number of women', he argued in the language of the public health hygienist, was not likely to prove 'fruitful': 'The conduct of this medical service, and especially where unwilling subjects are concerned, towards a worthwhile end, is very far from a simple undertaking. There must be no easy assumption that a woman can be brought up to a hospital or other centre at any hour and promptly certified to be free or not from venereal disease in an infective form.'[48] In conclusion he pointed out to the Chief Secretary that the draft regulations as they stood went far beyond the accepted public health position in Britain and amounted to a law to 'prohibit promiscuous intercourse'.

Young, like many of his medical colleagues, found such plans unacceptable. At the same time, however, he was troubled that there were no purely technical 'medical' remedies for the problem of sexually transmitted diseases. Treatment, even in the 1940s, was far from straightforward. Not only were there many different varieties of sexually transmitted diseases to deal with but diagnosis was often difficult and drug resistance frequent. Young, like many of his medical colleagues, saw a danger in the 'needle mentality' of African patients, which had begun with the success of the yaws campaigns in the 1920s. The anti-syphilis campaign, like the yaws campaign, was a process of 'blind, general bismuthization of the population', wrote Young. African patients, he argued, should ideally be treated only if they undertook to stay the whole course of injections in one place: 'The African is lax in his ideas of continuity and by and large is so primitive that he dimly regards European medicine as a form of magic: thus he comes along as a butterfly to flower, leaves and by chance calls again, but he seldom returns in conscious pursuance of a regimen.'[49] African patients, he seemed to be saying, would have to earn the right of non-interference in their sexual relations by demonstrating a clearer commitment to medical science.

The issue of the 'needle' subsumed many concerns of this period. In particular, there was a continuing tension between the 'moral' and 'technical' approaches to the problem of sexually transmitted diseases. As cures became more effective and less painful, so the issue for mission medics became more acute. Most mission hospitals, it seems, charged quite heavily for treatment with the new antibiotics, as a way of appeasing their own feelings of unease at the lack of a concerted effort to address what they saw as the moral causes of the problem. At the UMCA hospital at Likwenu in Nyasaland, the charges extracted from 'lordly libertines' who had contracted syphilis were used to subsidize the leper colony, a situation which Electra Dory, the nurse in charge, found acutely embarrassing.[50]

W. H. Watson (a government medical officer in Nyasaland and co-author of the report on insanity discussed in Chapter 5) was shocked by the moralistic attutude of the mission hospitals towards the treatment of sexually transmitted diseases. The Church of Scotland in Nyasaland in 1943 charged 10/6d for an 'M and B' injection, a situation which Watson considered outrageous. 'The combination of Calvin, Aberdeen, and if one believes Freud, subconscious guilt, so conditions my fellow countrymen', he wrote, 'that they believe that sin has to be paid for in this world as in the next'.[51]

These dilemmas were also discussed in the Colonial Office by the sub-Committee of the Colonial Advisory Medical Committee set up during the war to investigate the problem of sexually transmitted diseases in the colonies.[52] One of the effects of this Committee's deliberations was to call forth from medical 'experts' in the African colonies their characterizations of African sexuality. The old debate between mission and government medics reverberated around the Committee but in a new secular language. This was, of course, the debate between those who saw the solution as lying in a programme of social and moral reform, and those who thought attempts as such reform would be counterproductive and would tend to dissuade Africans from taking advantage of modern methods of treatment.

In 1943 the Secretary of State had sent a circular on the 'venereal disease' problem to all Colonial Governors. This, like the circular on the 'infertility' problem of 1930, had brought forth a range of statements on African sexuality from Directors of Medical Services. Some, like the Director of Medical Services for Kenya, A. R. Paterson, were not in favour of greater legal powers to control these diseases and argued that the real need was to make facilities for

treatment more readily and widely available.[53] Others, like the
Director of Medical Services for Uganda (H. S. de Boer), echoed the
earlier Ugandan debates by arguing that what was needed was a
reform of African sexuality: 'It is not suggested that the local African
is especially immoral or even that he is amoral but that his way of
looking at sexual contact is different from that generally accepted to
be that of the European Christian civilisation.'[54] 'Traditional morality', he argued in a familiar vein, had broken down, and Africans
were living in a kind of 'moral limbo', made worse by the war.
There was now no going back to an earlier morality, the way forward must lie in the development of a new. Giving evidence in
person to the Colonial Office Committee in 1944, he echoed Lambkin by arguing that 'in many parts of the country the customary
moral code had degenerated ... these areas being closely related to
areas in which mission influence and the spread of Christianity was
most marked'. The problem was, he said, that there was a 'time lag
between the destruction of an indigenous moral code and the
growth of a Christian code to replace it'.[55]

Quite how the 'new morality' could be spread, he was not sure,
but in the meantime it was clear to him that greater coercive powers
were called for. There should be frequent examinations of women
found soliciting, and compulsory detention of those found infected.
Qualms about such interventions were completely misplaced, he
said, as they took no account of the fact that 'the African's outlook
on sexual matters' was fundamentally different.

The Committee itself was divided on the issues of legislation and
'moral education'. There was much discussion of the example of
Nigeria, where far-reaching legislative powers had been taken to
control the spread of gonorrhoea, and there were differing views as
to the results of this. One member of the Committee, Sir Wilson
Jameson, took the view that 'the only propaganda that was worthwhile was quick and free treatment' and that 'nothing could be done
with the idea of chastity: it must be treated as a public health
problem and when enough of the population had been treated, V.D.
would disappear'. There was a price to pay for this strategy, as he
pointed out, for there was 'some risk of killing people with treatment'. This risk would have to be taken, he said, because it was 'a
choice between that and letting venereal disease spread'.[56]

This technocratic view was not shared by all on the Committee,
however. Others continued to argued that there were clear limits to
a purely medical approach and urged the medical profession to do
nothing which would 'interfere with any growing realisation and
acceptance of Christian standards of morality'.[57] Much reference
was made to the social problems of the West Indies, where the
'breakdown of the family' was felt to be particularly evident, and

the example of which was constantly held up before those whose concern was the African colonies.

One feature of the African 'epidemic' of sexually transmitted diseases was evident from all the replies to the Secretary of State's circular and occasioned much discussion in the Committee. Most Directors of Medical Services in the African territories reported that there was, amongst African subjects, very little, if any, sense of shame or stigma attached to infection with syphilis or gonorrhoea. Whether true or not, this was frequently cited as a 'fact' about African attitudes which engendered two different responses. Some medics and officials took the view that this was enormously useful as it meant that Africans came forward for treatment readily, making control of the diseases and the job of the medical officer very much easier than it might have been. Those who took this view also argued that the 'African attitude' to sexually transmitted diseases made legislation to control their spread unnecessary and inappropriate. In a situation in which patients needed no encouragement to come forward, it was the lack of funds to provide a widely available service which most embarrassed some medical officers. In these circumstances, argued the Director of Medical services for the Gold Coast, any attempt to make treatment compulsory would be likely to cause 'public discontent'.[58]

Others on the Committee, or giving evidence to it, argued more along the lines of the missionary medics, that a sense of 'shame' needed to be attached to these diseases if the 'new moral code', the only effective prophylactic, was ever to triumph. As a contribution to this discussion, members of the Committee were sent copies of an article by Morrison Rutherford, a Major of the Royal Army Medical Corps in West Africa. In it he discussed the absence of stigma attached to infection with gonorrhoea, and as evidence for this cited a Sierra Leonian newspaper obituary for an African clergyman which read, 'In spite of being a martyr to gonorrhoea for many years, he continued his work as a missionary to the end.'[59]

In general the Colonial Office, and most colonial medical departments, retained a cautious stance on the issue of 'morality', fending off an attempt by the British Social Hygiene Council to extend their operations in the colonies.[60]

The generally pragmatic approach of colonial governments and the medical profession did not prevent the articulation of a sense of frustration with the very rationality of African attitudes. Although there was a great fuss made about African indigenous healers 'fobbing off' sufferers with palliatives and creating in them a false sense of security, most evidence points to the fact that African patients regarded biomedical remedies for this particular set of diseases as

superior, and simply wanted greater access to treatment. In Nyasaland, concern at the activities of local healers gave rise to what might
have been a rather imaginative experiment at the Zomba African
Hospital. A local healer was invited to demonstrate his curative
powers on a control group, but the experiment had to be abandoned
when no patients would volunteer for his treatment.[61]

African readiness to come forward and be treated produced a
bemused and superior attitude amongst many European observers
exposing their own very contradictory views on the issue. This lack
of 'shame' was sometimes interpreted as evidence for the very per-
verse and dangerous nature of Africans' sexuality, and sometimes
(echoing another long strand of European thought on Africa)
evidence for their fundamental 'innocence'. The interpretation
depended on the circumstances. In settler colonies, like Southern
Rhodesia, the African was frequently depicted as a 'reservoir' of
many diseases, including syphilis and gonorrhoea. The whole question of inter-racial sex was itself fraught with guilt and difficulty,
and the association of sexually transmitted diseases with such relationships increased the paranoia. In the inter-war period, Europeans
in Southern Rhodesia called constantly for greater controls over
Africans suffering from sexually transmitted diseases, to prevent
their spread to what was represented as a basically innocent and
unsuspecting European population. Writing generally of the 'health
of the native' in 1930, the Director of Medical Services had this to
say about the dangers posed to the European: 'The native is the
reservoir of infective tropical disease, from which the European and
his family is subject to invasion. Unfortunately, the native carrier is
commonly a perfectly healthy looking individual, so that the European may not have the opportunity of realising until too late the
danger to which he is being subjected.'[62] The African, it was said,
might appear in a healthy guise, but the truth was that he (or she)
was really a source of infection. When it came to sexually transmitted diseases, the secrecy of the sexual act between the 'races'
and the lack of shame of the African made the danger all the more
acute.

But, in other contexts, amongst rural Africans who posed no
immediate threat to the boundaries of race and sexual relations
maintained by Europeans, there was little expectation that they
might associate sex with guilt, and syphilis with shame.

Take for instance the account by Evans of the Ba Ila reaction to
the massive venereal diseases campaign launched on the Kafue
River by the colonial government of Northern Rhodesia after the
war. This was a 'great campaign' on the lines of earlier colonial
campaigns to eradicate sleeping sickness and yaws, and was conducted in a self-consciously military fashion through the native

authorities. Examination and treatment were compulsory, but there was apparently little if any resistance to the campaign from the people. The Ba Ila attitude to venereal disease occasioned amused and derisory comment from Evans: 'When a headman is told to bring the people for treatment, they all come along quite happily and at first it was a constant source of amusement to see patients come out of the grass shelter after examination and announce that they were 'on treatment', each such announcement being greeted with cheers and laughter from their assembled friends awaiting their turn for examination.'[63] The Ba Ila were viewed as a 'primitive' and 'backward' rural group, and therefore their attitude to treatment could be constructed as evidence of innocence. 'Primitive sexual customs' were cited to account for the high rate of syphilis amongst them, whilst for other groups the 'degeneration' of customs continued to be viewed as the central problem.[64] As well as being 'primitive', the Ba Ila were also, however, described by Evans to be a 'painfully logical people'. They had, apparently, been impressed by drugs used against tsetse disease which allowed them to continue to graze their animals in fly-ridden areas. Now, 'with similar logic, what little fears they had of getting venereal disease have been allayed by the knowledge that there is an adequate and reasonably painless form of treatment available'.[65]

It was the acceptance, rather than resistance, of African patients to certain biomedical remedies which brought to the fore many of the contradictions inherent in biomedicine, and these contradictions were very clear in the debate over sexually transmitted diseases. African enthusiasm for, and belief in, the power of modern drugs was interpreted as evidence of their continuing belief in 'magic'. Implicitly (and sometimes explicitly) they were being asked to accept not only a set of remedies but also a set of ideas and social practice as part of the bundle which constituted 'modern medicine'. What these ideas might be, however, was partly obscured by the foremost amongst them, which was medicine's pretence at being scientifically 'neutral' and indifferent to social realities.

By the end of the Second World War the 'scientific' and universalizing strand of colonial medicine seemed to have won out in the discussion over sexually transmitted diseases in Africa. The idea that Africans were irreducibly 'different' in their attitudes to sexuality, though still articulated, was less evident than it had been before. The war had brought about a situation in which sexually transmitted disease was perceived as a problem for the Empire as a whole, white and black, with similar causes and similar solutions. In the process of producing health education material, however, the whole question of 'difference' was to come to the fore again. If such material were to be effective, it would seem to require that its readers (and viewers in the case of film) should identify with the images of 'the African' presented to them. In the next two chapters I examine the faltering attempts of doctors and communications 'experts' to create a later colonial African subject.

NOTES

1 Gilman (1985), p. 101.
2 See for a similar argument, White (1990).
3 Fanon (1986), p. 157.
4 Fanon (1986), p. 160.
5 Mort (1987); Weeks (1981). See also Davenport-Hines (1990). I am grateful to Richard Davenport-Hines for sending me the proofs of his book prior to its publication.
6 Mort (1987), p. 163; Russett (1989), pp. 67–74; Dijkstra (1986), chapter 7.
7 Davin (1978); Mort (1987), pp. 166–7.
8 For an interesting discussion of the ambiguities of the representation of female sexuality at this time see Poovey (1990).
9 For the history of the eugenics movement in South Africa see Dubow (1987).
10 Published as Lambkin (1908).
11 Lambkin's address, reported in *The Lancet*, vol. 2 of 1908 (1908), p. 1022.
12 *British Medical Journal (BMJ)*, vol. 2 of 1908, p. 1409.
13 *The Lancet*, vol. 2 of 1908, letter from Albert Tucker, 13.10.08.
14 *BMJ*, vol. 2 of 1908 (1908), letter from Albert Cook, 3.11.08, pp. 1780–1.
15 Public Record Office (PRO); CO 536/15: Uganda Correspondence, 1905 onwards: Colonel Lambkin's Mission to the Uganda Protectorate on the prevalence of venereal disease: summary of evidence.
16 Lambkin (1908), p. 344.
17 *Mercy and Truth*, no. 225 (1915): J. H. Cook, 'Pressing Problems in Uganda', p. 300.
18 Uganda Protectorate, *Annual Medical and Sanitary Report for 1913*: Uganda Protectorate (1914), p. 79.
19 Larsson makes a similar point concerning the Haya of Tanganyika, arguing that the incidence of sexually transmitted diseases was probably no higher in Buhaya than in many other parts of Tanganyika, but that attention was focused on Buhaya since it was an important coffee-growing area. Larsson (1987).
20 Uganda Protectorate, *Annual Medical and Sanitary Report for 1913*: Uganda Protectorate (1914), appendix III, p. 78. See also Zeller (1971), p. 200.
21 Zeller (1971), p. 289.
22 Uganda Protectorate, *Annual Medical and Sanitary Report for 1921*: Uganda Protectorate (1922), p. 68.
23 *Mercy and Truth*, no. 288 (1921), A. R. Cook, 'A Social Purity Campaign in Uganda', p. 298.
24 Uganda Protectorate, *Annual Medical and Sanitary Report for 1926*: Uganda Protectorate (1927): Mulago Hospital Report, p. 79.

25 Uganda Protectorate, *Annual Medical and Sanitary Report for 1927*: Uganda Protectorate (1928), p. 12.
26 Uganda Protectorate, *Annual Medical and Sanitary Report for 1932*: Uganda Protectorate (1933), p. 28.
27 Uganda Protectorate, *Annual Medical and Sanitary Report for 1932*: Uganda Protectorate (1933): report of the Lady Coryndon Maternity Training School, p. 49.
28 Uganda Protectorate, *Annual Report of the Medical Department for 1938*: Uganda Protectorate (1939), p. 28.
29 Davies (1956).
30 Vaughan (forthcoming 1991). On endemic syphilis see also Murray (1957); Willcox (1951); Murray, Merriweather and Freedman (1956); Willcox (1951); Merriweather (1959). On South Africa see Jochelson (1989). On the effects of yaws eradication in Kenya see Dawson (1987).
31 Musisi (1988).
32 MNA: M2/14/11: Circular from Secretary of State for the Colonies to Governor, Nyasaland, 8.3.30.
33 See Chapter 2 and Warboys (1988b).
34 Wilson (1942).
35 Richards (1939).
36 In the Belgian Congo, where the State was not so restrained by the need to be seen to be preserving 'custom', a much clearer and more interventionist position was taken over matters surrounding fertility. See Hunt (1988).
37 MNA: M2/24/7: Native Birth Rate, 1925–30.
38 MNA: M2/24/7: Sub-Assistant Surgeon, Fort Manning, to Director of Medical and Sanitary Services, 22.1.26.
39 ZNA: SEC 2/1297: Northern Province, Annual Report on Native Affairs, 1928, p. 61.
40 Jeater (forthcoming, 1991); Parpart (1988).
41 Luise White (1988); See also White's discussion of the question of male sexuality in colonial Kenya: White (1990).
42 Chanock (1987); Whitehead and Vaughan, eds (forthcoming, 1991); Ault (1983).
43 Kenya, *Annual Report of the Medical Department* (abbreviated) for 1942: Kenya (1943), p. 6.
44 Kenya, *Annual Report of the Medical Department* (abbreviated), for 1944: Kenya (1945), p. 1.
45 MNA: M2/5/56: Venereal Diseases: T. A. Austin (Director of Medical Services) to Brigadier Gormack, 10.6.44.
46 Mort (1987), p. 199. The colonial debates on intervention parallel directly those conducted in Britain from the 1920s onwards: Davenport-Hines (1990), p. 246.
47 Rhodes House, Mss. Afr.s.1519, W. A. Young papers: Box IV: East African Campaign 1941: Lecture on venereal diseases to the Hygiene School.
48 Young papers, Box V: Young to Chief Secretary, Tanganyika, 12.6.44.
49 Young papers, Box V: 'The Out-patient Approach to the Service of Public Health', n.d. [post-war].

50 Dory (1963), p. 77.
51 MNA: M2/5/21: W. Watson to Director of Medical Services, Nyasaland, 25.10.43.
52 PRO: CO 994/5: Colonial Advisory Medical Committee: Venereal Diseases Sub-Committee, 1943–7.
53 CO 994/5: DMS Kenya to Chief Secretary, Nairobi, 18.6.43.
54 CO 994/5: DMS Uganda to Chief Secretary, Entebbe, 5.10.43.
55 CO 994/5: Minutes of the 5th meeting of the Venereal Diseases Committee, 5.5.44.
56 CO 994/5: Minutes of the 6th meeting of the Venereal Diseases Committee, 19.7.44.
57 CO 994/5: Dr Letitia Fairfield to the 6th meeting of the Venereal Diseases Committee, 19.7.44.
58 CO 994/5: J. Balfour Kirk, Director of Medical Services, Gold Coast, 4.9.43.
59 CO 994/5: enclosure: Morrison C. Rutherford, 'Some Observations on Gynaecology and Obstetrics in Nigeria', *Journal of the Royal Army Medical Corps*, vol. LXXXIII (1944), no. 2, p. 60.
60 CO 859/30/15: Venereal Diseases: Relations with the British Social Hygiene Council.
61 CO 994/5: T. A. Austin, DMS Nyasaland, Comments on the Report of the Committee appointed to consider and make recommendations on the problem of venereal diseases in Nyasaland, n.d.
62 Southern Rhodesia, *Report on the Public Health for 1930*: Southern Rhodesia (1931), p. 19.
63 Evans (1950), p. 44. See also ZNA: NR 7/40, VD Campaign, Ba Ila, 1946–52.
64 See for example McElligott (1949).
65 Evans (1950), p. 44.

7 Hippo Happenings: Jungle Doctors, Children and Animals

The white doctor in Africa is an enduring hero-figure of western culture. From Livingstone through Schweitzer to the more recent figures of doctors and nurses working in the famine camps of Sudan and Ethiopia, there is a continuity in the images associated with the European biomedical endeavour in Africa. Self-sacrifice is one important element of the construction. In John Ford's film *Arrowsmith* (1931), and in Noel Coward's *Brief Encounter* (1942), the doctors, already constructed as heroes at home, end up by going to Africa in what Anne Karpf describes as 'that enduring emblem of altruism'.[1]

Of course the image of self-sacrifice is partly one which reflects the very real difficulties which biomedical personnel, both African and non-African, face in their work. These problems are almost as evident today as they were in Albert Cook's and Albert Schweitzer's time. Advances in biomedicine in the last fifty to one hundred years have been great, but for the average rural health worker, operating often in a situation of economic crisis and chronic underfunding of medical services, these advances may seem more theoretical than real. The difficulties facing the doctor, nurse and medical assistant in rural Africa are very real ones, but the European doctor-hero literature is not, by and large, concerned with the political economy of health in Africa so much as with constructing an image of that 'Africa' through a narrative of biomedical endeavour.

Jungle doctor memoirs

The 1950s and 1960s was a period when the doctor-hero was an increasingly popular figure both of film and of the new medium of television, in both Britain and North America.[2] The viewing public was, by the 1950s, familiar with the figure of the dramatic doctor-hero, usually a surgeon. As analysts of this popular genre have pointed out, doctors on film and television seem to spend an unrepresentative amount of time wielding the scalpel. The realism of these medical dramas and the degree of sensationalism involved were the subject of much heated debate between the professional medical associations, film-makers and government in both North America and Britain. Biomedicine, it seems, is not difficult to dramatize, and sensationalizing the practice of surgery proved particularly irresistible to writers and directors, and popular amongst the viewing public (just as long as there were not too many medical failures portrayed). Perhaps medical drama did not need Africa, or any other alien setting for that matter, when there was so much dramatic potential in the practice of biomedicine 'at home'. This dramatic potential relied on two aspects of biomedicine. Firstly, the humanitarianism and altruism associated with the medical role which has been a marked feature of the image of the medic in western culture in the twentieth century. The doctor is empowered to 'save' patients, and this is what he (it is almost always a he) does in the medical dramas. Secondly, there was great dramatic potential in the manipulation of technology. Medicine in television and film medical dramas is definitely 'high-tech': the more mundane practices of hospitals, and especially the more mundane nursing practices, are given much less attention than the life-support machines. Given the nature of the biomedical practices portrayed, and the heroic role accorded the biomedical personnel, it is clear that the viewer is expected to identify not with the patient but with the doctor. The doctors (and to a lesser extent nurses) are the powerful and enduring figures of these dramas, their technical knowledge enabling them to act on the world in a very powerful, but also benign, way.

The 1950s and 1960s also saw the publication of a large number of what I shall call 'jungle doctor' memoirs, though this was a publishing tradition which went back to the early years of the century and which has continued into the 1990s. These were books written by British and North American doctors, and to a lesser extent nurses, who had worked in colonial Africa. Many were written by ex-medical-missionaries who had spent twenty or thirty years practising medicine in rural Africa. Others were written by those who had been employed by colonial medical departments. Some of these books were published by Christian publishers and sold primarily through Christian bookshops, but there was also, it seems, a large secular market for 'jungle doctor' books, and many were published in popular travel and adventure book series.

These books clearly need to be read as part of the British and North American cult of the doctor-hero in popular culture, but they are also colonial and post-colonial narratives. Though, as many have argued, the very practices of biomedicine can be seen as alienating ones which objectify and distance the body and person of the 'patient',[3] the position constructed for 'Africa' and for the 'African patient' in these books is, I think, a particular one, and it is this construction which I will examine here.

In W. E. Davis's book *Caring and Curing in Congo and Kentucky* (published in 1984) the author, a mission doctor, describes his practice both in a poor area of Chicago and in the Congo.[4] In Chicago in the 1920s, obstetric practice amongst Czech immigrants presented Dr Davis with its own challenges. These were poor people whose living conditions brought serious health problems, but they were also regarded by Davis as 'aliens', with their own cultural practices and language. Davis represents his work amongst them as that of the missionary attempting to bring health, hygiene and order to a marginal and alien group. The 'foreignness' of the Czech community is represented as one of the constitutive elements of the medical problems he encounters. But when the narrative turns to Africa, there is a qualitative shift in the language. This is how he discusses his fiancée's decision to go to work as a nurse in Africa in the 1920s: 'And why Africa? Was there some strange attraction within her to the obscure and somber (she was always a cheerful and happy person) that drew her, inexorably, to the dark continent? ... She knew the conditions that were to be faced. Why did she choose to live in the midst of dirt and insects and squalor, far from the amenities of civilisation ...?'[5] Africa is clearly 'darker' then, than the slums of Chicago, and demands some greater level of altruism and self-sacrifice of the medical worker. Why, puzzles Davis, would a 'cheerful and happy person' choose to go there? If sensationalism has been a feature of most twentieth-century medical memoirs and medical dramas, it is especially evident in these 'jungle doctor' books. For one thing, publishers clearly felt that this was what the reading public looked for in such a book. The 'blurb' on the inside sleeve of *Leper Country* (London, 1963), written by the nurse Electra Dory reads like this:

> The African boy was sick because he had eaten food cooked by a woman who had had a miscarriage. In a few days he would be dead. It was a situation calling for White Magic, which had not been on the curriculum in England. During her arduous years in charge of a missionary hospital and a leper colony in Nyasaland the author learnt to handle such situations with ease. By then she was also combating disease and filth and barbaric initiation ceremonies practised by the fierce natives who seek to ensure the fertility of their tribe ... The setting is that loveliest part of the Central African Federation, the land which curls around the turbulent Lake Nyasa, but the beauty is stripped away when one has to struggle through the bush to the mud hut in the stifling heat of the day or the darkness of night ... the

crackle of twigs may be due to the tread of a leopard as the author hastens to do battle with superstitious old women and witches in a noisy hut over the exhausted form of a young woman about to become a mother. Physical suffering is not the only problem. The broad acres which have to supply the food are gay with scarlet devils, bright splashes among the whispering blue gums, which indicate the encroaching dustbowl. The struggles to restore the soil are hindered by floods, famines and fires, and a plague of worms munch their way through the crops. And when modern drugs help disperse the miasma of decay and death the natives use their energies for hatching spells and getting into matrimonial entanglements. That the natives and lepers remain happy and lovable is a living tribute to the author.

That the 'fierce natives' were soon to become citizens of an independent African country is not hinted at here, but all the elements of the 'jungle doctor' saga are present although, unusually, the author is a woman and a nurse. There is the trio of disease, filth and 'barbarism'; the beguiling beauty of landscape obscuring a deeper ugliness and evil; there is superstition and cruelty, immorality and the battle against an inhospitable environment, and there is the heroic figure of the white nurse who apparently ensures that even the lepers are happy. Biblical images are much in evidence – 'floods, famines ... fires, and a plague of worms' are all encountered, and the 'miasma of death and decay' which hangs over the African landscape must be dispelled. But the fearfulness of this picture (and thus the heroism of the nurse) lies not so much in the dangers and evils intrinsic to the landscape as in the actions of Africans who are 'fierce', 'superstitious', 'barbaric', and 'noisy'.

There are two themes here which recur again and again in the African 'jungle doctor' sagas. Firstly, there is a concern to construct and represent the essential nature of the African environment. Jungle doctors and nurses both do battle with, and stand in awe of, the African forest, bush and wilderness. Secondly, they do battle with witchcraft, superstition, ignorance and degeneracy. The production of disease is never a simple matter in these narratives, for it is located in both 'nature' and 'culture', and so the jungle doctor must get to grips with both. These two 'battles' are essential ingredients of the 'jungle doctor' book, even in the case of the memoirs of Michael Vane, who spent much of his working life in the very industrialized and urban settings of South Africa and the Copperbelt. 'The author', reads the cover of his book *Black and White Medicine*, 'spent thirty-five years in Africa and got to know over 100,000 Africans.' There had been 'adventure in his calling':

 ... with numerous cases: snakebites, injuries from crocodiles, lions and lightning, as well as plenty of traumatic surgery – fractures and lacerated wounds, head injuries and stab wounds and ruptures. Michael Vane's book is not wholly for the doctor or the surgeon; its story is vivid and exciting and goes beyond the operating theatre into this strange dark land of medicine men, thunder swears, illicit diamond digging and liquor brewings of African nurses, ancestor worship and pygmies.[6]

Potential readers of Vane's book, then, are assured by the publisher that there will be plenty of the 'real' Africa here – both snakes and crocodiles, and pygmies and ancestor worship – despite the fact that the author's experience had been in mining areas amongst urban Africans.

Encounters with 'nature', and especially with animals, are a feature of these books, as they are of most popular books by Europeans on the 'African experience'. Jungle doctors do all the things that other twentieth-century European visitors to Africa do – they hunt, they collect, they photograph, they explore the 'wilderness', and they enjoy the sensation of power which the encounter with the African natural environment gives them.[7] The representation of this 'nature' does, however, vary. Many early medical missionary pioneers felt that they were doing battle with nature itself, and that this nature was fearful indeed. In Albert Schweitzer's Lamberene, this took the dramatic form of literally fighting off the ever-encroaching forest. 'We live', he wrote, 'between the river and the virgin forest, on three hills, which every year have to be secured afresh against the invasion of wild Nature, who is ever trying to get her own back again.'[8]

The early medical missionary fought disease only by fighting with the very nature of Africa, it seemed. Schweitzer leaves us in little doubt that he was genuinely fearful of the 'nature' around him, and this fearfulness and humility are what make his memoirs so powerful.

Later jungle doctors may have also been fearful, but they try not to show it, rather they give us an obligatory chapter on the hunt for a man-eating lion, or tussle with a lethal snake. Their 'nature' is tamer by far than that of Lamberene, and consequently they are ever in search of the 'real' wilderness which is Africa.

The American doctor Pascal Imperato, like many others, discovers his 'real' Africa not when working in a hospital but when on leave and walking in the Northern Territories of Kenya:

> Baboons swung from the trees and beautiful Colobus monkeys chattered inquisitively at us, as we stood on the rim of what we knew to be, without doubt, Lake Paradise. A leopard coughed, and from below in the crater there arose a crescendo of cries from the ducks, coots, herons and egrets who swam at the lake's edge ... All was

quiet in this timeless Garden of Eden. Only the forest knew what had
transpired here long ago.[9]

In this Africa, where the white doctor is alone but for the animals,
nature is dissociated from images of darkness, death and disease.
When on leave, the jungle doctor can revel in, rather than do battle
with, nature, the only battles he engages in being the ritualized ones
of the hunting party. The European man is alone in the wilderness,
and Africans are rendered invisible in these accounts. Imperato's
early morning trek, for instance, is silent but for the 'shrill cry of a
lonely hyaena coming up from the forested valley below', and the
'rhythmic crunching of my heavy boots on the jungle floor'.[10]

Animals, both wild and tame, are central to many of these
accounts. Electra Dory walks through the bush on the way to a
difficult midwifery case and is surprised by the sound of what
might, or might not, be a leopard. Snakes are a recurring problem,
and victims of snake bites and crocodiles seem to people the wards
of the hospitals in which jungle doctors and nurses work. But jungle
doctors often befriend the local wildlife, forming relationships with
monkeys and chimpanzees which only serve to emphasize their
distance from the Africans they live and work with.[11] The German
doctor Werner Junge, for instance, not only establishes a leper colony (see Chapter 4) but also sets up a private zoo in his garden in
Liberia, and self-consciously sets out to impress the local population
with his ability to tame the wild. His daughter plays with chimpanzees rather than dolls, dressing them up and taking them for walks;
his wife keeps a cage full of leopards, which occasionally escape, to
the horror of local people.[12]

Jungle doctors, like most European subjects in narratives on Africa, are distinguished by their ability to bring 'nature' under control,
whilst admiring and preserving the wilderness. But there is always a
little bit of the untamed held in reserve to give that extra edge to his
heroism. Jungle doctors must face fearful natural obstacles unknown
in British or North American hospital wards – a trek through a forest
at night to reach a patient, for instance, a bolt of lightning in a
tropical storm, or a surprise attack from a man-eating lion.

In Paul White's 1960 illustrated 'coffee-table' book *Jungle Doctor
Panorama*, he sums up Jungle Doctor's Enemies thus:

> Battle is everywhere in a Jungle Doctor Hospital.
> Air attacks come from those mighty killers the mosquito, the house-fly
> and the tsetse fly.
> From the water angle comes
> the sly aggression of bilharzia, hookworm and the typhoids.
> ... The guerilla warfare of venereal disease, drink, hashish, leprosy and
> epidemics

like smallpox, combined with the fifth column of
witchcraft, native medicine, ignorance, apathy and
prejudice
makes formidable opposition . . .[13]

Jungle doctor's 'battle' begins, then, with the products of the environment, those air-borne killers that quite literally drop out of the sky. It continues with the 'sly', less visible, water-borne sources of disease, slides into a 'guerilla warfare' with a range of problems from sex to smallpox, ending with the 'formidable' opposition of 'witchcraft, native medicine, ignorance, apathy and prejudice'. In this short narrative, then, we have moved from 'nature' to 'culture', from environmentally to socially produced problems. The former, though formidable, are visible and straightforward, the latter are more intractable, it seems.

Just as jungle doctor sagas always contain a chapter on a hunt or a wildlife safari, so they also always have a chapter on the encounter with a 'witchdoctor'. This is the jungle doctor's other line in heroism, for not only must he contend with the forces of nature but he must also contend with 'superstition', and 'ignorance'. As well as fighting off the pathogens, he has to deal with the sometimes overt, sometimes subtle, hostilities of the potential patients.

African patients, as we have seen throughout this book, are rarely represented as the hapless victims of disease but are more often implicated in some way in their own misfortune. Though jungle doctors may enjoy the 'natural' wilderness of Africa, they seem more nervous when they encounter their patients. Pascal Imperato, for instance, took great pleasure in being a lone European in the forest ('the silence . . . was broken only by the rhythmic crunching of my heavy boots on the jungle floor'), but was less enthusiastic about being alone with the sounds of human activity: 'That night as I lay in my bed, enveloped in a solitary world of mosquito netting, I could hear the rumbling of the distant drums and the din of the incessant chanting, as they floated up from the valley below. The feast celebrating the circumcisions continued well into the night . . .'[14] The 'origins of circumcision in the Dark Continent', writes Imperato, 'lie hidden somewhere in the antiquity of Africa', but this is a very differently framed antiquity to that of Lake Paradise where he had revelled in the knowledge that 'only the forest knew what had transpired here long ago' (p. 192).

As we have seen, colonial medical discourse on Africa did not have a unitary or unchanging view of culture or 'custom'. At times, and most notably in the missionary discourse, 'traditional' African culture and society was constituted as the major enemy of social and medical progress, and was often represented by the figure of the 'witchdoctor'. At other times, and especially in areas experiencing directly the effects of industrialization, it was the 'degeneration' of 'tradition' and the corruption of the African by modernity that was seen as the more serious, and disease-producing, problem. Jungle doctor memoirs reflect both of these views, but the images which dominate, even in the more recent of these texts, are those of the battle of science and reason with ignorance and superstition. The 'witchdoctor' features prominently on book covers and chapter headings, implying that the reading public expected to find him there somewhere.

This scene from Imperato's book is typical of the dramatic encounters which jungle doctors have with their 'witchdoctor' enemies:

> I threw the door open and flashed the beam of my flashlight across the small room, until it rested upon a tall, still figure, which threw a grotesque shadow upon the whitewashed wall.
>
> He was dressed in a cloak of multicoloured strands of long grass, which touched the floor. His face was covered by a mask carved with bizarre patterns, and it was attached to a leopard-skin cap that covered his entire head. Strings of bells and various charms hung from his wrists, and in his right hand he held a long giraffe tail. This he was waving slowly to and fro when the beam of the light fell on him.[15]

In this encounter, as in many others, the contrast between light and darkness is a recurring emblem. There is nothing very subtle or nuanced about the representation of the 'witchdoctor' in most of these books. 'Witchdoctors' and traditional midwives occupy dark huts or inhabit the shadows; jungle doctors inhabit the reassuring light of the hospital ward at night, they carry torches, and when they encounter the 'witchdoctor' head-on, they do so by casting light on him. 'Witchdoctors', emphasizes Paul White, are often up to no good very close by:

> Not a stone's throw from the main road
> we came upon a medicine man in ritual black concocting his brew.
> I could almost hear his rumbled,
> 'Double, double, toil and trouble;
> Fire burn and cauldron bubble ...'[16]

The need to portray a 'black and white' picture of the encounter between medical systems in Africa is evident in the literary style of these books, their titles, and the pictorial representations of their contents. Michael Vane's book *Black and White Medicine* not only carries this very uncompromising title but also has a cover featuring a stylized witchdoctor's mask and feather headdress, and beneath this a syringe lying crossed over a simple knife. Again it seems that such an image was thought necessary for the promotion of the book, for in fact Vane's account of his encounters with the 'witchdoctor' is a much more interesting and complex one than this image would indicate.

Vane worked as a mine-doctor in South Africa and the Belgian Congo, and then moved on to Sierra Leone and the Gold Coast. In each of these places he encountered the 'witchdoctor' but, as the photographs in his book indicate, the 'witchdoctors' he met came in very varied guises. On the frontispiece is a photograph of a serious young man, staring straight into the camera. He is dressed elaborately in a cloak and headdress of skins, and hanging around his neck are dense layers of shell necklaces. In his hands he is apparently holding some bones, for the caption reads 'the witchdoctor prepares to "read the bones"'. Further on in the book we are given another picture of a 'witchdoctor', this time actually throwing his 'bones' (which are in fact pieces of marked wood). He is crouched on the ground, hands outstretched, and wears nothing but a short piece of cloth around his waist, and a strip of cloth on his head. Another picture shows a stylishly posed young man dressed in overcoat and trilby, who holds a smart briefcase and is standing in the doorway of a building. Beside him, hanging from the wall, is an array of what appear to be bones, animal skins and horns. The caption reads 'Almost as respectable as his European counterpart; a witch-doctor with expensive clothes and brief-case'. Between these two images – the near-naked bone-thrower and the sophisticated city medicine man – lies another. The photograph of 'The South African Medicine Man, M'bongo, who provides witchdoctors with roots, bones and skins on a wholesale basis' shows a broadly-smiling man dressed very ornately and regally in a leopard-skin cloak and hat, decorated with beads holding in his hands the open jaws of an animal skull. Immediately behind him on the wall is a set of pigeonholes, each marked clearly with a number, and each containing small boxes and phials, neatly arranged. The man's ornate 'traditional' dress, is thus juxtaposed with what looks like a very 'scientific' classification system.

Despite the 'black and white' of his title, then, Vane's book illustrates many shades of grey. Vane, like other 'jungle doctors', expresses frustration at the fact that so many of his patients (and African medical colleagues) cling to 'irrational' beliefs, but he does not feel obliged to portray himself as having done any heroic 'battle' with these beliefs. Rather, he is a pragmatist, playing on and with local ideas of medicine and disease causation in order to achieve his own medical ends. Unlike many medical missionaries he is not, for instance, worried about portraying his own medicine as another form of 'magic':

The belief in magic sometimes increases the difficulty of treating the tribal native; it is useless trying to argue with him about anything in which he believes. But, though rationalization is ineffective, there is fortunately an alternative approach. He believes that the white man also has his own form of magic, and he may be willing to try it – may even have great faith in its potency – sometimes more than it merits. A boy was admitted to my hospital with a fractured pelvis, for which he was X-rayed with a small portable machine. When the apparatus had been moved away, thinking that he was now cured, he decided to take a walk down the ward to prove the matter beyond doubt. He had walked rather unsteadily some twenty yards before he was noticed, and was much surprised when ordered to stop. Fortunately, his mis-guided faith had caused no further displacement of the fragments.[17]

Werner Junge describes in his memoirs his rather more reluctant manipulation of local beliefs in Liberia. Fighting a losing battle against a smallpox epidemic, he intervenes when local people attempt to spear the body of a hunchbacked woman (Uata) who had died of the disease:

> The stabbing of Uata with spears was, of course, more than I could tolerate. I told the boys to go home and report at once as out-patients if they were afraid. I would give them a magic drink, and the dead would have no power over them. So at the hospital we mixed a bucket of water with a little trypaflavine, a harmless greenish-yellow fluoresc-ent liquid, and gave hundreds of disturbed and excited natives a good gulp of our 'funk-medicine'. The effect was highly successful.[18]

Junge recounts how his ultimate lack of success in dealing with the epidemic, combined with his willingness to tolerate local practices, actually earned him respect. His confrontation with the 'witch-doctor' is much more reminiscent of Livingstone's. The community of the 'medical profession', it seems, could exert an immense power:

> It seemed to give my black colleague, the medicine-man, special satis-faction that I was as helpless as he in face of this outbreak of smallpox. The confession that even my power had limits lost me my nimbus of omnipotence, but gained me the medicine-man's esteem as a man and a colleague. The hatred which the superior white intruder had drawn upon himself by undermining their prestige vanished when they found that there were sicknesses which put us on the same level of competence, or of incompetence.[19]

Junge goes on to describe how he gradually 'won over' the com-munity to his methods. Tolerance had its limits. His attempt to introduce western midwifery techniques involved not only the train-ing of local midwives (whom he calls 'Bush-mistresses'), but also legal action against the untrained. The final chapter of his book is entitled 'The Defeat of the Medicine-Man'. Success in the 1930s was marked by the fact that, increasingly, patients came not only to be rescued in extremity but for 'medical attention of the most expert and specialized kinds'. Junge successfully replaces a nose with a plastic substitute and cures a case of hysterical paralysis through hypnotism. After these 'triumphs', the community apparently pronounced that the local 'medicine-man' was 'old-fashioned', and he shut up shop: 'This was precisely what I had been striving for. It was for them to see for themselves that their ideas of sickness and magic and enchantment were old-fashioned. The tyranny which the primeval forest and the black medicine-man exercised over their souls and bodies had been broken.'[20] But we are back to an invocation of 'nature' again when Junge, in the final pages of his book, expresses some ambivalence over his very success in 'winning' people to biomedicine. 'I have often wondered', he writes, 'whether the battle against all that the primeval forest meant, and the inculcation of progress, were the right thing for these primitive savages . . . Was it not worse to be awakened than to dream on in the green twilight of the forest.'[21]

In a reiteration of a common colonial theme, Junge ponders over the question of whether his African patients might, after all, have been better left alone in their 'primeval forest'.

The confrontation between the 'jungle doctor' and the 'witch-doctor' as depicted in these accounts, then, is not as black and white as the iconography of these books would suggest. Though the heroism of the jungle doctor is constructed through the 'battle with ignorance and superstition', the idea that these cultural obstacles to 'progress' might in fact be 'natural' to inhabitants of the 'primeval forest' and best left alone, like the 'wilderness', is also articulated by some of them. As with 'nature', so with 'culture', the jungle doctor can afford to romanticize and regret interference only when his power has been very clearly established.

What is produced through all these accounts of confrontation with local cultures, however, is the notion of the African patient as decidedly 'difficult'. African patients might sometimes be overly impressed by 'white magic', but they also often insist on retaining a degree of control over their therapy which is largely denied the recipient of twentieth-century biomedical care. Jungle doctors, these memoirs tell us, are frequently frustrated and exasperated. Though, on the one hand, their knowledge and position in the colonial state gives them an undeniable power, on the other hand they do not always succeed in exerting it, for African patients are constantly calling it into question. It is not difficult to 'read against the grain' in a jungle doctor memoir and find that the 'battle against ignorance and superstition' is in fact a confrontation with scepticism and resistance.

In *Black and White Medicine*, Vane describes a scene which sums up a great deal of this. An elderly woman in Sierra Leone is prepared for an operation but, before she can be anaesthetized, gets up from the operating table and escapes. Vane is exasperated: '... on this occasion I cursed the Africans in my thoughts for their stupidity, ignorance, unreasonableness, obstinacy, and 'Africanness' generally, assuring myself that there was nothing I should like better than to get away from this detestable accursed continent for ever and ever.'[22]

The difficulty with African patients then, in Vane's words, is their 'Africanness', an attribute which Vane does not think requires definition, but which appears intimately associated with 'stupidity', 'ignorance', 'unreasonableness' and 'obstinacy'. This is not the passive victim of disease or the passive patient of biomedicine. Jungle doctors, it seems, encountered criticism, scepticism and outright resistance from some of their patients, but this resistance was portrayed in their accounts as part of the age-old battle between black and white medicine, between rationality and superstition. In Christian versions of the jungle doctor story, this 'battle' was, quite explicitly, taken to represent a battle between Christianity and evil, and therefore could stand as a parable with much wider significance. The opportunities for exploiting the jungle doctor story for wider Christian pedogogic purposes were eagerly taken up in a sub-genre – the jungle doctor story for child readers.

Jungle doctors and child readers

Shortly after the outbreak of the Second World War, Dr Paul White, a missionary doctor who had been working in rural Tanganyika, found himself in Ceylon contemplating his future. He was on his way home to Australia with his wife, whose ill-health, it seemed, would prevent any return to work in Africa. With time on his hands, he began writing about his African experiences, producing the draft of his first book, *Doctor of Tanganyika*.[23] Back in Australia the book was published and, rather to his surprise, quickly became a best-seller. White emerged as something of a celebrity, broadcasting on 'jungle doctor' themes over the Australian air-waves, 'on thirty-five stations from Perth to Sydney'. He produced new books in quick succession, responding to the growing, and increasingly international, demand for his stories. By the late 1950s his books had been translated into French, German, Norwegian, Spanish, Portuguese, Swedish, Dutch, Urdu and Chinese. More translations were to follow. In 1959 White celebrated the sale of his millionth copy and launched a 'Jungle Doctor' television series. As of 1988, Paul White was still producing 'Jungle Doctor' books, which now come in a confusing proliferation of series. There are Jungle Doctor 'Books', Jungle Doctor 'Novels', Jungle Doctor 'Adventures' and Jungle Doctor 'Story Fables', as well as Jungle Doctor audio-cassettes and Jungle Doctor film strips. Sold in Britain primarily through Christian bookshops, and directed at a young audience, White's Jungle Doctor stories are essentially Christian fables with an African setting. Jungle Doctor stories catalogue the joint triumph of Christianity and bio-medicine over the multitude of 'evils' encountered in the 'jungle' of rural Africa. They are also health education manuals, for whilst they relentlessly address moral issues, they also deliver health messages.

If the message of these stories is simple, the manner of their telling is often quite complex, as is the positioning of the reader. This is the opening of one of the books in the Jungle Doctor Adventure series, entitled *Crooked Dealings*:

The flames of the camp fire threw huge shadows on the walls of the jungle hospital.

From the dispensary door I could see young Goha. He stood in the background, but his deformed face and the unsightly lumps on his back were clearly visible.

Daudi whispered, 'How long before we can do his operations, Bwana?'

'Everything depends on how he responds to the new medicines. Mosquitoes have done much harm to his blood'.

Lying at Goha's feet was Seko, his small dog, who seemed to have the ability to smile.

Daudi grip[p]ed my elbow. 'Look at that dog, doctor'.

Seko's ears were flat. He trembled all over.

'Seko, come here!' ordered Goha, but instead of obeying the dog tried to creep under a three-legged stool.

Goha put one hand over the twisted side of his face and moved forward to pick up the little animal.

It all happened in a second. A brown, hunched-up shadow came rocketing out of the darkness. Snarling, it grabbed the small dog by the scruff of the neck and shot off again into the gloom of the night.

Daudi jumped to his feet. 'Mbisi, the hyaena! Quickly, after the brute!'

I snatched my torch. Its beam followed the sound of the little dog's howling as I swept the corn garden systematically with light.

'Save him, Bwana!' gasped Goha as we dashed through the gate.[24]

Crooked Dealings was first published in 1959, has been reprinted several times since, and was revized in 1988. Virtually all the features of the earlier Paul White Jungle Doctor stories are contained within these opening pages. The 'I' of the story is the (white) Jungle

Doctor himself, immediately placed in an heroic role, both by his medical knowledge (he may, it seems, be able to 'transform' Goha), and by his dashing off into the bush after the hyena – 'Save him, Bwana'. His faithful medical and evangelical assistant, Daudi, goes with him. The child patient, in this case Goha, is another central character of these books, and one who often carries many of Jungle Doctor's moral messages. Children are represented to the child readers of these books as basically innocent, but as very vulnerable to the forces of corruption in the 'jungle'. Animals are even more important in these books than they are in the adult 'jungle doctor' memoirs we have surveyed. They come in two basic varieties – the wild and the tame, with the wild most often symbolizing the danger and evil of the 'jungle', while the tame (in this case Goha's smiling dog) share in the attributes of those 'saved' through Christianity.

In *Crooked Dealings*, as in White's other books, and in many of the 'jungle doctor' memoirs, evil influences, whether in the form of animal, human being or pathogen, emerge from the darkness of the bush, whilst all that is wholesome and good stays within the light of the hospital, or is illuminated by the flickering flames of the campfire. In this opening sequence of *Crooked Dealings*, Jungle Doctor directs the beam of his torch into the darkness of the bush, just as Imperato reported himself casting his torch beam on the shape of the 'witchdoctor'.

The pervasiveness of evil, even amongst the innocent children of Africa, is a theme graphically expressed in this story by Goha's physical deformities. The boy has both a 'twisted' face, and a hunched back. He pleads with the doctor to perform an operation to remove the swelling: 'Bwana, first remove the ipu, the swelling that is in my back ... It irritates, it is in the way. I can't rest properly while it is there, Bwana.'

Jungle Doctor, never one to miss the opportunity to deliver a moral message, seems to imply that Goha's physical disability might be associated with a deeper problem when he replies: 'Sin is exactly like that, Goha. It twists, it irritates, it grows and disturbs your rest. It's a cruel, cramping, crippling thing and, strangely enough, people don't bother about it. They shrug and pretend it isn't there.'[25] Disease in White's books rarely has a 'natural' aetiology but is relentlessly connected with sin. Even poor Goha, a 'good' child, does not escape this association.

There is little doubt about the ways in which White's early Jungle Doctor stories are to be read. As in the adult versions that we have surveyed, the white doctor is very definitely the hero of these stories, and the child reader must presumably identify with him in his adventures. But if Jungle Doctor's moral messages are to be successfully conveyed, then the child must also identify to some degree with the children of the stories, and their struggles to remain 'good'. This is slightly more problematic, for although there are children in these books who show courage and fortitude and humour, they would be nothing but for the doctor who continually rescues them from teetering over the edge into the 'wilderness' which is Africa. Furthermore, these early books are written in an explicitly colonial setting. The doctor-hero is white, he is surrounded by African servants and subordinates, and his patients are Africans. Evil, in the form of the 'witchdoctor', also comes in the shape of an African. The adventure story and moral story components of these books are structured in such a way as to make it almost obligatory to read as a 'white', to identify with Jungle Doctor's struggles over Africa and Africans.

But White seems always to have different audiences in mind, for each story also carries a health education message, and none of these messages would make much sense to the average white child reader of Britain, France or Australia in the 1950s and 1960s. In *Crooked Dealings* the message is on the dangers of bilharzia, while other books convey health messages on smallpox and bubonic plague. As health education texts, these stories seem to assume a young rural African readership. It is the dual nature of White's books which makes them interesting, and the way in which they move from the objectification of Africans to their manipulation as subject-readers.[26]

The white imperial child of the 1950s and 1960s might have read the Jungle Doctor books as modern versions of the David Livingstone story which had occupied space in school textbooks and Sunday School tracts for a hundred years. More recently, British children's comics had also provided a vehicle for modern versions of this medical missionary adventure story. Children had been an important constituency of the fund-raising and propaganda efforts of the medical missionary movement from its beginnings. The journal of the Medical Missionary Association, *Medical Missions at Home and Abroad* (later *Conquest by Healing*) had, since its foundation in the late 1890s, featured a 'Children's Corner'. The 'Children's Corner' was edited by the MMA's Children's Secretary, whose job it also was to facilitate the establishment of local fund-raising branches amongst British children. Foremost amongst these were the bands of girls with names like the 'Gosport Bluebells' and the 'Blackheath Roses', whose fund-raising achievements were catalogued in the 'Children's Corner'. There was even a 'Babies Band' to which the new-born could become subscribers and thus embark on a life of good works from their first moments.[27] In the early days of the medical missionary enterprise, Africa was a marginal place in terms of the numbers

of medical missionaries operating there, but the symbolic significance which Livingstone had helped to create for healing in Africa
was always evident.[28]

In the late 1890s and 1900s the readers of the Children's Corner
were treated to many a story of sin, disease and poverty from
China, the East End of London, the Middle East, India, and, less
frequently, from Africa. In 1898, for example, they could read an
account of the 'winter treat' at the Islington Medical Mission, at
which poor children ('How nice their mothers have made them look
...') were given tea followed by a magic lantern display of medical
missionary work amongst the children of China, Persia and India.[29]
If the children of the East End of London were objects of a mixture
of pity and abhorrence to the Blackheath Roses and the Gosport
Bluebells, they were, it seems, given the opportunity of projecting
some of these feelings on to the alien others of the far corners of the
world.

In all these 'dark corners', from the gin palaces and synagogues of
the East End to the 'harems' of the Orient, medical missionary work
was represented as a battle against evil in which the white Christian
child must join through prayer, work parties and the collection box:

> There's always work in plenty for little hands to do,
> There is something waiting every day that none may try but you;
> Little burdens you may lift and happy steps that you can take,
> Heavy hearts that you may comfort for the blessed Saviour's sake.[30]

But despite some essential similarities in these representations, Africa and 'the African' were allotted a particular place, and a more
prominent place in the 1910s and 1920s as the medical missionary
enterprise gained ground there. In the Children's Corner of this
period, variants of an Orientalist discourse were restated through
constructions of the 'cruel Chinese' and the 'caste-ridden' Indian,
but Africa and the African, the child reader was told, were peculiarly 'dark', their essential evil being obscured by what at first
sight appeared to be an engaging closeness to nature. Fearful
unmaskings of this innocence were catalogued on the pages of
Conquest by Healing. Take this example from a description of early
medical missionary work in southern Africa:

> A little light is seen amid the thick darkness. When I arrived at
> Khocene the life of the natives, simple, heedless, natural, under the
> great blue heavens or by the brilliant light of an African moon,
> appeared to me full of poetry. On a superficial glance, one was
> inclined to range oneself on the side of Rousseau. But wait and see; all
> the charm disappears. These big children of nature are often its vic-
> tims. And what wretched mortals?[31]

The development of this medical missionary discourse on Africa I have outlined in more detail in Chapter 3 and its influence has been seen in the jungle doctor medical memoirs surveyed earlier in this chapter. The point to be made here is that in Britain (and presumably in other 'white' parts of the Empire) many of the participants in this discourse were children.

When White's books began to appear after the Second World War they must have struck a number of familiar chords to the white child reader, familiar with the story of Livingstone, with imperialist adventure stories of children's comics, and with the doctor-hero of British film and television. Both this background and the structure of the text would have lead to a reading in which the white child identified with the white doctor hero.

But taken as a whole White's Jungle Doctor books require a more complex analysis for, as I have suggested, White seems to have at least two different kinds of audience in mind, one of which is an African child readership. All of White's narratives are interspersed with bits of pseudo-vernacular and 'African' English. This becomes more noticeable in his later books, though it is a stylistic device present from his earliest stories. On the opening pages of *Jungle Doctor on the Hop* (first published in 1957), there are several examples of this device in use. A group of young boys are enjoying a feast of roasted rat. They invite Jungle Doctor to join in the feast:

'Will you come and eat with us, Bwana?'
'Truly, Great One, it's a sikuku of great merit'.
Another voice chimed in. 'There is no meat as sweet to the palate as that of Panya'.
Out of the corner of my mouth I asked my African assistant. 'As the meat of what, Daudi?'
'Panya, the rat, Bwana', he murmured . . .
. . . I turned to the boys. 'This is an invitation of great kindness but I would not rob you of your feast'.
A chorus of answers came:
'Ng'o, Bwana, there is plenty for all'.
'We caught a great heap of them'.
'There are eighty-seven, Bwana'.
'It would bring joy to your stomach.'
'Truly, they're delicious roasted.'
It was hard to keep a straight face.
'Yoh, behold it's a thing of sadness to me that the flesh of Panya, the rat, brings little joy to my stomach. Rather than reduce the size of your feast, let me add to it with another bringer of happiness'.[32]

This passage provides an example of White's use of vernacular and a stereotyped 'African English' to provide what can only be described as 'local colour' in his early texts. The reader who is being provided with this 'local colour' seems to be a non-African. Jungle Doctor, who has himself to be provided with a 'cultural translation' of the boys' feast by Daudi, his assistant, confides in the reader in an aside ('It was hard to keep a straight face'), and involves the reader in his dilemma over the boys' invitation to join the feast. Jungle Doctor suppresses his smile so that the boys cannot see it, but the reader shares in his mixture of amusement and abhorrence at the idea of eating roasted rat. But Jungle Doctor is presented to us as sensitive to, rather then codemnatory of, this bit of cultural difference. A great manipulator of language, he turns to address the boys politely in what the reader must assume to be 'African English'.

There are moments, however, even in the earlier books, when White's repeated use of Swahili phrases indicates the possibility of another agenda. White does not provide a glossary, and although he does sometimes make clear the English meanings of the Swahili words he uses, he also frequently leaves them hanging in the air, without explanation. If the readers are the white imperial children we have been imagining, then a fairly high degree of competence in 'textual analysis' seems to be expected of them in passages such as the following:

> 'Heeh!' Simba broke in, 'this is trouble talk indeed.'
> 'Ngheeh, and now suddenly Sumbuli has the sneezing disease. Yoh, he is a fundi at sneezing, even rivalling the Bwana here'.
> 'Kah! The sneezing disease, hay fever, is not produced by spells but by pollen from grasses!'
> 'But, Bwana, this sneezing comes suddenly, and spells are a convenient way of explaining that mapepo, evil spirits, are attacking'.[33]

In some passages it seems that White is injecting words of Swahili and apparently 'African' turns of phrase not in order to provide 'local colour' for the white reader but in order to foster an identification of an African reader with the African subjects of the stories.

The African reader which White creates in these narratives is a young person who must have some degree of Christian education, and who, of course, will be literate in English.[34] This young person needs to be informed on certain health issues (the choice of which makes this aspect of all the stories irrelevant to a non-African readership) in quite a direct way. The African reader is also presented with African subjects like her or himself who are educated and Christian, but who are constantly battling against sin and temptation. 'Good Africans' and 'bad Africans' are produced in these narratives, and the reader is shown the ultimate benefits of remaining 'good'.

Figure 8 Dr Paul White and the Rev. Dan Mbogoni (Daudi of the Jungle Doctor books) in 1967.

There is a tension inherent in White's narratives, then, between their different roles. On the one hand they are imperial 'jungle doctor' stories of white heroism, dependent on identification with the white doctor-hero and objectification of African characters. On the other hand, they are both health and morality manuals for young educated Africans, providing them with guidance through their identification with the African subjects of the stories.

In White's Animal Fable series, the ambiguous positioning of the reader is partly overcome by making the central characters animals rather than human beings. White exploits the apparent universality of the animal fable genre of children's story to get his messages (on both health and morality) across. Animals are centre stage in these books, but at the beginning and end of every animal fable we have (in italics) a setting of the story-telling scene, and a drawing out of morals from the text. Though animal fables may be a widely-understood story form for children in many parts of the world, the rest of the text seems explicitly designed for a young African readership. In *Hippo Happenings*, for example, the teller of the fables is Daudi, Jungle Doctor's assistant, rather than Jungle Doctor himself. (This foregrounding of Daudi is made even more explicit in other later books, as we shall see.) Jungle Doctor is not entirely absent, however, for it is he who suggests to Daudi that he might tell the children some stories about smallpox, a disease which is threatening to reach epidemic form in the area: 'Jungle Doctor's voice came over Daudi's shoulder, "Daudi, these young friends of ours could be very useful in what we're planning to do. Why not tell them about it and ..." He dropped his voice.'[35] The group of children, then, are to be recipients and transmitters of two messages – one is a health education message on the benefits of vaccination, the other a Christian message on the healing of the soul, and both these lessons are drawn out at the beginning and end of every chapter in discussions between the children and Daudi when he has finished telling a fable. Within the fables the animals are themselves low-key transmitters of moral messages, though they are never allowed the status of being Christians themselves! In one chapter of *Hippo Happenings*, however, Punda the donkey seems to be expressing White's own dilemma over the nature of his readership and subject when he finds himself to be both black and white.

Later books in the series Jungle Doctor Adventures are more explicit in the creation of an African reader position. *Jungle Doctor in Slippery Places* was first published in 1973 by the African Christian Press as *Yakobo in Slippery Places*, then reissued in 1988 by Anzea Books as *Jungle Doctor in Slippery Places*. A foreword to this second edition is entitled 'Introducing Jungle Doctors':

> Since 1934 there have been a number of Jungle Doctors working in Mvumi Hospital, Tanzania, East Africa – some Australian, some British, a West Indian and of recent years a number of East African Jungle Doctors.
>   This story introduces one of these African doctors, Dr Daudi Matama.[36]

The scene is set, then, for a post-colonial narrative. The habitual reader of the Jungle Doctor Adventure series is being warned, no less, that the leading character of the book is an African, Daudi. Daudi seems to have been promoted from medical assistant to fully qualified doctor, though there remains some ambiguity about whether he qualifies as a Jungle Doctor. The 'blurb' on the back cover of the book seems to imply that, although Daudi might be the central heroic figure of this story, only the author and creator, Paul White, is eligible for the title of Jungle Doctor: 'Another thrilling adventure from Paul White, the Jungle Doctor'. As in *Hippo Happenings*, the white doctor seems to be peering over Daudi's shoulder, unwilling to disappear altogether.

The basic messages of White's later books remain very similar to those of his earlier stories, as does the structure of the texts. Daudi, however, has replaced the white Jungle Doctor, and this does repre-

sent a shift in the construction of the reader, if not in the content of
the message. White has updated his message and produced a more
'suitable' hero for a post-colonial African audience. Class has largely
taken the place of race as providing the level of objectification
needed of the 'bad' African in order for the message of the book to
be conveyed, and the 'bad' African is now constructed not solely as
someone immersed in superstition and witchcraft but as someone
corrupted by greed, money and modernity as well.

Slippery Places tells the story of Yakobo, a medical assistant who is
persuaded by a criminal associate to steal a supply of antibiotics
from the mission hospital in which he works, and to tour the
countryside selling injections to those who want them. Yakobo is
aided and urged on in his new life of sin by 'Arab' and 'Pakistani'
traders, who seem to have been created as a repository of degeneration and corruption. Many of the devices used in *Slippery Places*
remain familiar from earlier books. When, for example, Yakobo
leaves the hospital with his 'loot', he leaves 'light' for 'darkness':

> Always keeping in the shadow, he chose a seldom used path which
> went steeply downhill. Gradually the lights of the hospital dis-
> appeared. He grunted with relief. Before anyone realised he had gone
> he would be far away.
>   In the darkness, he smiled with satisfaction. It really had been easy.
> Dolla was right. You had only to make your plans and . . . Hooked
> thorns tore into his leg. He gasped, bent down to free himself and
> dropped his torch. Again thorns stabbed at him as he groped in the
> gloom. When he pressed the switch no light came.
>   He muttered in disgust. 'Now I must walk in darkness.'[37]

As in earlier books, the 'African jungle' continues to be the repository of danger and evil, but a new 'frontier' has also been created. In
Slippery Places, Africa has been transformed into a place divided into
the 'developed' and the 'undeveloped'. The African heroes, Dr
Matama and his friend the Area Commissioner, unambiguously
inhabit the 'developed' and 'civilized' world. Whereas in earlier
Jungle Doctor stories the wilderness was all around, and only the
white Jungle Doctor ventured into it with his torch, in *Slippery Places*
the wilderness has a more explicit geographical location. Where
'Africa' was the frontier, it is now a place called Malenga country (or
the Slippery Place). The Slippery Place is a marshy and unproduc-
tive area inhabited by a mixture of 'unimproved' farmers, poachers
and marijuana suppliers. It is also an unhealthy place, prone to
famine and infested with malarial mosquitoes. In *Slippery Places*
medicine and 'development' are part of the same modernizing project being pursued by Dr Matama and his Area Commissioner
friend. The place of Jungle Doctor's friend and ally, previously

occupied by children and tame animals, is partly taken over by a
benign and friendly technology. A central character of *Slippery Places*
is Pili Pili, the driver of an earthmoving machine, which the affec-
tionately addresses as Punda: 'Punda here, who is an animal of
understanding and obedience, will save your feet still further . . .
Just watch her cleverness . . . Pull this: she bends her neck. Push
that: she opens her mouth.'[38] Together Matama the doctor, the Area
Commissioner, and earthmoving machine, a boat and an aeroplane,
set about 'civilizing' Mulenga country, and do battle with those
degenerate forces of corrupt modernity. The symbolism of the specifically medical project which was prominent in earlier Jungle Doctor
Adventures is very much subdued here. Perhaps only a white Jungle Doctor was able to carry that symbolism, for in *Slippery Places*
Daudi is not so much a doctor as just one representative of the
modern African Christianity which has harnessed the forces of technology for good rather than for evil ends.

This chapter has examined different types of 'jungle doctor' story in
order to analyse some of the ways in which the medical encounter in
Africa has been represented, and how it represents itself, through
the pens of white doctors and nurses. In the case of the 'jungle
doctor' memoirs, which had an adult readership in Britain and
North America, we can see the endurance of the heroic image of the
white doctor facing, single-handedly it seems, enormous physical
obstacles and dangers, but also cultural ones. Jungle doctors,
through their own accounts, do battle with both 'nature' and 'culture' in their encounters with the mosquito, the witchdoctor and
African patient. Jungle doctor memoirs are little different from most
popular twentieth-century British and North American books on
Africa, with their chapters on big game or its preservation, and with
their emphasis on adventure. The fact that their heroes are medics,
however, does give them a certain distinctive power. Many seem
to set out to shock their readers through lurid accounts of the most
gory of medical episodes. But these are not mere medical horror
stories, they are also vehicles through which a fear and often an
abhorrence for Africa can be expressed. Disease, in these accounts,
does not simply attack the people of Africa, rather it *is* Africa. Of
course this does not mean that many of these writers of these
memoirs were not, in their way, truly heroic figures, who worked
with humility and humanity in very difficult circumstances. Rather it
is that when faced with the task of summarizing their lives for a
European audience they found themselves locking into, reproducing
and conveying long-standing images of Africa as the 'dark continent' which held a fearful attraction.

Paul White's Jungle Doctor books are, of course written with a

Figure 9 Illustration from Dr Paul White's autobiography, Alias Jungle Doctor, captioned 'The funniest thing I've read since Darwin'.

different purpose and different audience in mind. They employ many of the same images as were used in the jungle doctor memoirs, but with a much more conscious exploitation of their significance in Christian morality. Thus light and dark, black and white, are employed to express not only the individual jungle doctor's encounter with Africa but also the larger encounter between Christianity and paganism. In these stories both children and animals contain within them possibilities for both good and evil, while only the white jungle doctor seems to have the power to influence whether good or evil will triumph. A physically powerful figure, he is never entirely replaced by his African successor, Daudi, the character of which seems unable, in White's later narratives, to fully bear the medical and moral symbolism. These later post-colonial narratives, then, which consciously set out to create an African reader-position, end up, tellingly, as rather neo-imperial narratives, with the white doctor-author unable to make a complete exit. Perhaps, as White's publishers put it, 'we have to realise too the possibility that stories about Africa are more interesting to those outside than those inside'. Certainly in the later stories White draws back from creating a black medical hero in the mould of his white predecessor, and Daudi becomes less a doctor and more a general emblem of the benefits of a Christian version of modernity.

White's stories are primarily Christian fables, and only secondarily health education manuals. How successful they were in the latter role is not clear (particularly since most of their readership lived outside Africa), but it is clear that the author regarded the moral and the medical messages as in some sense intertwined. Colonial health education films of this period also sometimes employed fictional narratives and sought to create African audience-positions, and this attempt is the subject of the next chapter.

NOTES

1 Karpf (1988), p. 182.
2 Karpf (1988); Turow (1989).
3 See discussion in Chapter 1.
4 Davis (1984).
5 Davis (1984), p. 16.
6 Vane (1957).
7 MacKenzie (1988).
8 Schweitzer (1948), p. 27.
9 Imperato (1964), p. 192.
10 Imperato (1964), p. 64.
11 See Haraway (1989).
12 Junge (1952), p. 153.
13 White (1960).

14 Imperato (1964), p. 63.
15 Imperato (1964), p. 50.
16 White (1960), pp. 98–9.
17 Vane (1957), p. 41.
18 Junge (1952), p. 57.
19 Junge (1952), p. 97.
20 Junge (1952), p. 207.
21 Junge (1952), p. 208.
22 Vane (1957), p. 184.
23 White (1977).
24 White (1988a), pp. 7–8.
25 White (1988a), p. 25.
26 White's publishers, Anzea Press in Australia, point out that few copies of his books are sold in Africa, though White considers Africa to be an important market for his books. A large number of translations have, however, been produced by mission societies in Africa, most commonly of the 'Story Fable' and 'Comic' series: 'The usual problem is that various missionary printing presses are strapped for funds. Maybe we have to realise too the possibility that stories about Africa are more interesting to those outside than those inside.' Letter to the author from Jeffrey Blair, General Manager, Anzea Publishers, New South Wales, 6 April 1990.
27 *Medical Missions at Home and Abroad*, vol. VII, nos 1 and 2 (1898), p. 172.
28 In 1898, for example, of the forty-four British medical missionary doctors sent overseas by the Church Missionary Society, only four were in Africa, whilst fourteen were in India, and thirteen in China. The proportions were similar for the Free Church of Scotland, the London Missionary Society, and for other denominations. *Medical Missions at Home and Abroad*, vol. VII, no. 4 (1898).
29 *Medical Missions at Home and Abroad*, vol. VII, no. 6 (1898), p. 91.
30 *Medical Missions at Home and Abroad*, vol. VII, no. 9 (1898): 'Work to Do', pp. 142–3.
31 *Medical Missions at Home and Abroad*, vol. VII, no. 10 (1898), p. 154.
32 White (1988b), p. 7.
33 White (1988b), p. 24.
34 But, as White's publishers indicate, a great many 'informal' translations of White's books have been made. See note 26.
35 White (1988c), p. 7.
36 White (1988d), preface.
37 White (1988d), pp. 20–1.
38 White (1988d), p. 41.

8 'Seeing is Believing': Colonial Health Education Films and the Question of Identity

During the Second World War, selected African audiences in Northern Rhodesia and Nyasaland were shown a film on venereal disease entitled *Mr Wise and Mr Foolish Go to Town*. This was an edited version of *The Two Brothers*, made by the African Film Production Company in South Africa before the war, and sponsored by the South African Red Cross. Both the original and the edited versions were silent films, to which commentary in the appropriate vernacular was to be added at each viewing.

The story was a simple one, tracing the fate of two brothers, each of whom contract syphilis during a spell as labour migrants in Johannesburg.[1] The film opens with scenes of village life in South Africa, beginning with a shot of women, in 'traditional' Zulu dress, collecting water. The viewer is then introduced to each of the 'two brothers', whose respective identities as 'Mr Wise' and 'Mr Foolish' are fairly quickly established through the courtship scenes which follow. Mr Wise, dressed in an animal skin and holding a spear, is seen approaching a woman who is collecting water. He talks to her at some length, whilst she smiles shyly. He is later presented by her with a string of beads, in an apparent act of betrothal. Mr Foolish, by contrast, is seen evidently getting up late, emerging from his hut and yawning. He spots a young woman carrying a water pot and approaches her in an overtly seductive way. In the next scene both men are being instructed by an older man to go off to earn money in the town before they can be finally married. Dressed now in jackets, trousers and hats, they set off on foot from the village, the women waving goodbye to them as they go.

The following scene opens with a shot of Johannesburg and a pan of the urban horizon. Mr Wise has got a job as a cleaner at a block of flats and is seen scrubbing floors. Mr Foolish has a job at a garage, where he is shown working. In the next scene he is at a beer hall, laughing rather drunkenly, with his arm around a woman. The film then cuts to Mr Wise who is chatting at length to a young woman in a nurse-like uniform, then back to Mr Foolish who is now very evidently drunk and is handing over money to a woman and disappearing into her room. Mr Wise meanwhile appears to have successfully seduced the young woman and is shown disappearing into a room with her.

'SOME WEEKS LATER' and the two brothers are shown together at Mr Wise's lodgings. Mr Foolish seems to be in some pain as he sits down, and points to his groin as being the location of the trouble. Mr Wise indicates that he has a similar problem. Both are shown lowering their trousers (shot ends at the waistline) and apparently comparing notes. A friend of Mr Wise calls in. They describe the problem to him, and demonstrate it by letting down their trousers again. The friend shakes his head and appears to admonish them. The brothers look shocked at what they are being told. The friend produces from his pocket a leaflet entitled 'Syphilis', and seems to be giving them instructions. Mr Foolish is very upset and angry and leaves the room. Mr Wise appears to be thanking his friend for the advice.

The next scene takes place in a 'witchdoctor's' surgery, bedecked with skins, horns and bottles. The witchdoctor is shaking up a bottle of liquid, which he then gives to Mr Foolish, with instructions as to how much to take. Mr Foolish thanks and pays him, and we are shown a close-up of the coins on the witchdoctor's palm, and a parting shot of him counting the money.

The following scene is set outside the hospital where Mr Wise is waiting his turn for treatment. The filming technique changes and we are shown direct and close shots of a number of evidently very advanced cases of syphilis, and of children with congenital syphilis. Mr Wise looks very shocked and unhappy, especially when his eyes fall on a small boy with no nose. Finally he is called into the hospital and shown into a room with a white doctor and African assistant. The white doctor shakes his finger at Mr Wise and appears to admonish him, then gives him an injection into the arm and, with a smile and some instructions, bids him goodbye.

'SOME MONTHS LATER' and we are shown a meeting of the two brothers. Mr Wise seems to be saying that he is now cured and will be returning to the village to marry the woman to whom he is betrothed. He points to the marks on his brother's face, recalls for him the horrors of syphilis he has witnessed at the hospital (flashbacks are employed here) and appears to advise him to go there for treatment. Mr Foolish becomes angry and leaves the room.

In 'CURED', Mr Wise is seen consulting the white doctor again. The latter looks through his notes and appears to be telling him that he has completed his treatment. Mr Wise looks very happy and offers the doctor money, which he declines. The doctor, smiling, shakes hands with Mr Wise, who is then seen leaving the clinic.

The final scene of the film, entitled 'TEN YEARS LATER', is set in the village of the opening scene. Mr Wise, his wife and two children are seen outside their house looking prosperous and happy. They seem to have a good crop of maize and plenty of cattle. The family then go off to visit Mr Foolish and his family in the same village, carrying with them plates of cooked food and calabashes of milk. Mr Foolish is seen crouched outside his very poor house, and appears to be very sick and blind. His wife, who then appears from the hut, is also sick and has lesions on her face. A small child is also shown, emaciated and blind. Mr and Mrs Wise look pityingly at Mr and Mrs Foolish and hand over their gifts.

If we were to try and locate *Mr Wise and Mr Foolish* within the colonial debate over venereal disease which I have outlined in Chapter 6, it would fall towards the 'biomedical' rather than the 'moral' end of the spectrum of opinion. The main purpose of the film seems to be to impart information on the nature of syphilis and, most importantly, its treatment. It is, of course, also a moral tale. The contrast between Mr Wise and Mr Foolish is made explicit from the very beginning of the film, when Mr Wise, up bright and early, appears to be following a 'traditional' courtship ritual, while Mr Foolish, who has overslept and is therefore missing the most productive part of the rural day, is seen making an unseemly dive for a passing woman. The contrast is maintained as the film moves to depict the sexual involvements of the two men in Johannesburg, but here a twist in the 'plot' is made evident. Mr Wise goes to bed with a respectable-looking girl, who is dressed in an almost clinical uniform, while Mr Foolish gets very drunk and pays to sleep with a prostitute. Both men, however, contract syphills, and this is an important component of the health education message. Even a respectable-looking girl in a uniform, it seems, can be infected with syphilis, leaving Mr Wise and Mr Foolish in the same boat. All sorts of women (or at least urban women) are, according to the film, potentially dangerous, and the disease which they carry does not discriminate between the wise and the foolish. Though the film is explicit on the dangers of sexual relations in town, it is not heavily moralistic on the issue of sexual activity. Where the moral tale is really taken up in force, and where the real contrast between the two brothers is driven home, is over the issue of treatment.

Moral superiority is, in this film, reducible to being 'sensible' and believing in the effectiveness of biomedicine. Mr Wise proves himself superior to Mr Foolish, not through evidencing any great sexual restraint but through following the instructions of his friend and going to the hospital for treatment. He is duly rewarded, at the end of the film, with health, fertility and prosperity. Mr Foolish, meanwhile, is not punished so much for having slept with a prostitute as for being stubborn and wilful in the matter of treatment and persisting with a superstitious belief in the efficacy of the witchdoctor. *Mr Wise and Mr Foolish* represented one type of health education film made for African audiences in the colonial period – that is, the fictional tale. Whilst other health education films more straightforwardly imparted medical information, with the minimum of 'story line', *Mr Wise and Mr Foolish*, though a simple story, clearly relied for its effect in part on the creation of an 'audience-position' and an identification with the characters of the film. In order to understand the message of the film it was important that the audience should recognize the two brothers as distinctive 'types', and, in following through the story to the end, recognize that Mr Wise's approach to his infection was the right one. Though fictional, this is hardly a complex film, however: the contrast between the fates of the two men, and the 'horror shots' of patients with syphilis, leave the audience with very little option as regards their identification with Mr Wise.

Films about the dangers of venereal disease were, of course, not an exclusively colonial phenomenon. Annette Kuhn has described both the context of production and the content of anti-venereal-disease propaganda films in Britain and the United States between the wars.[2] In particular, she examines the discourses on morality, sexuality, health and nationhood constructed through these films, and the literal 'embodiment' of these discourses through the representation of the sexual body of the characters. As Kuhn points out, these VD propaganda films, though employing the narrative fictional form, do not in general create fully 'rounded' characters but rather characters who are representatives of social types and moral positions, and in which 'Moral position is constructed in terms of characters' sexual practices and placement in relation to discourses around the body and its health'. The moral positions available in these films are limited ones (though perhaps not quite as limited as those offered to African audiences) and determined by the films' 'fundamental imperative of rectifying lack of knowledge'. As Kuhn points out, what all the victims of venereal disease in these films have in common is their lack of knowledge or ignorance. It is this, rather than their moral failings, which the films emphasize, for 'while codes of (say) iconography and music may construct a particular character as morally deficient, the narrative's drive towards knowledge will tend to position that character not as "bad" but merely as ignorant or misinformed'.[3]

Mr Wise and Mr Foolish clearly follows many of the lines of the inter-war VD propaganda film as analysed by Kuhn, though the 'colonialization' of the delivery of the message is nevertheless evident. In *Mr Wise and Mr Foolish* there is little or no reference to the 'shame of discovery' which seems to have been a theme of many British and American VD films. It is not the spectre of discovery and shame which haunts Mr Wise but the prospect of sterility. Little comment is made on the morality of African sexual relations in this film, and there is an inevitability about the scenes of sexual encounter. Sexuality and the body, as represented in *Mr Wise and Mr Foolish*, are constructed as 'natural' to such an extent that they appear quite disconnected with any other aspect of the characters. The scene in which both brothers lower their trousers in order to diagnose 'the problem' constructs their sexual bodies as remote, almost separate, from themselves as people. African bodies, this film seems to be saying, are functional things, to which few meanings are attached by their owners.

If Mr Wise and Mr Foolish both occupy very simple and limited moral positions, the women characters barely occupy any moral position at all. Whereas in films for British and American audiences there were at least a limited number of rounded female characters conveying moral and educational messages,[4] in *Mr Wise and Mr Foolish* there are no such characters and women are mere transmitters of, or receptacles for, the disease. No moral–tragic tale is constructed around the nursemaid who apparently infects Mr Wise, nor around the fate of the prostitute. Though the audience might feel regret for the fate that befalls Mr Foolish's wife in later years, this fate is represented entirely from her husband's perspective. There is no 'women's point of view' in this film. Designed as it was for male audiences, it presented urban women as the source of the disease but made no attempt to educate them in the facts of the disease – a reflection on the curious reasoning of health education on this subject.

Though *Mr Wise and Mr Foolish*, with its simple medico-moral message, can hardly be said to have constructed any complex 'audience-positions', it was nevertheless amenable to a certain amount of re-interpretation and resistant 'reading', as its screening in Northern Rhodesia and Nyasaland demonstrated. In 1945 the film was shown to selected African audiences in Lusaka. W. V. Brelsford, then Information and Public Relations Officer for the Northern Rhodesian administration, was asked by the Rhoasa Sub-Area Anti-Venereal Disease Committee to analyse audience reaction to the film.[5] It was shown to four distinct audiences, all of which were exclusively male. The first was a 'mixed adult audience' of one hundred people who were gathered in the Welfare Hall in Lusaka. The second audience consisted of two hundred soldiers stationed in Lusaka; the third of four hundred teachers and pupils at the Jeanes School, and the fourth of fifteen chiefs from all over the country who were attending a course in Lusaka. In addition to gauging audience reaction whilst the film was being shown, Brelsford also organized an essay-writing competition (a favoured colonial method of eliciting literate African opinion) on the subject of the film and awarded prizes for the best entries.

Mr Wise and Mr Foolish, according to Brelsford, could not be considered an 'outstanding success' when shown to the audiences in Lusaka. The first problem lay in establishing a suitable atmosphere of seriousness at the beginning of the showing. When shown to the audience of 'mixed adults' in the Welfare Hall the opening scenes caused a great deal of laughter 'and set the film off in a wrong atmosphere'. At the Jeanes School the film was 'half-way through before the audience became serious', and when shown to the audience of soldiers the opening scenes 'brought the house down'. Mr Foolish's attempts at courtship and seduction were thought to be particularly hilarious.

Brelsford's explanation for this reaction was a common one at the time. It seemed to him that the problem arose because of the ethnic conservatism of African audiences. The film was, after all, 'laid in an unfamiliar South African setting with people of a strange tribe dressed in strange clothes', and this inevitably gave rise to a great deal of laughter. But the evidence which he himself presented from the essays written by viewers would seem to point to a rather more complex analysis, and one which I shall attempt here.

Most films, as I have already indicated, need to create 'audience-positions' if they are to be successful, and this is as much the case with health propaganda films as with any other type of film. In the previous chapter I have tried to show how Paul White's Jungle Doctor books moved away from a straightforward objectification of Africans and their health problems to the creation of an African subject position for the reader. This was partly achieved, as we saw, through the replacement of the white 'jungle doctor' by his African counterpart. In colonial Africa it was often asserted that the creation of this subject position through film was a hazardous business. African audiences, it was implied, could not understand the concept of a fictional tale which, whilst being fictional, was not a 'fairy-tale' but conveyed a real and factual message. The Lusaka audiences clearly had no difficulty in grasping this concept. As Brelsford pointed out, many of them were regular cinemagoers, who were accustomed to viewing both fictional and educational films. The real problem seemed to lie in their refusal to identify with the images of Africans presented before them on the screen, and their refusal thereby to adopt the audience-position on which the power of the film seemed to rest.

Whilst Brelsford saw this as evidence of a kind of ethnic conservatism and implied that any film, to be successful, would have to be acted by members of the ethnic group to whom it was to be shown, much of his evidence seems to indicate that it was a lack of class identification rather than ethnic identification which really mattered. Education was an important component of this class identification. Brelsford's essayists were, by definition, literate, though many of them did not write in English but in their vernacular. They were also almost all either involved in full-time education or were employed as soldiers or civilians. The essay writers from the 'mixed adult' audience, for example, numbered seven pupils from a training school, two postal clerks, two medical orderlies, two compound clerks, one police sergeant, one shoemaker, one office boy, one personal servant, one printing compositor and only one who was unemployed.[6] Though not an homogenously 'middle-class' group, they nevertheless represented a relatively privileged and educated section of the African working class.

The film, as I have already indicated, followed the pattern described by Kuhn of creating centrally an audience-position of ignorance. But many members of the Lusaka audiences had already been 'bombarded', as Brelsford put it, with information on venereal disease, and therefore could not easily adopt this audience-position of ignorance. What they appear to have been resisting, however, was more than a construction of their ignorance on the matter of venereal disease. They rather appear to have been resisting the whole construction of 'the African' shown before them on the screen.

This resistance began with their reception of the opening scenes, which were considered not only funny but also offensive. As one medical orderly put it, 'It is never interesting to see the African exposed as he (or she) is in this film. Most if not all Africans can clothe well now and exposing their pictures roughly clothed or even without any, is a disgrace to many.'[7] Mr Wise and Mr Foolish were both regarded by many essayists as being hopelessly ignorant and unsophisticated. During one showing it was loudly remarked that Mr Foolish's job of washing down cars in the garage would only earn him fifteen shillings a month. His lack of education called forth a great deal of comment. As one essayist remarked scathingly, Mr Foolish would have to see 'experimental films for a year before he would understand about syphilis', and another that 'Africans differ from one another, there are some who think and some who do not'. Some viewers moved from a lack of identification with the characters to an objectification of them as 'Africans'. One police sergeant, for example, wrote at some length about the problems of controlling 'African' sexuality:

> It is a very hard task to control Africans from running about with native girls in towns and villages. The custom of kissing with girls should cease and this can be done if all Africans are educated. There is no other way in which Africans, though married, will stop making sexual intercourse with other women unless educated ... The slow progress of influence of education among the Africans will help the bad habits every minute until Northern Rhodesia is civilised.[8]

Projected before him on the screen then, the police sergeant saw 'Africans', but did not see himself. In much the same way, Frantz Fanon described his shock when, attending the showing of a Tarzan film in France, he realized that he was expected to identify with the 'negro', whereas he had always assumed an identification with the hero.[9]

It was not resistance, however, but rather misunderstanding that the colonial health film-makers saw as the source of their problems, and this seemed to be borne out by the reception given to the film in Nyasaland, where it was shown to a much less 'film-literate' audience of chiefs. Their 'reading' of the film, as recounted by a reporter for the *Nyasaland Times*, under the heading 'Propaganda Awry', was thought to be much more typical of the problems faced by the colonial film maker:

> The screening of a hygiene film lent by the Durban City Health Department at a convention of native chiefs ended in uproar when one of the characters acting the part of a man suffering from venereal disease was recognised by the chairman. 'That is my nephew', he cried in astonishment, 'What is he doing in a film like this? I never knew that he had been sick'. 'He's related to me too' called out the general secretary, 'It's a disgrace to our family'. The uproar continued until at the order of the president of the Native Congress the film was stopped. The lights went up, and there sitting on the platform was the offending member of the family, who is Secretary of the Bantu Sports Club in Johannesburg. He explained that the film was purely health propaganda and that he had never had a day's sickness in his life. Nor had his brother who also took part in the film.
> But many of the simpler country chiefs would not believe him, 'We've just seen the history of your sickness with our own eyes', they

protested, 'How can you tell us such lies?' If, as he said, the film was
purely a fairy tale, what was the use of showing it as though it were
true?, they demanded.[10]

This somewhat implausible, or at the very least embellished,
account of a health film screening incorporates much colonial 'com-
monsense' knowledge of African psychology and behaviour. Whilst
it was known that Africans were 'irrational' and 'superstitious', they
were also thought to have a 'child-like' literalness, and an inability
to distinguish between 'fact' and 'fiction'. Hence it would not have
come as any surprise to readers of the Nyasaland Times that the
message of Mr Wise and Mr Foolish was lost on the African audience,
whose literal reading of the film had caused so much confusion. In
contrast to the Lusaka audiences, which had seemed to be consciously resisting taking up the subject position offered to them
by the film, the Nyasaland audience suffered from an over-
identification with, and identification of, the main characters of the
film. In order for them to understand the health message it was
essential that they should first understand the nature of the fictional
narrative form. But far from understanding this they seemed, to the
Nyasaland Times reporter, to have so completely confused 'fact' and
'fiction' that they could accuse the colonial administrators of 'telling
them lies'.

The need for simplicity and explicitness was, by the late 1940s, an
article of faith amongst many colonial film-makers.[11] A theory of
'African' film-viewing began to be elaborated on the pages of the
Colonial Film Unit's journal, Colonial Cinema, a theory heavily influenced by contemporary notions of African psychological development, and one which was largely blind to those class differences
which we have seen to have been so crucial to the reception of Mr
Wise and Mr Foolish.
    Health education films for Africans had, in fact, been produced
for some time before the growth of the Colonial Film Unit and the
elaboration of an African film-viewing theory in the 1940s and 1950s.
A health official in Nigeria, William Sellers, had been producing
health education films for Africans since 1929. In that year he
produced Anti-Plague Operations in Lagos (re-issued in 1937), a film
designed to combat a plague epidemic in the city.[12] Though not
a fictional film, compared to many health education films of the
period, this was a visually and conceptually elaborate film, featuring
what would later be held to be 'confusing' and unconventional
shots. It begins, for example, with an aerial view of a Lagos slum,
before 'zooming in' on a rat scurrying amongst rubbish. A later shot

of a white man pumping gas into a rat-hole, viewed as he is only at knee level, would also have been regarded by other colonial film-makers as potentially confusing for African audiences. The narrative development is also elaborate. After showing attempts to eradicate rats from the slum, the film switches to a scene in the Lagos Town Planning Department, and the viewer is shown plans for a new housing development. From here the film turns to shots of African women waiting their turn in a baby clinic, and to extensive scenes of Lagos Health Week (itself the subject of a separate Sellers film), and to a baby-show. Finally we are shown the new housing area, with clean streets and well cared-for children.

A great number of health education messages, then, were being conveyed in this one film. Not only were measures against rats and plague being demonstrated (with a characteristic emphasis on the white man's technology), but connections were being made with a variety of health and welfare issues, from how to bath a baby to how to construct a latrine. In the extended shots of the Lagos Health Week Exhibition the levels of representation become quite complex. Central to the exhibition were model houses, model baby clinics and model babies – some real and others not – and African visitors to the exhibition are seen acting out the roles of perfect housewife and mother, sometimes with miniature props. Much health education would, indeed, have seemed to have been highly ritualistic. In this case the film merely documented an already elaborate colonial ritual, and connected it, albeit rather tenuously, with the problems of plague, poverty and housing.

William Sellers's other films from this period were less ambitious and more single-minded in the conveyance of their messages. *Yaws*, for example, was fairly typical of the 'factual' health education film. It showed an anti-yaws campaign in operation in a village and, like *Mr Wise and Mr Foolish*, featured long and explicit shots of the ravages of the disease.[13] Like many of these films it placed great emphasis on the nature of biomedical technology, and showed Africans employing this technology under the direction of white men. The whole process of the sterilization of needles in the yaws film was examined at length and in detail, as was the administration of injections.

In Sellers's 1933 film *An African Hospital*, the techniques of slow pace and careful continuity which were to become a feature of later health education films were already present. The film showed an accident occurring between a lorry and a cyclist, and the latter being taken by ambulance to hospital with a splint on his right leg. The sequencing of scenes was slow and careful, the viewer following the patient through his hospital experience. Sellers's editing let him down at one crucial point, however, since the accident victim is shown lying in a hospital bed with his left, rather than his right, leg in plaster![14]

In East Africa at the same period the International Missionary Council was funding the Bantu Educational Kinema Experiment (BEKE) under the direction of G. C. Latham.[15] Latham was impressed by the ability of rural Africans to follow film narratives, even when they apparently had relatively little experience of recognizing and interpreting pictures. Typical of the BEKE health education films directed to a mass, rural audience was *Tropical Hookworm*, which attempted to impart information both on the nature of the hookworm and on the social context of its transmission. It featured a carefully sequenced and explicit narrative showing how transmission came about, but also showed shots of the hookworm under a microscope. The opening scene was designed to aid recognition of the symptoms of hookworm infestation. A man is shown talking to his friend, and their dialogue appears on the screen: 'My head goes "Pouff Pouff"', says the first man, 'My face and ankles are swollen.' He puts his tongue out for his friend (and the audience) to see, and this is followed by a close-up shot of his swollen feet. Having demonstrated the symptoms, the ultimate cause of the problem is then explained by the film: 'If you could see inside his intestines', the screen reads, 'you would see little worms that are the cause of the disease.' And this is followed by shots of hookworms under the microscope.

Hookworm, however, as the film goes on to make clear, is a complex and multi-faceted health problem. Not only had the circumstances of transmission to be explained (this was done through explicit shots of defecation), but so had the dangers of re-infection to be demonstrated. The need for both prevention and cure had to be shown – the infected had to go to get the appropriate medicine from the African dispenser, but also had to be urged to build latrines. Even when cured, however, the patient was likely to be anaemic, so a nutritional message had also to be given: 'Green vegetables will help to improve the weakened blood. For example – 20 leaves of cassava daily.' Finally, the role of footwear in preventing infection was explained, and 'simple ways of making sandals from old tyres and hides' were demonstrated at length, ending with a shot of a man wearing the rubber tyre sandals he has just made, and laughing.[16]

Many health messages were, by their nature, complex. By the 1940s, however, just as more rural Africans were being exposed to both commercial and educational films, the view was being increasingly expressed that Africans had great difficulty in 'reading' a film message, especially when, as in the case of the hookworm film, this involved any form of abstract representation (hookworm under microscope). George Pearson, the film director who worked with Sellers in the Colonial Film Unit in London, recounted a common story of African film 'mis-reading', or rather, of the literalness of African film reading:

an overseas unit had made a film on malaria in which the menace of the mosquito was shown to an utterly backward audience in the bush. After a while a greatly enlarged picture of the ugly insect filled the screen, in order, presumably, to give a more intimate knowledge of its structure. The instant reaction was ruinous to the film's purpose; these bush folk said that there was no need to worry about the tiny mosquitoes that they knew, for these in the film were enormous and terrible things, as big as elephants, quite different from those of their country.[17]

Similar stories abounded on the colonial circuit and were clearly told with great glee. Brelsford, making a similar point, gave the example of the showing of a 'big game film' to an audience of 'village natives': 'The next morning some of the women were back at the place of showing looking on the ground for the spoor of the game.'[18]

Such stories are not, of course, implausible. Both Pearson and Brelsford made the reasonable assumption that film-viewing and interpretation were skills which had to be acquired, and could not just be assumed. It was quite possible that the women in Brelsford's example were genuinely looking for evidence of the presence of the 'big game' they had seen on the screen the night before, especially if this had been their first viewing of a film. On the other hand, George Pearson's mosquito example is surely open to interpretation other than that which stressed the supposed literalness of African viewing. African audiences, it seems, were never credited with the potential for ironic comment.

Pearson and his colleagues in the Colonial Film Unit moved from their assumption that 'reading' film was an acquired skill to a condescending view of African audiences which seemed to imply that they would never learn to 'read' more than the most simple film.

Modern cinema methods for literate audiences follows a highly developed formula of brief scenes carrying the story forward, with all the time and space gaps covered by screen conventions of mixes, wipes, montages, and fades ... All the conventional methods of short-circuiting time and place are utterly confusing to the illiterate, with the possible exception of the 'fade'. His experience of the approach of darkness and dawn helps him to the understanding of the fade-out or fade-in as an indication of an ending or beginning of something.[19]

Despite the care which he held to be essential in producing simple narratives for illiterate audiences, Pearson was enthusiastic about the educational and cultural possibilities of film in Africa. Not only could the 'motion picture' do battle with 'the curse of the locust, the tsetse fly, malaria, yaws, leprosy, smallpox, dysentery and tuberculosis', but it also had the power to stir 'human emotions', and to inspire a new African pride in things African: 'It is their Pride of Race that matters', he wrote, 'for that implies character building ...'[20]

Pearson and his colleagues saw the potential of film to create 'new Africans', who would retain a pride in their own cultural traditions,[21] but this could only be achieved slowly, since Africans had a limited ability to 'read' and interpret film correctly.

Many of the films produced by the CFU for African audiences during the war seemed designed to prove Pearson's point in their emphasis on the strangeness and difference of life in Britain which positively invited misunderstanding. Wartime films presented 'simple explanations of strange inventions' including the aeroplane, the tank, the barrage balloon, the searchlight, the air-raid warden, the Home Guard and the Fire Brigade. Pearson argued that films comparing 'English and African life' would serve to draw the two peoples 'closer together in understanding', but it is hard to avoid the impression that it was difference rather than similarity which he was keen to stress. Scenes would include 'an African mother with her baby wrapped to her back, an English mother with her baby in her arms or in a cradle ... an African market-place with its squatting bargainers, an English market with its covered stall ...'[22]

Both the theory and the practice of film-making for colonial Africans, then, stressed cultural difference. Not only were Africans less able to read film because of this cultural difference (and implied simplicity), but they also were themselves different, and this could be demonstrated to them by showing them images of their British equivalents in the film version of a distorted mirror.

Pearson's theory and approach did not, however, go unchallenged. An article by an African film-maker, G. Odunton, published in Colonial Cinema in 1950, took him to task. 'What a lot has been written about the illiterate African and films', Odunton wrote, 'How little solid sense, how many debatable theories, and how much high-falutin nonsense!'[23] Odunton went on to complain that there was, despite assertions to the contrary, no conclusive scientific evidence to show whether 'the illiterate African sees things differently', and complained that the 'assumption that Africans see things differently' had led to the development of a stultifying film technique, in which there was 'no scope for the free play of imagination': 'Anything more intricate than a rudimentary and simple plot was avoided; the seamy side of life was never shown, and the moral was always painfully obvious. The goody-goody type who did everything right always won (without effort), and the foolish man who did everything wrong was duly penitent and saw the error of his ways.'[24] Such films were accompanied by 'patronising commentaries' which did not credit the audience with any degree of 'intelligence' or 'discernment', and were therefore unlikely to leave any mark. In an effort to break out of this mould, he went on, he and his colleagues in the Gold Coast Unit had begun making educational and instructional films (*Amenu's Child* on malnutrition, for instance) in the local idiom of the story-teller, and with the determination 'not to make our films dull': 'We want to appeal to the emotions of our audiences, rather than their reason, for what is art if it fails to appeal to their feelings?'[25]

Pearson's reply to Odunton's assertions was bitter and contemptuous,[26] Norman Spurr's somewhat more measured.[27] The problem was, wrote Spurr, that if one produced films with an emphasis on 'emotional reaction', this would necessarily limit their direct teaching role.[28]

Spurr had himself been involved in measuring the impact of Walt Disney health educational films on African audiences in Western Uganda, an experiment designed to test out many of the assumptions made about the nature of African film-viewing.[29] These cartoon films had been made originally for South American audiences and lent by the American Consulate in Nairobi. It was generally feared that, given the supposed lack of sophistication of the audiences, cartoon depictions of health problems would prove utterly confusing. The Disney *Hookworm* film was used to test out this assumption, and an experiment set up, with two observers watching and recording the reactions of the audience during the viewing. As with most health education films, its success was to be measured by whether it conveyed both the social and the scientific message adequately. In other words, it was hoped that by the end of the film viewers would understand something of the nature of the hookworm itself, and also the social context in which it became a health problem.

Spurr's description of the contents of the film was as follows:

The film is a teaching film with a central character called 'Careless Charlie'. Using the personal commentary method, the commentator tells Charlie why he is ill, how he can be cured, and how he can remain cured. In order to remind the audience that the film is not a record of actuality, the artist's brush is introduced into the picture frame, and is shown forming the outline of the figure. A simplified diagram of Charlie's intestine is drawn, and hookworms are shown therein. The effect of the medicine upon them is vividly illustrated. The final part of the film showing the digging of the latrine follows the traditional cartoon method. A spade appears in the sky, the hole is dug in one fantastic whirl, the shelter builds itself, and the grass for the roofing and sides of the hut, falling out of Charlie's hands as he trips over a stone, miraculously wraps itself round the framework of the hut to form the finished shelter.[30]

Spurr's major objective was to note the audience reaction to the cartoon technique. A microphone linked to a recorder was placed over a section of the audience with the purpose of 'listening in' to their reactions, but the 'jumble of voices and mixture of tongues' rendered this part of the experiment a near failure. A few comments were, however, overheard and translated as follows:

> Aha, this monster widens its mouth.
> It wants to swallow him.
> Look at its big teeth.
> What a wonder those intestinal creatures have teeth.
> This huge thing baffles me still.
> He is going. No, he has postponed his journey, hopeless man! (This last remark was made when Charlie refused to leave the tree to go for treatment)
> and finally,
> I swore for it this morning.[31]

Spurr concluded that as long as the film followed a 'reasonably normal narrative tradition', or explained itself when it departed from this, 'e.g. when Charlie's skin is removed and his intestines revealed', then the audience 'accepted' the cartoon technique. But when the film introduced a 'traditional cartoon comedy approach', in the building of the latrine, for instance, this was put down to 'European magic'.

A similar experiment on audience reaction to *Hookworm* had been conducted around the same time in the Gold Coast, and also reported that original misgivings over the use of cartoon films proved largely unfounded.[32] The very 'magical' and abstract quality of the cartoon could, it appeared, be a definite asset rather than a disadvantage for 'the devotion to simplicity and the avoidance of visible characteristics attributable to any one people make it relatively easy, with the vernacular commentary, for the audience concerned to identify themselves with the story of the film'.[33]

The images produced by the cartoon technique apparently made a deep impression and conveyed the salient points in a 'vivid and unforgettable manner'. The very potency of the images, however, meant that these films should only be used with the greatest care;

They are too important to be used indifferently. Inquiries in the Gold Coast of audiences who had seen, discussed, and thoroughly understood *Hookworm* a few weeks earlier revealed that in most cases the visual images remained, but out of sequence, and the lesson had been lost. Most dangerous, the effort to reconstruct the action from the images produced grossly distorted ideas. Again, the effort to understand more than one film simultaneously produced a confusion of causes, symptoms, disease and methods of infection which increased with the passage of time. Further, and more grave, in a few cases, intense as had been the initial reaction, it was short-lived and belief had given way to scepticism.[34]

Films, as many writers on health education pointed out, had a glamour and attraction which brought thousands to view them, but which needed to be supported by other forms of instruction if they were to be effective in implanting their message.

A number of issues are, I think, raised by the discussions which were carried on in the 1940s and 1950s over the production of health education films for Africa.

Firstly, despite the confidence which health educators had in the correctness of their various 'messages', a number of ambiguities inherent in biomedicine come to the surface over the representation of these messages on film. Though, as Donna Haraway and others have pointed out, medical and scientific narratives are stories like any others, the pretension is that they merely reflect and relay the 'truth'.[35] A certain amount of unease was therefore evident over the necessity to make 'stories' out of medical 'facts', for this might give the wrong impression to colonial peoples as to the nature of biodicine. It was 'their' medicine which was supposed, after all, to be 'magical' and superstitious, and for this reason the Disney films had to be treated with the utmost care lest they convey the impression that biomedicine was 'magical' too. For this reason, those colonial health education films which I have viewed lay enormous stress on the role of biomedical technology, with sometimes seemingly endless shots of technical procedures, and a special emphasis given to the evidence of the microscope. Representing this 'evidence', however, always ran the risk of misinterpretation (would Africans think that mosquitoes were six feet wide?), though it usually appeared that African audiences were well able to understand the concept of cinematic representation and enlargement.

The constant strain within biomedicine between what one might call its social and scientific paradigms is also evident in these discussions, and in the films themselves. In order to prevent the spread of some diseases (tuberculosis, hookworm, leprosy, and venereal diseases, for example), it was clearly important not only to explain the biological foundations of these diseases (where they were understood) and to present these in comprehensible narratives but also to stress the social contexts of transmission. As we have seen in previous chapters, biomedicine in Africa was shot through with social assumptions and constructions, so this was not a feature only of film-making. In making health educational films, however, the question of how far disease was a social and how far a 'natural' phenomenon had to be faced in the choices which were made concerning its representation. If the 'social' was to be stressed, as it clearly had to be to some extent, then the whole question of identification with the characters in the film, whether real or fictional, became crucial. For the social message to be put across, an 'audience-position' would have to be created for the viewer. One of Odunton's complaints about the CFU's techniques was precisely this, that the characterization of Africans was simplistic, patronizing and implausible, and liable to render the film useless from an educational point of view. 'Art', he argued, would have to be used to convey the story of 'science', if people were to absorb and believe the messages that were being promoted.

George Pearson and others at the CFU were not unaware of the need for audiences to identify with characters in the films but they were more concerned with the possibilities for misinterpretation. Subversive interpretation of film material was always a great colonial bogey, as discussions of the 'corrupting' influence of Hollywood films testify.[36] Instead of tackling the whole complex question of identification and 'audience-position', Pearson and others fell back on the notion that African viewers were, as a whole, different – they received images differently, they saw differently, and hence great care had to be taken not to confuse them. Whilst films, it might be argued, provided biomedicine with the greatest opportunity to exercise 'bio-power', through the creation of new notions of subjectivity and the body, to a large extent colonial film-makers drew back from this role, preferring instead to represent simple stereotypes of 'the African' and of the African audience. As the various receptions given to Mr Wise and Mr Foolish indicated, the role of class in forming late colonial African subjectivities could be particularly important since it could give rise to a 'resistant' viewing of the film (though it did not, in this case, seem to impair understanding of the basic health message contained in it).

Analysing these films, then, once again brings us to the question of the nature of colonial power as exercised through biomedicine. The power to create new subjectivities, through the creation of new ideas about the body and sexuality, whilst not totally absent in these films, is far from immediately evident. There is no doubt that colonial medical departments did wish, at some level, to change African

notions of the body and to create new ones. It was seen as important, for instance, that Africans, both rural and urban, learnt new
hygiene regimes, and indeed this was a vital ingredient of 'modernization'. The films, whilst imparting messages about the necessity to build latrines and to use them, and the need for different
regimes of personal hygiene, did not, for the most part, present the
kind of rounded characterization of people which would enable
viewers to identify with the bodies on the screen. Changes in African notions of the body and bodily self-perception were, almost
certainly, occurring in the 1940s and 1950s when many of these films
were made, but they would have been, to a large extent, class-
related changes. The role of the soap industry and its advertising
in creating, amongst better-off urban Africans, new ideas about
hygiene and new bodily needs, may have begun to produce a new
'modern' African body at this time.[37] The potential for building on
these new, class-related, differences in body perception was in film-
making, however, once more circumscribed by the colonial impulse
to construct 'the African' as undifferentiatedly 'different'.

There were, of course, some versions of the biomedical message
which had, from the earliest medical missionary days, sought not
merely to convey a technical message but also to effect changes in
the meaning of the body. Mother and child welfare was, as I have
already noted, an important vehicle for this wider biomedical message in which cleanliness, morality and prosperity were closely intertwined. The films made of Health and Baby Week in Lagos
needed to do nothing more than record what was an extraordinary
colonial event. Elaborate as this event had been when filmed in
1936, by 1956 its rituals were even further developed, showing
colonial medicine as an imperialistic animal, expanding into the
realms of housing, cookery and bed-making. The 1956 Health
Queen sat, as her predecessor had in 1936, on her float, dressed in
finery and surrounded by her attendants, each of whom carried a
placard carrying a variety of slogans from 'Vaccinate that child' to
'Kill that Mosquito', and 'Health is Wealth'. A whole parade of floats
followed on behind her: one (sponsored by Lux soap) featured a
man playing cricket, whose health message was rather obscure,
another showed St George fighting off the dragon of 'ignorance,
filth and disease and superstition'. Schoolchildren, babies, mothers
from welfare clinics, all followed on behind, as the oversized 'key to
health' made its slow progress from the hands of one dignitary to
another.

Once this extraordinary carnival of health was over, the baby
competitions began, and the health show was declared open. Lagos
city dwellers were then free to wander into stands where they could
pretend to wash babies (under the watchful eye of a white matron),

or they could view the 'model house' and its contents, play with a stove, and flush a water closet.

There is no simple health message to be read from this event, or from watching the film of the event, but a complex bundle of representations of beauty, hygiene, gender, morality, class and race. The association between 'health' and 'wealth', for example, was repeatedly emphasized not only in the slogans on the floats, but also in the connections drawn between a 'healthy' lifestyle and the ability to purchase new commodities. Health was also associated with a particular, and competitive, concept of 'beauty'. Healthy babies, each individually groomed by mothers and fathers, were considered both to be beautiful and to be a physical indication of their parents' prosperity. The 'Health Queen', meanwhile, seemed not only to be following 'The path to loveliness' through using Lux soap, but also appeared, through following the rules of hygiene, to have, symbolically, turned 'white'. Here, in this ritual, then, colonial biomedicine for once offered not only to cure but to transform its subjects.

NOTES

1 The following description of the film is based on my own viewing of the unedited version, *The Two Brothers*. As far as I can ascertain from Brelsford's description of *Mr Wise and Mr Foolish*, the changes made to the film by the Colonial Film Unit were minimal.
   I would like to thank Tony Muscat, of the Overseas Film and Television Service, for uncovering this film and screening it for me.
2 Kuhn (1985), chapter 5: 'A Moral Subject'. In this chapter, Kuhn analyses in detail a number of venereal disease propaganda films, the best known of which is *Damaged Goods*, produced in Britain in 1919.
3 Kuhn (1985), p. 109.
4 See, for instance, Kuhn (1985), pp. 99–100.
5 Brelsford (1947), pp. 7–22.
6 Brelsford (1947), p. 9.
7 Brelsford (1947), p. 11.
8 Brelsford (1947), p. 11.
9 Fanon (1986), p. 152, footnote 15.
10 *Nyasaland Times*, 29 October 1945, quoted in Brelsford (1947), pp. 20–1.
11 Rosaleen Smyth has written illuminatingly on the history of colonial film-making for Africa, and on the development of these ideas. See Smyth (1988). Also Giltrow and Giltrow (1986).
12 This account is based on a viewing of the 1937 version of the film held at the National Film Archive, London. I would like to thank the staff of the National Film Archive, and especially Fiona O'Brien, for their help.
13 *Yaws* was produced by Sellers in the Gold Coast in 1944. The film was viewed at the Overseas Film and Television Centre, London.
14 Notes made on *Progress in the Colonies*, a re-make of *An African Hospital*, in the files of the National Film Archive.

15 See Notcutt and Latham (1937).
16 *Tropical Hookworm: its Causes, Prevention and Cure* (1936). Viewed at the National Film Archive.
17 Pearson (1957), p. 211.
18 Brelsford (1947), p. 19.
19 Pearson (1957), p. 222.
20 Pearson (1957), p. 225.
21 Pearson (1957), pp. 224–5.
22 Pearson (1957), p. 205.
23 Odunton (1950), p. 29.
24 Odunton (1950), p. 29.
25 Odunton (1950), p. 31.
26 G.P., 'Re ... One Step Ahead' in Pearson (1950).
27 Spurr had been an education officer in East Africa where he had made a number of films.
28 Spurr (1950), p. 33.
29 Spurr (1951).
30 Spurr (1951), p. 28.
31 Spurr (1951), p. 30.
32 Pickering (1954).
33 Pickering (1954), p. 52.
34 Pickering (1954), p. 53.
35 Haraway (1989).
36 Smyth (1988); Lawman (1952); Franklin (1950).
37 This is a subject currently being researched by Tim Burke of Northwestern University, Chicago.

9 Conclusion: The Changing Nature of Biomedical Discourse on Africa

In the late 1920s, the missionary Georgina Gollock was writing a health education book for Africans, entitled *Heroes of Health*. The book, which detailed the heroic triumphs of medicine from Ancient Greece onwards, was written in part to inspire literate Africans to become medical personnel, a calling which was, in her words, great enough 'to quicken the pulses of those sprung from warrior tribes'.[1] Originally Miss Gollock had intended her book to deal only with the medical problems of Africa, but a conversation with the Ghanaian educator (and member of the Phelps–Stokes Commission) Dr James Aggrey, had changed her mind. Aggrey had suggested, respectfully, that she include stories 'drawn from many lands', for 'Africans ... do not like their country to be looked upon as the only hotbed of disease'.[2]

Aggrey's fears that Africa would come to be looked on as 'the only hotbed of disease' seem, in retrospect, to have been well-founded. Rather than leave the image intact, however, I have tried in this book to deconstruct it, and most importantly to delineate the complex process of its production in the specific historical circumstances of British colonial Africa.

I have argued that the biomedical discourse on Africa was not a monolithic or unchanging one, and certainly not without its own internal contradictions. In part this is because biomedicine itself was, and is, an unstable and evolving body of theory and practice. It is not so much that its scientific foundations conflicted with its social and cultural assumptions but rather that the scientific and the social aspects of medicine were born of the same European historical circumstances, and were therefore, at one level, inseparable.

Colonialism was an important feature of those historical circumstances in which biomedicine evolved, from the late nineteenth century through the twentieth century. Colonialism provided much 'raw material' on which the new scientific biomedicine drew for the elaboration of its theories, and also provided a 'surgery' for the evolving practice of medicine. Often this 'raw material' was used not to develop a more effective and appropriate healing system for Africa, but rather to contribute to some larger metropolitan debate. So, as we have seen, in the nineteenth century the physical features and illnesses of the peoples of Africa were often studied not for their own sake but for what they supposedly helped to demonstrate on the question of the differences between the sexes in Europe (see Chapter 1).

I have argued that, in the course of the period surveyed here (*c.*1890s–1950), there were discernible shifts in the biomedical discourse on Africa. Some writers have seen the bacteriological 'revolution' as the central feature of this history, marking a major change from a nineteenth-century sanitarian and environmental science to a more reductive, socially blind and 'magic bullet'-oriented twentieth-century biomedicine. Though this change was indeed significant, in the context of colonial Africa other shifts were equally important. In particular, I have tried to delineate the shifting relationship between 'nature' and 'culture' as it evolved in the biomedical discourse, and as it affected practice. As conquest gave way to colonialism, and particularly to the management of industrial capitalism, so a new theory of difference was elaborated.

The biomedical discourse on Africa had always been centrally concerned with difference, but in the earlier period this difference was seen to be a product of a larger natural environment. By the 1920s and 1930s, however, biomedicine in East and Central Africa was contributing to and participating in a discourse on difference in which 'culture' became the central marker. In this discourse Africans were conceived of as members of collectivities, the features of which could be defined and delineated, and which in large part accounted for the differential incidence of diseases on the continent.

There were two ways in which culture was used as an explanatory variable by biomedics in Africa. On the one hand there was a long tradition, elaborated by Christian missionaries, but not only by them, which viewed the 'primitiveness' of African societies as a factor predisposing them to certain diseases. Africans got sick, in this model, because their societies were fundamentally sick. The associations which Gilman has drawn our attention to between sickness, blackness, sexuality and madness were all elaborated in this discourse, as I have tried to demonstrate in my discussion of missionary medicine, leprosy, sexuality and 'jungle doctor' memoirs.

But there was another version of the theory which saw culture as centrally implicated in disease. This was the theory of 'deculturation' which we have seen being elaborated in many of the discussions on insanity, sexually-transmitted disease, leprosy and industrial diseases. In the inter-war period in British colonial Africa the problems of dealing with rapid but uneven industrialization and urbanization were foremost in the minds of many administrators. Social disintegration and loss of control were feared to be the consequences of the system of labour migration, and the changes which capitalism was bringing to rural African societies (Chapters 5 and 6). Biomedicine contributed to a discussion of the effects of 'modernization' which was, in many ways, reminiscent of those of nineteenth-century Britain but which had its own particular features. In elaborating a theory of the differential incidence of disease, the idea was formulated that the disintegration or 'deculturation' of societies was a central factor. Though many medics in colonial Africa were aware that the material circumstances of people's lives, and in particular the new patterns of poverty, were responsible for changing disease patterns, there were others who found in the idea of 'deculturation' a ready peg on which to hang their theories. In this version of the role of culture in producing disease, Africans got sick essentially because they had forgotten who they were, they had ventured across boundaries of difference and chaos had ensued.

Difference, then, was central to both versions of the biomedical discourse on Africa in the mid twentieth century. Leading on from this I have argued that the history of 'bio-power' in colonial Africa was rather different from that described by Foucault for Europe. The fundamental difference was that Africans were always conceived of as members of a collectivity as colonial people, and beyond that as members of collectivities in the form of 'tribes' or cultural groups. Consequently, when classification systems were elaborated to account, for instance, for the incidence of insanity in Africa, the psychiatric categories became secondary to the 'ethnic' categories, and beyond that to the overriding difference ascribed to colonial people, the signifier of which was skin colour. The colonial African literature on psychiatry is, as I have shown, more centrally concerned with the description of a 'normal' African psychology than it is with the 'abnormal'. The madwoman and madman in colonial Africa did not then occupy the same space as their equivalent in modern Europe, since the 'normal' African psychology was viewed as pathological.

Biomedical discourse in Africa operated through the specification of the features of groups, rather than through the minute specification of the features of individuals which Foucault held to be so central to the operation of modern systems of power. Though colonial biomedicine, and colonial states more generally, 'unitized' their subjects, they did not 'individualize' them for, as I have argued, there was a strong strand of thinking which held that Africans were, by definition, hardly capable of being individuals at all.

Related to this, of course, is the question of how far colonial power operated through the production of subjectivities at all, and how far it relied on the kind of 'repressive' power which Foucault sees as characterizing pre-modern regimes. Did colonial biomedicine 'subjectify' at all, or did it merely 'objectify' through its elaboration of a discourse on 'the African'? This, as I have indicated, is perhaps the more important question, but one which, given the limitations of my method, I cannot fully answer.

Africa was not, as I have tried to indicate throughout this book, a blank slate on which biomedicine drew its designs, notwithstanding some of its more dehumanizing practices, including the chalking of prescriptions on the skin of the patient. African people were engaged with the practices of biomedicine, and at times engaged in the elaboration of the biomedical discourse on Africa. Biomedicine, we must remember, was practised not only *on* Africans, but *by* Africans, and is therefore, in some senses, as African as other healing systems practised on the continent. But how far engagement with biomedical practices made a difference to people's understandings of themselves, their bodies and their identities is, I think, more difficult to gauge, and would require a very different kind of study. I have indicated a number of points at which the engagement of individual Africans in both the discourse and the practice of bio-medicine would seem to have been significant. In the chapter on insanity, for example, the court assessors contributed to an evolving legal definition of African criminal insanity; in the area of sexually transmitted diseases there were always individuals and groups who invested in and contributed to colonial ideas about the dangers of sexuality.

But, as the discussion of health education films in Chapter 8 indicates, the fact that Africans participated in the colonial bio-medical discourse does not necessarily indicate compliance. Indeed, participation was often a necessary step towards resistance, and the forging of new identities through resistance. As I have tried to indicate in that chapter, by the late colonial period class became an important element of identity for some Africans, though it was largely unacknowledged in a colonial discourse which remained tied to the notion of ethnic difference. It was class, rather than ethnic difference, which, in my view, gave rise to the 'resistant reading' of *Mr Wise and Mr Foolish*. More direct resistance to public health measures could also help to forge a rather different collective iden-tity in the form of nationalism. Here new differences could be

submerged for a time in the struggle against the overriding
difference of being a colonial person.

The experience of colonialism and the formation of subjectivities
through that experience is, of course, not a process which is directly
accessible to me as a product of an imperial country, but I have tried
to hear what has been said about this experience by those directly
involved. Being positioned as the site of Otherness and difference
was, for Fanon, an experience liable to create a profound sense of
fragmentation and dissonance. Engagement with the discourses and
practices of colonialism meant that one stepped outside the 'Other'
that one was supposed to be, at the risk of total dissolution and
madness. As I have indicated, interpreting such an account of the
subjective experience of colonialism is made more complicated by
the fact that the colonial discourse was so heavily permeated with
the idea of 'deculturation' and of the dangers of disintegration. In
the colonial account such disintegration would lead to an unsettling
of boundaries of difference and a loss of control. For colonial peoples, however, such disintegration could in fact be part of the process of the forging of new identities beyond those ascribed to them
as 'Others', and the process of liberation.

With the current popularity of postmodernist theories of the subject it is important, I think, to reassess the experience of colonialism
in its own right. There is a sense, as I have indicated in the Introduction, in which colonial peoples and marginal groups in metropolitan
societies discovered the postmodernist subject long before a postmodernist theory of subjectivity was elaborated in academic and
literary circles. The experience of being a fragmented and fluid self
was, if Fanon is correct, a common experience of colonial people as
it was, according to many feminist writers, a common experience for
women in western societies. Discussions on the question of how to
deal with the consequences of this fragmented subjectivity have
long been current amongst participants in the debates of Afro-
American literary criticism. For many people in Africa the fluidity of
identity and the necessity of constructing new individual and collective identities for political purposes are real and immediate experiences. Nationalism, after all, was and is about just such processes.

Though, as Fanon indicates, the experience of colonialism could
be a profoundly fragmenting and painful one, we need to be cautious about how we represent this experience. It is important not to
provide a pathologizing account of it since, as I have indicated in
this book, such pathologization itself contributed importantly to that
fragmentation. The power of the biomedical discourse on colonial
Africa lay in exactly this ability to describe poverty, subordination
and exploitation in terms of the 'sickness' of African peoples who
were subjected to these processes, a 'sickness' for which they could

then be held largely responsible. Nevertheless, whilst postmodernist theories have described fragmentation as a universal experience, and have tended sometimes to celebrate it, we need to be aware that there are different degrees of fragmentation, and that the colonial experience was, for some, not an experience to be celebrated. The 'fragmented self' of postmodernist theory may, as I have indicated in Chapter 1, be a luxury which only those who have previously experienced the unified self can afford.

If the experience of fragmentation should not be pathologized, neither should that of difference. In the colonial biomedical discussions I have described in this book, difference was either pathologized or denied entirely. Liberal critics of the reification of difference found themselves arguing for no differences at all, and indirectly for a biomedicine which would be totalizing and universalizing. The denial of difference, or rather of differences, does not seem to me to offer an answer to the problem of accounting for this particular history. Colonialism did produce differences, and not only the overriding difference of 'Otherness'. It produced individuals with varying investments in a range of identities, including gender identities, sexual identities, class identities, religious identities and ethnic identities.

This was not a unique feature of colonial peoples, but the 'package' of available materials from which to build identities was particular to the historical circumstances of colonial Africa. To maintain that such differences are not real, because they are constructed rather than 'essential', is to deny colonial peoples any role in the making of their own history.

It is because of the power of the biomedical languages of pathologization and the history of its application to colonial Afica, that finding a new language with which to describe differences is so important. Of course African writers, film-makers and artists have been doing just this for a long time, but in the area of biomedicine the colonial history I have outlined retains a strong, and even at times imprisoning, influence.

Recent literature on the problem of AIDS in Africa demonstrates this in a startling and shocking way. In Europe and North America, both medical and journalistic accounts of AIDS in Africa indicated once again the durability of that European cultural tradition which sees Africa as synonymous with disease, death, and uncontrolled sexuality. Africans, it seems, in this socio-medical discourse, never get sick innocently.

Africans have, of course, responded vigorously to this assault. Some African commentators hold to the view that AIDS is largely a 'western' health problem, which has been skilfully blamed on Africa and Africans.[3] This analysis denies the existence of AIDS as a serious medical problem in Africa, arguing that it is a disease associated with the degeneracy of the West, and particularly with the 'exotic' practice of homosexuality, reminding us that it is not only western societies which formulate visions of 'Otherness'. In an inversion of the colonial discourse on Africa, then, this analysis of AIDS constructs Africa as a place of social stability and morality, in which sexuality is still ordered by a set of traditional norms. Against this are positioned the societies of Europe and North America, exporting to Africa a disease brought about by their own sexual degeneracy.[4]

Other commentators and health workers, however, have steered away from this inversion. Rather than denying AIDS as a medical problem and projecting back on some other 'Other', they emphasize rather the politico-economic context which has facilitated its spread in Africa.[5] As AIDS is, in part, a sexually-transmitted disease, this project will involve utilizing the self-representations which African culture has produced to forge a new discussion of sexuality. To be effective such a discussion will rest not on European constructions of African sexuality nor solely on the denial of those constructions but rather on the real experiences of women and men.

As the AIDS example shows, the medical discourse on Africa, which I have tried to outline and dissect in this book, has left its legacy. However powerful this discourse may have been, it has, as I have attempted to show, never been all-powerful and never gone unchallenged. African societies have also had their visions of 'the Other', and the cultures of healing and the representations of disease and health which these societies have produced remain, ultimately, much more powerful and important than the memoirs of 'jungle doctors' or obscure articles in journals of tropical diseases. These cultures of healing and self-representations, however, have been forged not in total isolation from the discourses and practices of biomedicine, but rather alongside them, sometimes through them, and sometimes in reaction against them.

Perhaps more important than this is the fact that biomedicine is practised by Africans, that biomedical research is carried out by Africans, and that Africans edit and contribute to biomedical journals. In the late twentieth century, then, biomedicine is an African healing system. The extent to which this fact will alter the dominant images constructed of disease in Africa remains to be seen.

NOTES

1 G. A. Gollock, *Heroes of Health* (London, 1930), p. vii.
2 Gollock, *Heroes of Health*, p. vii.

3 For this argument see Chirumuuta and Chirmumuuta (1987).
4 For a discussion of the phenomenon of 'blaming others' in the AIDS epidemic, see Sabatier (1988).
5 Packard (1989) provides a useful critique of current social science research on AIDS in Africa and suggests a political-economic analysis.

Bibliography

Books and articles

Albino, R. C. and V. J. Thompson (1956), 'The Effects of Sudden Weaning on Zulu Children', *British Journal of Medical Psychology*, vol. 29, pp. 177–210.

Arnold, David (1988), 'Smallpox and Colonial Medicine in Nineteenth Century India', in Arnold, ed. (1988), pp. 45–66.

Arnold, David, ed. (1988), *Imperial Medicine and Indigenous Societies*, Manchester.

Ashcroft, Bill, Gareth Griffiths and Helen Tiffin (1989), *The Empire Writes Back: Theory and Practice in Post-colonial Literatures*, London.

Ault, James (1983), 'Making "Modern" Marriage "Traditional": State Power and the Regulation of Marriage in Colonial Zambia', *Theory and Society*, vol. 12, pp. 181–210.

Bartlett, F. C. (1937), 'Psychological Methods and Anthropological Problems', *Africa*, vol. 10, pp. 401–20.

Beinart, William (1989), 'Introduction: the Politics of Colonial Conservation', *Journal of Southern African Studies*, vol. 15, pp. 143–62.

Ben-Tovim, David I. (1987), *Development Psychiatry: Mental Health and Primary Health Care in Botswana*, London.

Berry, W. T. C. (1984), *Before the Wind of Change*, Halesworth.

Brelsford, W. V. (1947), 'Analysis of African Reaction to Propaganda Film', *Nada*, vol. 24, pp. 7–22.

Brown, James W. (1978), 'Increased Communication and Epidemic Disease in early Colonial Ashanti', in Gerald W. Hartwig and K. David Patterson, eds, *Disease in African History: an Introductory Survey and Case Studies*, Durham, N.C., pp. 180–207.

Bryder, Linda (1988), *Below the Magic Mountain: a Scoial History of Tuberculosis in Twentieth Century Britain*, Oxford.

Bury, M. R. (1986), 'Social Constructionism and the Development of Medical Sociology', *Sociology of Health and Illness*, vol. 8, pp. 137–79.

Carothers, J. C. (1953), *The African Mind in Health and Disease*, Geneva.

Carothers, J. C. (1954), *The Mind of Mau Mau*, Nairobi.

Catanach, I. J. (1988), 'Plague and the Tensions of Empire: India, 1896–1918', in Arnold, ed. (1988), pp. 149–72.

Chanock, Martin (1987), *Law, Custom and Social Order: the Colonial Experience in Malawi and Zambia*, Cambridge.

Chirumuuta R. C. and Chirumuuta, R. J. (1987), *Aids, Africa and Racism*, Burton-on-Trent.

Churchill, Caryl (1989), *Cloud Nine*, London.

Cochrane, R. (1931), 'Leprosy in Uganda', *Leprosy Review*, vol. 2, pp. 59–63.

Comaroff, Jean (1982), 'Medicine: Symbol and Ideology', in Wright and Treacher, eds (1982), pp. 49–69.

Comaroff, Jean (forthcoming, 1991), 'The Diseased Heart: Medicine, Colonialism and the Black Body', in Margaret Lock and Shirley Lindenbaum, eds, *Analysis in Medical Anthropology*, Dordrecht.

Cook, Sir Albert (1945), *Uganda Memories*, Kampala.

Cooter, Roger (1982), 'Anticontagionism and History's Medical Record', in Wright and Treacher, eds (1982), pp. 87–109.

Critical Inquiry, vol. 12, no. 1 (1985), Special issue on 'race', writing and difference, edited by Henry Gates.

Curtin, Philip (1961), '"The White Man's Grave": Image and Reality', *Journal of British Studies*, vol. 1, pp. 94–110.

Curtin, Philip (1965), *The Image of Africa: British Ideas and Action, 1780–1850*, London.

Davenport-Hines, Richard (1990), *Sex, Death and Punishment*, London.

Davidson, Capt (1949), 'Psychiatric Work among the Bemba', *'Rhodes–Livingstone Institute Journal*, vol. 7, pp. 75–86.

Davies, J. N. P. (1956), 'A History of Syphilis in Uganda', *Bulletin of the World Health Organisation*, vol. 15, pp. 1041–55.

Davin, Anna (1978), 'Imperialism and Motherhood', *History Workshop*, vol. 5, pp. 9–65.

Davis, W. E. (1984), *Caring and Curing in Congo and Kentucky*, North Middletown.

Dawson, Marc (1979), 'Smallpox in Kenya, 1880–1920', *Social Science and Medicine*, vol. 13B, pp. 245–51.

Dawson, Marc (1987), 'The Anti-Yaws Campaign and Colonial Medical Policy in Kenya', *International Journal of African Historical Studies*, vol. 20, pp. 417–37.

de Groot, Joanna (1989), '"Sex" and "Race": the Construction of Language and Image in the Nineteenth Century', in Susan Mendus and Jane Rendall, eds, *Sexuality and Subordination*, London and New York, pp. 89–131.

Deleuze, Gilles and Félix Guattari (1984), *Anti-Oedipus: Capitalism and Schizophrenia*, trans. Robert Hurley, London.

Dieterlen, G. ed. (1973), *La Notion de la personne en Afrique Noir*, Paris.

Dijkstra, Bram (1986), *Idols of Perversity: Fantasies of Feminine Evil in Fin-de-Siècle Culture*, Oxford.

Dory, Electra (1963), *Leper Country*, London.

Dreyfus, H. L. and P. Rabinow (1982), *Michel Foucault: Beyond Structuralism and Hermeneutics*, Brighton.

Dubow, Saul (1987), 'Race, Civilisation and Culture: the Elaboration of

Segregationist Discourse in the Inter-war Years', in Shula Marks and Stanley Trapido, eds, *The Politics of Race, Class and Nationalism in Twentieth Century South Africa*, London, pp. 71–95.

East African High Commission (1949–53), East Africa Medical Survey, *Annual Reports*, Nairobi.

Ernst, Waltrund (1988), 'The European Insane in British India, 1800–1858: a Case-study in Psychiatry and Colonial Rule', in Arnold, ed. (1988), pp. 27–45.

Etherington, Norman (1987), 'Missionary Doctors and African Healers in mid-Victorian South Africa', *South African Historical Journal*, vol. 19, pp. 77–91.

Evans, A. J. (1950), 'The Ila V.D. Campaign', *Rhodes–Livingstone Journal*, vol. 9, pp. 40–7.

Fanon, Frantz (1986), *Black Skin, White Masks*, London (first published 1952).

Federation of Rhodesia and Nyasaland (1955), Federal Assembly, *Votes and Proceedings of the Federal Assembly, 1st Session, 1st Parliament*, Salisbury.

Feierman, Steven (1985), 'Struggles for Control: the Social Roots of Health and Healing in Modern Africa', *African Studies Review*, vol. 28, pp. 73–147.

Field, Margaret (1960), *Search for Security: an Ethno-psyciatric Study of Rural Ghana*, London.

Figlio, Karl (1982), 'How Does Illness Mediate Social Relations? Workmen's Compensation and Medico-Legal Practices, 1890–1940', in Wright and Treacher, eds (1982), pp. 175–225.

Follereau, Raoul (1968), *Love One Another*, trans. Barbara Wall, London.

Ford, John (1971), *The Role of Trypanosomiasis in African Ecology*, Oxford.

Ford, John (1979), 'Ideas which have Influenced Attempts to Solve the Problem of African Trypanosomiasis', *Social Science and Medicine*, vol. 13B, pp. 269–75.

Fortes, M. with R. Horton (1983), *Oedipus and Job in West African Religion*, Cambridge.

Fortes, M. and D. Y. Fortes (1966), 'Psychosis and Social Change among the Tallensi of Northern Ghana', *Cahiers d'Etudes Africaines*, vol. 6, pp. 5–40.

Foskett, R., ed. (1964), *The Zambesi Doctors: David Livingstone's Letters to John Kirk*, Edinburgh.

Foucault, Michel (1976), *The Birth of the Clinic*, London.

Foucault, Michel (1979a), *Discipline and Punish*, Harmondsworth.

Foucault, Michel (1979b), *The History of Sexuality*, vol. 1, London.

Foucault, Michel (1980), *Michel Foucault: Power and Knowledge*, ed. C. Gordon, Hassocks, Sussex.

Foucault, Michel (1989), *Madness and Civilisation*, London.

Franklin, H. (1950), 'The Central African Screen', *Colonial Cinema*, vol. 8, no. 4, pp. 85–8.

Fraser, Nancy (1989), *Unruly Practices: Power, Discourse and Gender in Contemporary Social Theory*, Oxford.

Fuss, Diana (1989), *Essentially Speaking: Feminism, Nature and Difference*, New York and London.

Gelfand, Michael (1964), *Lakeside Pioneers: a Socio-medical Study of Nyasaland, 1850–1920*, Oxford.

Gilman, Sander (1985), *Difference and Pathology: Stereotypes of Sexuality, Race and Madness*, Ithaca, N.Y.

Giltrow, D. R. and P. M. Giltrow (1986), 'Cinema with a Purpose: Films for Development in British Colonial Africa', paper presented at the African Studies Assoication (U.K.) meeting, University of Kent, 17–19 September.

Gordon, H. L. (1935–6), 'An Inquiry into the correlation of Civilisation and Mental Disorders', *East African Medical Journal*, vol. 12, pp. 327–35.

Gould, S. J. (1977), *Ontogeny and Phylogeny*, Cambridge, Mass.

Greenless, T. D. (1895), 'Insanity among the Natives of South Africa', *Journal of Mental Science*, vol. 41, pp. 71–81.

Haraway, Donna (1989), *Primate Visions*, New York and London.

Harris, Marvin (1968), *The Rise of Anthropological Theory*, New York.

Harstock, Nancy (1987), 'Rethinking Modernism: Majority vs Minority Theories', *Cultural Critique*, vol. 7, pp. 187–206.

Harstock, Nancy (1990), 'Foucault on Power: a Theory for Women?', in Linda Nicholson, ed., *Feminism/Postmodernism*, New York and London, pp. 157–76.

Hooks, Bell (1984), *Feminist Theory from Margin to Center*, Boston.

Hunt, Nancy (1988), '"Le Bébé en Brousse": European Women, African Birthspacing and Colonial Intervention in Breast Feeding in the Belgian Congo', *International Journal of Afrian Historical Studies*, vol. 21, pp. 401–32.

Iliffe, John (1987), *The African Poor: a History*, Cambridge.

Imperato, Pascal (1964), *Bwana Doctor*, London.

Jacobus, Mary, Evelyn Fox Keller and Sally Shuttleworth, eds (1990), *Body/ Politics: Women and the Discourses of Science*, London.

Janzen, John (1978), *The Quest for Therapy in Lower Zaire*, Berkeley and London.

Jeater, Diana (forthcoming, 1991), 'The Pointing Finger: Ascriptions of Blame in the Debate over Adultery in Southern Rhodesia', in Whitehead and Vaughan, eds (1991).

Jochelson, Karen (1989), 'Patterns of Syphilis in South Africa, 1880–1940', unpublished paper, South African Research Seminar, Oxford University.

Jordan, June (1989), 'En Passant', in June Jordan, *Lyrical Campaigns: Selected Poems*, London, p. 97.

Jordanova, Ludmilla (1989), *Sexual Visions*, Hemel Hempstead.

Junge, Werner (1952), *African Jungle Doctor: Ten Years in Liberia*, London.

Karpf, Anne (1988), *Doctoring the Media*, London.

Kenya (1943), *Annual Report of the Medical Department* for 1942, Nairobi.

Kenya (1945), *Annual Report of the Medical Department* for 1944, Nairobi.

Kjekshus, Helge (1977), *Ecology Control and Economic Development in East African History*, London.

Kuhn, Annette (1985), *The Power of the Image: Essays on Representation and Sexuality*, London.

Lambkin, F. J. (1908), 'An Outbreak of Syphilis in a Virgin Soil', in D'A. Power and K. Murphy, eds, *A System of Syphilis*, London. vol. 2.

Lambo, T. A. (1955), 'The Role of Cultural Factors in Paranoid Psychosis among the Yoruba Tribe', *Journal of Mental Science*, vol. 101, pp. 239–66.

Lambo, T. A. (1957), 'Some Unusual Features of Schizophrenia among Primitive Peoples', *West African Medical Journal*, vol. 1, pp. 147–52.

Lambo, T. A. (1960), 'The Concept and Practice of Mental Health in African Cultures', *East African Medical Journal*, vol. 37, pp. 464–71.

Larsson, Birgitta (1987), 'A Dying People? Women, Church and Social Change in North-Western Tanzania under British Rule', unpublished paper.

Laubscher, B. J. F. (1937), *Sex, Custom and Psychopathology: a Study of South African Pagan Natives*, London.

Lawman, Tony (1952), 'Information Research: an Experiment in Northern Rhodesia', *Colonial Cinema*, vol. 10, no. 3, pp. 56–61.

Littlewood, Ronald and Maurice Lipsedge (1989), *Aliens and Alienists: Ethnic Minorities and Psychiatry*, London, second edition.

Lyons, Maryinez (1987), 'The Colonial Disease: Sleeping Sickness in the Social History of Northern Zaire, 1903–1930', PhD. thesis, University of California.

Lyotard, Jean-François (1984), *The Postmodern Condition*, trans. G. Bennington and B. Massumi. Manchester and Minneapolis.

McElligott, G. L. M. (1949), 'The Venereal Disease Problem in Tropical Africa', *The Practitioner*, vol. 162, pp. 390–5.

McKelvey, J. J.(1973), *Man Against Tsetse: Struggle for Africa*, Ithaca, N.Y.

MacKenzie, John (1984), *Propaganda and Empire: the Manipulation of British Public Opinion, 1880–1960*, Manchester.

MacKenzie, John (1988), *Empire of Nature*, Manchester.

McKeown, T. (1979), *The Role of Medicine: Dream, Mirage or Nemesis?*, Oxford.

MacLeod, Roy and Milton Lewis, eds (1988), *Disease, Medicine and Empire: Perspectives on Western Medicine and the Experience of European Expansion*, London and New York.

Mannoni, O. (1956), *Prospero and Caliban*, London.

Manual, P; Fani-Koyode, R; and S. Gupta (1989), 'Imaging Black Sexuaity', in Michelle Reeves and Jenny Hammond, eds, *Looking Beyond the Frame: Racism, Representation and Resistance*, Oxford, pp. 44–53.

Martin, Emily (1989), *The Woman in the Body*, Milton Keynes.

Marwick, M. (1944), 'Review', *Journal of the Rhodes–Livingstone Institute*, vol. 11, pp. 69–76.

Memmi, Albert (1990), *The Colonizer and the Colonized*, London, first published 1957.

Merriweather, A. M. (1959), 'Endemic Syphilis – "Dichuchwa" – in the Bechuanaland Protectorate', *Central African Journal of Medicine*, vol. 5, pp. 181–5.

Mews, Stuart (1982), 'The Revival of Spiritual Healing in the Church of England, 1920–1926', in W. J. Shiels, ed., *The Church and Healing*, Oxford, pp. 299–333.

Miller, C. L. (1985), *Black Darkness: Africanist Discourse in French*, Chicago.

Minde, M. (1956), 'Early Psychiatry in Natal', *South African Medical Journal*, vol. 30, pp. 287–91.

Minh-ha, Trinh T. (1989), *Woman, Native, Other*, Bloomington and Indianapolis.

Mohanty, Chandra (1988), 'Under Western Eyes: Feminist Scholarship and Colonial Discourse', *Feminist Review*, vol. 30, pp. 61–88.

Mort, Frank (1987), *Dangerous Sexualities: Medico-moral Politics in England since 1830*, London.

Mudimbe, V. Y. (1988), *The Invention of Africa: Gnosis, Philosophy and the Order of Knowledge*, Bloomington.

Mullings, Leith (1984), *Therapy, Ideology and Social Change: Mental Healing in Urban Ghana*, Berkeley.

Murray, J. F. (1957), 'Endemic Syphilis or Yaws?: a Review of the Literature from South Africa', *South African Medical Journal*, vol. 31, pp. 821–4.

Murray, J. F., A. M. Merriweather and M. L. Freedman (1956), 'Endemic Syphilis in the Bakwena Reserve of Bechuanaland Protectorate', *Bulletin of the World Health Organisation*, vol. 15, pp. 975–1039.

Musisi, Nakanyike (1988), 'Buganda: the Rise and Maintenance of Irresponsible Polygamy, 1856–1962', paper to the Workshop on the Crisis over Marriage in Colonial Africa, Nuffield College, Oxford, December.

Nicholson, Linda, ed. (1990), *Feminism/Postmodernism*, New York and London.

Northern Rhodesia (1949), *Annual Report of the Health Department for 1946*, Lusaka.

Notcutt, L. A. and G. C. Latham (1937), *The African and the Cinema*, London.

Nyasaland Protectorate (1910), *Blue Book*, Zomba.

Nyasaland Protectorate (1912), *Blue Book*, Zomba.

Nyasaland Protectorate (1952), *Annual Report of the Medical Department for 1951*, Zomba.

O'Brien, Brian (1962), *That Good Physician*, London.

Odunton, G. (1950), 'One Step Ahead', *Colonial Cinema*, vol. 8, no. 2, pp. 32–3.

O'Hanlon, Rosalind and David Washbrook (1990), 'After Orientalism: Culture, Criticism and Politics in the Third World'. Unpublished paper.

Orley, J. (1970), *Culture and Mental Illness: a Study from Uganda*, Nairobi.

Ortigues, M. C. and E. Ortigues (1966), *Oedipe Africain*, Paris.

Packard, Randall (1989), *White Plague, Black Labour: Tuberculosis and the Political Economy of Health and Disease in South Africa*, Berkeley and London.

Palmer, Richard (1982), 'The Church, Leprosy and Plague in Medieval and Early Modern Europe', in W. J. Shiels, ed., *The Church and Healing*, Oxford, pp. 79–101.

Parin, P., F. Morgenthaler and G. Parin-Matthey (1980), *Fear Thy Neighbour as Thyself: Psychoanalysis and Society among the Anyi of West Africa*, trans. Partricia Klamerth, Chicago.

Parpart, Jane (1988), 'Sexuality and Power on the Zambian Copperbelt, 1926–1964', in Sharon Stichter and Jane Parpart, eds, *Patriarchy and Class: African Women in the Home and the Workforce*, Boulder, pp. 115–39.

Parry, Benita (1987), 'Problems in Current Theories of Colonial Discourse', *Oxford Literary Review*, vol. 7, nos 1 and 2, pp. 27–58.

Pearson, George (1957), *Flashback: an Autobiography of a British Film-maker*, London.

Piault, C., ed. (1975), *Prophetisme et Thérapeutique: Albert Atcho et la Communauté de Bregbo*, Paris.

Pickering, K. (1954), 'Another Walt Disney Experiment', *Colonial Cinema*, vol. 12, no. 3, pp. 50–3.

Poovey, Mary (1990), 'Speaking of the Body: Mid-Victorian Constructions of Female Desire', in Jacobus et al. (1990), pp. 29–47.

Porter, Roy (1987), *A Social History of Madness: Stories of the Insane*, London.

Power, A. D. (1939), 'A British Empire Leprosarium', *Journal of the African Society*, vol. 38, pp. 465–8.

Prins, Gwyn (1989), 'But What Was the Disease? The Present State of Health and Healing in African Studies', *Past and Present*, vol. 124, pp. 159–79.

Ramasubban, Radhika (1988), 'Imperial Health in British India, 1857–1900', in MacLeod and Lewis (1988), pp. 38–61.

Ranger, Terence (1981), 'Godly Medicine: the Ambiguities of Medical Mission in Southeast Tanzania', *Social Science and Medicine*, vol. 15B, pp. 261–77.

Ranger, Terence (1982), 'Medical Science and the Pentecost: the Dilemma of Anglicanism in Africa', in W. J. Shiels, ed., *The Church and Healing*, Oxford, pp. 333–67.

Reismann, Paul (1985), 'The Person and the Life-Cycle; African Social Life and Thought', paper to the African Studies Association meeting, New Orleans, November.

Richards, Audrey (1939), *Land, Labour and Diet*, London.

Riley, Denise (1988), *'Am I That Name?': Feminism and the Category of 'Woman' in History*, Basingstoke.

Ritchie, J. F. (1943), *The African as Suckling and Adult*, Rhodes–Livingstone Paper no. 9, Livingstone.

Russett, Cynthia Eagle (1989), *Sexual Science: the Victorian Construction of Womanhood*, Cambridge, Mass.

Subatier, Renée (1988), *Blaming Others: Prejudice, Race and Worldwide AIDS*, London.

Sachs, Wulf (1933), 'The Insane Native: an Introduction to a Psychological Study', *South African Journal of Science*, vol. 30, pp. 706–13.

Sachs, Wulf (1937), *Black Hamlet: the Mind of an African Negro Revealed by Psychoanalysis*, London.

Said, Edward (1978), *Orientalism*, New York.

Schweitzer, Albert (1948), *On the Edge of the Primeval Forest*, London.

Showalter, Elaine (1987), *The Female Malady: Women, Madness and English Culture, 1830–1980*, London.

Simons, H. J. (1985), 'Mental Disease in Africans: Racial Determinism', *Journal of Mental Science*, vol. 104, pp. 377–88.

Sivadon, Paul (1958), 'Problèmes de santé mentale en Afrique Noire', *World Mental Health*, vol. 10, pp. 106–20.

Smartt, G. (1956), 'Mental Maladjustment in the East African', *Journal of Mental Science*, vol. 102, pp. 441–66.

Smith, Edwin W. (1946), *Knowing the African*, London.

Smyth, R. (1988), 'The British Colonial Film Unit and Sub-Saharan Africa, 1939–1945', *Historical Journal of Film, Radio and Television*, vol. 8, pp. 285–98.

Social Science and Medicine, (1989), vol. 28, Special Issue on the Political Economy of Health in Africa and Latin America.

Southern Rhodesia (1931), *Report on the Public Health for 1930*, Salisbury.

Sow, I. (1977), *Psychiatrie dynamique africaine*, Paris.

Spivak, Gayatri Chakravorty (1986), 'Imperialism and Sexual Difference', *Oxford Literary Review*, vol. 8, nos 1–2.

Spivak, Gayatri Chaykravorty (1987), *In Other Worlds*, London.

Spurr, Norman (1950), 'Odunton's Article', *Colonial Cinema*, vol. 8, no. 2, p. 33.

Spurr, Norman (1951), 'A Report on the Use of Disney's Hookworm Film with an African Audience in the Western Province, Uganda', *Colonial Cinema*, vol. 9, no. 2, pp. 28–33.

Stirling, Leader (1947), *Bush Doctor: Being Letters from Dr Leader Stirling*, London.

Stirling, Leader, (1977), *Tanzanian Doctor*, London.

Stocking, George W. (1969), *Race, Culture and Evolution*, New York.

Stott, Rebecca (1989), 'The Dark Continent: Africa as Female Body in Haggard's Adventure Fiction', *Feminist Review*, vol. 32, pp. 69–89.

Swanson, Maynard (1977), 'The Sanitation Syndrome: Bubonic Plague and Urban Native Policy in the Cape Colony, 1900–1909', *Journal of African History*, vol. 18, pp. 387–410.

Szasz, Thomas (1971), *The Manufacture of Madness*, London.

Tooth, G. (1950), *Studies in Mental Illness in the Gold Coast*, Colonial Research Publication, no. 6, London.

Trant, Hope (1970), *Not Merrion Square: Anecdotes from a Woman's Medical Career in Africa*, East London (Canada).

Turner, Bryan (1987), *Medical Power and Social Knowledge*, London.

Turow, Joseph (1989), *Playing Doctor: Television, Story-Telling, and Medical Power*, Oxford.

Turshen, Meredith (1984), *The Political Ecology of Disease in Tanzania*, New Brunswick.

Uganda Protectorate (1914), *Annual Medical and Sanitary Report for 1913*, London.

Uganda Protectorate (1922), *Annual Medical and Sanitary Report for 1921*, Entebbe.

Uganda Protectorate (1927), *Annual Medical and Sanitary Report for 1926*, Entebbe.

Uganda Protectorate (1928), *Annual Medical and Sanitary Report for 1927*, Entebbe.

Uganda Protectorate (1933), *Annual Medical and Sanitary Report for 1932*, Entebbe.

Uganda Protectorate (1939), *Annual Report of the Medical Department for 1938*, Entebbe.

Vane, Michael (1957), *Black and White Medicine: a Mine Medical Officer's Experience in South Africa, the Belgian Congo, Sierra Leone and the Gold Coast*, London and Edinburgh.

Vaughan, Megan (1988a), 'Measuring Crisis in Maternal and Child Health: an Historical Perspective', in Marcia Wright et al., eds, *Women's Health and Apartheid*, Columbia University, New York, pp. 130–43.

Vaughan, Megan, (forthcoming, 1991), 'Syphilis in Colonial Africa: the Social Construction of an Epidemic', in T. O. Ranger and P. Slack, eds, *Epidemics and Ideas*, Cambridge.

Vint, F. W. (1932), 'A Preliminary Note on the Cell Content of the Prefrontal Cortex of the East African Native', *East African Medical Journal*, vol. 9, pp. 30–55.

Walls, A. F. (1982), '"The Heavy Artillery of the Missionary Army": the Domestic Importance of the Nineteenth Century Medical Missionary', in W. J. Shiels, ed., *The Church and Healing*, Oxford, pp. 287–99.

Worboys, Michael (1988a), 'Manson, Ross and Colonial Medical Policy: Tropical Medicine in London and Liverpool, 1899–1914', in MacLeod and Lewis, eds (1988), pp. 21–38.

Worboys, Michael (1988b), 'The Discovery of Colonial Malnutrition Between the Wars', in Arnold, ed. (1988), pp. 208–26.

Waxler, Nancy (1981), 'Learning to be a Leper', in Elliot G. Mishler et al., *Social Contexts of Health, Illness and Patient Care*, Cambridge, chapter 7.

Weeks, Jeffrey (1981), *Sex, Politics and Society: the Regulation of Sexuality since 1800*, London.

White, Luise (1988), 'Domestic Labour in a Colonial City: Prostitution in Nairobi, 1900–1952', in Sharon Stichter and Jane Parpart, eds, *Patriarchy and Class: African Women in the Home and the Workforce*, Boulder, pp. 139–61.

White, Luise (1990), 'Separating the Men from the Boys: Constructions of Gender, Sexuality and Terrorism in Central Kenya, 1939–1959', *International Journal of African Historical Studies*, vol. 23, pp. 1–25.

White, Paul (1960), *Jungle Doctor Panorama*, London.

White, Paul (1977), *Alias Jungle Doctor*, Exeter.

White, Paul (1988a), *Jungle Doctor's Crooked Dealings*, Homebush West, NSW. First published 1959.

White, Paul (1988b), *Jungle Doctor on the Hop*, Homebush West, NSW. First published 1957.

White, Paul (1988c), *Jungle Doctor's Hippo Happenings*, Exeter. First published 1966.

White, Paul (1988d), *Jungle Doctor in Slippery Places*, Homebush West, NSW.

Whitehead, Ann and Vaughan, Megan, eds (forthcoming, 1991), *Marriage, Sexuality and Colonial Discourse*, London and New York.

Willcox, R. R. (1951), 'Endemic Syphilis in Africa: the Njovera of Southern Rhodesia', *South African Medical Journal*, vol. 25, pp. 501–4.

Wilson, Godfrey (1942), 'An Essay on the Economics of Detribalization in Nothern Rhodesia', *Rhodes–Livingstone Paper*, no. 6, Livingstone.

Woolcock, Helen (1988), '"Our Salubrious Climate": Attitudes to Health in Colonial Queensland', in MacLeod and Lewis, eds (1988), pp. 176–94.

Wright, P. and Treacher, A., eds (1982), *The Problem of Medical Knowledge: Examining the Social Construction of Medicine*, Edinburgh.

Zahra, A. (1956), 'A Yaws Eradication Campaign in Eastern Nigeria', *Bulletin of the World Health Organisation*, vol. 15, pp. 911–35.

Zeller, Diane L. (1971), 'The Establishment of Western Medicine in Buganda', PhD. thesis, Columbia University.

Periodicals (used as primary sources)

Mercy and Truth: a record of the Church Missionary Society Medical Missionary Work, London, 1897–1916.

Central Africa: a monthly record of the work of the Universities' Mission to Central Africa, London, 1883–1959.

The Children's Tidings (later *African Tidings*): Universities' Mission to Central Africa, London, 1885–1928.
Uganda Notes (later *Uganda Church Review*), 1903–1950.
Leprosy Review: British Empire Leprosy Relief Association, London, 1930–58.
Without the Camp: Quarterly Magazine of the Mission to Lepers, London, 1914–18.
Medical Missions at Home and Abroad: Medical Missionary Association, London, 1898–1907.
Conquest by Healing: Medical Missionary Association, London, 1924–28.

Archival sources

1 *Malawi National Archives (MNA)*
S1/326/19: Bubonic Plague, 1919.
S1/1243/19: Smallpox, 1919–20.
M2/5/6: Smallpox, General, 1929–32.
M2/5/49: Smallpox, 1946–8.
M2/5/15: Relapsing Fever, 1934–8.
M2/14/1: Medical Surveys, 1930–6.
M2/14/2: Medical Surveys, 1937–8.
S1/470/20: Leprosy, 1914–22.
M2/5/12: Leprosy, 1922–8.
S1/512(1)/24: BELRA, 1924–37.
BS1/2/5: Native Criminal Cases, Ncheu, 1912–13.
S1/1191/24: Native Criminal Cases, 1924.
BA3/9/1: Lunacy Cases, Blantyre, 1929–34.
M2/11/1: Central Asylum.
M3/1/12: Central Asylum Report, 1930.
M2/14/11: Native Birth Rate, 1930.
M2/24/7: Native Birth Rate, 1925–30.
M2/5/56: Venereal Diseases, 1940–4.
M2/5/21: Venereal Diseases, 1932–4.
M2/5/6: Cerebro-Spinal Meningitis.
M3/4/3: Report on an investigation concerning mental disorder in Nyasaland natives, 1935.
S1/470/20: Leprosy, 1914–22.

2 *Zambia National Archives (ZNA)*
NR 7/187: Chitokoloki Leprosy Settlement, 1952–8.
NR 7/89: Luapuala Leprosy Settlement, vol. VI (1953–5).
SEC 2/1297: Northern Province, Annual Report on Native Affairs, 1928.
NR 7/40: VD Campaign, Ba Ila, 1946–52.

3 *Kenya National Archives (KNA)*
MD 47/252: Native Lunatics (Harmless).
MD 47/195: Birth of a child by a female lunatic, 1917–21.

4 *Public Record Office, London (PRO)*
CO 536/15: Uganda Correspondence.

CO 994/5: Colonial Medical Advisory Committee.
CO 859/30/15: Venereal Diseases: relations with the British Social Hygiene
   Council.

5   Rhodes House, Oxford
Mss. Afr.s.1519: W. A. Young
Mss. Afr.s.1872(16): A. Brincklow.
Mss. Afr.s.1872(2): Barbara Akinyemi.
Mss. Afr.r.97: J. B. Davey.
Mss. Afr.s.476: Hugh Stannus.
Mss. Afr.s.1091: C. J. Baker.

Index